Discussion with a New Spanish Mestizo

Jensen Cox

Published by Flood, 2023.

DISCUSSION WITH A NEW SPANISH MESTIZO

First edition. July 3, 2023.

ISBN: 979-8223083757

Written by Jensen Cox.

Table of Contents

"Those of the Kingdom of Mexico were in no way more civilized and more artistic than were the other nations there.

So they judged, like us, that the universe was near its end, and took as a sign of it the desolation that we brought there.

[...] What they estimate of the manner in which this last Sun will perish, my author has learned nothing. »

Michel de Montaigne, *The Essays* , III, "Coaches".

- I was expecting you. What did you have in mind when you started writing Indian history?

– I wanted to use the clearest possible language to talk about things that seemed to me worth knowing, and I sometimes used the terms that the Indians use in their language.

– For Montaigne, the Indians believe that "the universe is close to its end".

– Yes, they are convinced that there must be another end and that this one will come by fire: the earth will open up, it will swallow up men, and then the world and the whole universe will be set ablaze[1].

– Who will trigger this apocalypse?

– The gods and the stars will come down from the sky [...]. The gods themselves will destroy men, they will annihilate them. The stars will become like wild beings. This is the ultimate end that awaits the world.

– Did the Indians interpret the invasion of the conquistadors in this way?

– When ours[2]arrived in this province [...] the Indians understood that the end had come, for the signs and all the things which they saw were evident and indisputable.

" *Who told them?* "

– Our God, who is also our supreme good, took such pity, such mercy for such a great multitude of people that in his infinite goodness he took care to send messengers and celestial signs to announce to them the coming of the Spaniards. And dread spread throughout the New World[3].

– *Why this panic?*

“Because all these signs and other things they saw announced to the Indians their end and their annihilation. It was said that the whole world would disappear and be consumed. New peoples would be created and other inhabitants of the world, new beings, would arrive.

" *In what state were the Indians?"*

– The Indians were sinking into desolation. They were appalled and did not know what to think of these unprecedented events, of these things so strange and so unheard of.[4].

- *And what happened?*

- Everybody knows it. It is well known: on April 20, the Friday of Holy Week known as Good Friday, in the year 1519, Cortés landed at the head of his invincible and illustrious captains at the port of San Juan de Ulúa.

– *The world of the Indians collapsed, it was absorbed by ours.*

– [It had to be] in order to be able to convert these new peoples everywhere and thus bring down and defeat the demon, who is the enemy of the human race.

" *Are you talking about the Indians of Mexico?"*

– From all the nations of the world[5]!

The man we are interviewing is called Diego Muñoz Camargo. He is a contemporary of Michel de Montaigne. He was born in Mexico during the Renaissance period. So it's been four good centuries since he's been gone. As we do not disturb the dead for nothing, we must begin by justifying ourselves. When the great Brazilian novelist Machado de Assis collects the *Posthumous Memoirs of Brás Cubas* , he lets his hero express himself according to his imagination, because fiction gives him free rein.[6]. The historian is more constrained. And its audacity is only worth the safeguards that surround it.

1. Diego Muñoz Camargo, *Descripción de la ciudad y provincia de Tlaxcala* , René Acuña ed., Mexico City, UNAM, 1981, fol. 152v° (now D152v°).

2. The Spaniards.

3. D158v°.

4. D161v°.

5. D68v°.

6. J.-M. Machado de Assis, *Posthumous Memoirs of Brás Cubas* , Paris, Métailié, 2000. The original edition came out in 1881 in Rio de Janeiro (Tipografia nacional).

CHAPTER I

A Renaissance American

“Deprived [...] of the instructions and landmarks that defined my place in the world, I no longer knew how to situate myself, or what I had come to do on earth. »

Simone de Beauvoir, *Memoirs of a Tidy Young Girl*[1].

"So they judged, like us, that the universe was near its end", wrote Montaigne. Five centuries ago, for a Christian eye convinced of the importance of the event and anxious to give it meaning, the conquest of America and the upheavals it brought sounded the biblical and last supper hour, “the ultimate times so close to the end of the world[2]". Christian and colonial, the society which absorbed the conquered populations one by one then presented itself as the culmination of History.

The end is late. Five centuries later, the accomplishment has come, but the world has not been Christianized. The West seems to have burned all of its metaphysical fuel. It destroyed biodiversity and liquidated the Christian foundations for its construction and expansion as the planet became westernized. And now today is falling apart last cabin that we call modernity. Modernity is the time of the end and the last of the worlds since, by definition, nothing can succeed it.

What to relate to in this West in decline while the planet continues to globalize and shows countless signs of poor health? To try to answer this question, we will substitute for the analysis of contemporary realities the listening of a life that appeared in a distant century, on the other side of the Atlantic.

The history that we will survey is that inaugurated by Iberian globalization, this first stage of the expansion of the West during which Spain and Portugal built empires that linked or "connected" the four parts of the world.[3]. THE XVI he century of the Iberians is the time when everything began for us who live in XXI century in Europe and elsewhere. The setting in motion of Western Christianity and the sprawling progression of Europeans multiplied shocks and series of short-circuits which affected most of the great civilizations and great religions of the globe.

"Shocks", "short circuits", "connected worlds", these words point to gigantic processes without explaining to us the way in which they were experienced by the women and men of the time. And yet there are sources. Contacts, landings and invasions set off chain reactions among all those who were confronted with the intrusion of Europeans. Some have left written traces thanks to which we can today imagine how beings took their mark and evolved, even survived, in contexts upset by the irruption of the colonizers, then by the continual shocks it caused.

At XVI th century, processes as uncontrollable as they were unpredictable transformed the lives of invaders and invaded alike. If the idea of Westernization suggests the magnitude of the changes triggered by this globalization, it remains abstract. It designates a planetary project with complex dynamics, but what does it teach us about the awareness that individuals had of these transformations?

The question echoes our concerns: what do we grasp of globalization apart from the flow of discourse that it constantly arouses in the media? What impact does it have on our memories, on our way of living with each other? How do we react to such an extension of our horizons, to this abolition of space? What keys or what tools do we have to face this change when the certainties that the XIX he European century had given itself and which it believed it could instill in the rest of humanity? The question of benchmarks is therefore crucial. We forge landmarks, but we can just as easily lose them. Their erasure, always lamented, is in tune with the times. In France, have we not explained the disarray of the new generations by their disappearance and proposed to remedy it – big deal! – by establishing a universal national service?

A Renaissance American

THE XVI he Iberian century is a mirror that cannot be overlooked in European memories. It is at the same time a mine, richer than all those of Peru and Mexico combined, because it is full of human, indigenous, European, African, Asian and mainly mestizo experiences. Visiting them immerses us in a universe that in some respects anticipates ours because the mixture of men and women very early on reached an intensity and scale hitherto unmatched. Immersion causes a distancing since we move away from the surface of the water and the things of our world. As it facilitates listening and reflection, even, over time, empathy with other lives.

It is for these reasons that we interviewed an American from XVI th century. This American is called Diego Muñoz Camargo. “Born in this New World[4]», probably around 1530, he is an inhabitant of Mexico, which then bears the name of New Spain. Her father is a conquistador and her mother an Indian. He appears in the history books as the author of a Spanish document dated 1583, which is called a "geographical relation".

In the last quarter of XVI th century, the crown of Castile, anxious to know better its American possessions, had an impressive list of questions drawn up embracing all sorts of subjects. They are at the origin of a gigantic investigation on American soil, aimed at informing the sovereign about the riches of his Indian kingdoms.[5]. The king is Philip II; the kingdom which concerns us, New Spain. The leaders of the various constituencies of the country got down to the task and their more or less nourished answers flowed to the Council of the Indies. For the first time in modern times, a distant region of the world had to answer to a European nation.

In the heart of the Mexican Altiplano, in Tlaxcala, the highest local authority, the *alcalde mayor* , entrusts this task to Diego Muñoz Camargo. The latter gets caught up in the game and writes a long document in which he takes stock of the province: he recounts its past, draws up an inventory of its resources and, of course, evokes its military participation in the Spanish conquest. Diego could have limited himself to sending brief and stereotyped answers, as they abound in the other reports written at the time. He prefers to deviate from bureaucratic routines and the language of wood, even if it means going long, so long that he ends up transforming this pensum into a history book.[6].

Why improvise as a historian of your region, of Mexico and even of part of the world? The challenge is big. Especially since Diego Muñoz Camargo, promoted interpreter of an embassy of Tlaxcaltec Indians in Madrid, will hand over a particularly careful copy of the document to Philip II. Was it this exhilarating prospect that encouraged him to redouble his efforts and to outbid what was asked of him? Diego left Mexico in 1584 and returned in 1586[7]. The visit to the king is said to have taken place between March and May 1585[8]. For historian Charles Gibson, the two men even met several times[9]. If the detail is authentic, one is surprised at the interest that a sovereign so overwhelmed by his tasks was likely to find in Diego's conversation. Who could be this singular man born in the other world[10]?

Why Diego?

Diego lives in an America dominated by Christian Spain. We must keep in mind the context of the early 1580s: from Florida to Chile, a new form of domination was now exercised on an intercontinental scale and American. An economic order with planetary aims is in the process of being put in place while millennial legacies are disintegrating in whole sections, like icebergs devoured by melting. With the backdrop of the revolution in alphabetic writing and books, which is well worth our digital revolution in terms of its impact.

Diego takes us to the heart of a dual process: the construction of the first colonial society in modern Europe – Mexico – and the rise of Iberian globalization. What benchmarks, what defenses did he forge to survive – even live fairly well – in colonial Mexico at the end of the XVI th century? His career and his writings force us to review our binary vision of this era, fossilized in a confrontation between Spaniards and Indians. The clichés that clutter the history of Mexico are legion, especially in the debates on the fate of the natives where the questions asked are not always the right ones, when they do not strike condemnations that reassure our worried consciences on good account. Economic, demographic or social frameworks are certainly essential, but they imprison the past in a rigidity that it never had. *Political correctness* obliges, Indians, Spaniards, Blacks or mestizos, these convenient categories end up feeding ready-made ideas that sacrifice the complexity of colonial societies and turn them into anonymous, exotic and distant universes. It is with men and women of XVI century that I seek here to dialogue, not with figures or statistics. Globalization can be measured on a human and individual scale, and therefore necessarily on a local level, even if at the same time it manifests itself through intercontinental processes.

The inner man

Marguerite Yourcenar speaks of "inner man" when Montaigne is concerned with discovering "private moods": "I have a singular curiosity to know the soul and the naive judgments of my authors[11]. What is the relationship between what Diego writes and what he thinks? The circumstances of his death escape us. We don't know anything about his features, the color of his skin, his inclinations, not to mention the way he expresses himself since we only know him through his writings. So why persist in knowing "what he thought he was, wanted to be and what he was[12]» ?

"One of the best ways to recreate a man's thought is to reconstitute his library, to project other lights, other shadows onto this existence.[13]wrote Marguerite Yourcenar about Zénon, the hero of *L'Œuvre au noir* . Like the novelist playing the historian, I tracked down Diego's readings in the hundreds of pages he left behind. As for lights and shadows, these are the different contexts he has gone through and the contradictions that surface in his words.

I will therefore take a liberty with the rules of academic history by giving him the floor. At my own risk. Listening again to Marguerite Yourcenar: "In conversations with the prior, the words themselves are placed in the prior's field of reference, even when Zeno contradicts him, and we see only one face of the character, the angle of refraction and angle of incidence with its time[14]. It should not be forgotten that Diego's words - and therefore in part his thoughts - reflect or divert the questions of an investigation intended for the crown of Castile. The two signed texts in our possession, the *Description de Tlaxcala* and the *Histoire* , give us only one facet of the character, "the angle of refraction and the angle of incidence with his time". They compile direct or indirect answers inspired by the requests of the royal agents. It's a lot for this distant time and it's also very little[15].

In any case, it's enough to imagine the questions he wanted to answer, or that he asked himself. This conversation with Diego gives flesh to his writing. It helps to better distinguish what he actually said and what stems from my interventions and interpretations. This does not eliminate the risk of anachronistic or inappropriate questions. But what reading can be situated outside of time? We must keep this limit in mind, even take advantage of it, because the conditioning of today, our globalized world, encourages us to approach the past with another look.

To make Diego speak, we will be led to dismantle his texts, without reassembling the pieces in the sequence in which they reached us. Breaking the linear succession of his writings, confronting them with other passages, sometimes brings new or unexpected insights.

We will therefore distinguish between the themes on which Diego spoke and those he did not address. Even if it means imagining what is of the order of withholding information or simple political prudence in the face of oblivion or, even more impenetrable, the unthought. How to identify the intellectual and emotional limits of the character? How to cross the screens of his (false) modesty? How to separate what in a society, in a social environment and in a time is relevant from what is insignificant or accessory?

1. *Memoirs of a quiet young girl*, Paris, Gallimard, 1958, p. 63.

2. Gerónimo de Mendieta, *Historia eclesiástica indiana*, Joaquín García Icazbalceta ed., Mexico, Conaculta, t. I, 1997, p. 119.

3. Serge Gruzinski, *The Four Parts of the World. History of globalization*, Paris, La Martinière, 2004.

4. D1r°.

5. Serge Gruzinski, *The Time Machine. When Europe began to write the history of the world*, Paris, Fayard, 2017, p. 253-263.

6. On the manuscript, ms. Hunter 242, *Historia de Tlaxcala*, preserved in Glasgow, http://special.lib.gla.ac.uk/manuscripts/search/detail_c.cfm?ID=34997.[1]

7. Ana Díaz Serrano, "La república de Tlaxcala ante el rey de España", *Historia mexicana*, vol. 61, 3, January 2012, p. 1049-1107, here p. 1091.

8. The manuscript is kept in the Royal Library of the Escorial until the death of Philip II (1598). Passing from hand to hand, it ends up ending up in the library in Glasgow. It is a copy of an original that has now disappeared, lacking the signature of the *alcalde mayor*. It is likely that the author remained in possession of a copy, or even of the original that he would have reworked to write his *History of Tlaxcala* until 1592.

9. Charles Gibson, "The Identity of Diego Muñoz Camargo," *The Hispanic American Historical Review*, vol. 30, 2, May 1950, p. 203.

10. D1st. Sur les autres écrits de Diego Muñoz Camargo, see the introduction of the *Description of the city and province of Tlaxcala*, facsimile edition of the Glasgow manuscript with a preliminary study by René Acuña, Mexico, UNAM, 1981, p. 21-31.

11. Michel de Montaigne, *Essais*, Pierre Michel ed., t. II, Paris, Le Livre de poche, 1965, p. 43.

---

1. http://special.lib.gla.ac.uk/manuscripts/search/detail_c.cfm?ID=34997

12 . Marguerite Yourcenar, *Ouvres romanesques* , Paris, Gallimard, «La Pléiade», 1982, p. 536.

13 . *Ibid* ., p. 524.

14 . *Ibid* ., p. 875.

15 . Writings of Diego Muñoz Camargo are lost while he integrated into his *Description* pieces that do not belong to him. Here we have preferred to stick to its two major texts, the *History* being an amplification of the *Description...*

CHAPTER II

A mestizo in Tlaxcala

"To take a known, completed life, fixed (as much as they can ever be) by History, so as to embrace the entire curve at a single stroke. »

Marguerite Yourcenar, *Notebooks of "Memoirs of Hadrian"*[1].

In 1582 Diego resided in Tlaxcala. At this date, the Conquest is already only a distant memory. Most of its actors have disappeared from the scene: Hernán Cortés passed away in Spain in 1547, almost forty years earlier; his conquistadors and native allies preceded him or joined him in the grave. If they are still of this world, the men and women who were twenty years old at the time of the invasion are no longer very numerous nor very valiant.

In 1521, out of the ruins of Mexico City, the kingdom of New Spain arose with forceps. It integrates the indigenous province of Tlaxcala within a political entity of unprecedented dimensions: since 1580, the Catholic Monarchy has dominated Europe and part of the globe since the Spanish Empire and the Portuguese Empire are united under the same crown. . Tlaxcala like Seville and Lille, Antwerp like Naples and Milan, Goa like Macao and Manila obey King Philip II.

Where is Mexico in 1580?

The Spanish crown subjected the vanquished to a political and legal system, to institutions, to forms of economic exploitation, but also to a universe of certainties and beliefs of Iberian origin. The Church intervened in the colonization of minds and bodies [2]. Mexico has gone through unprecedented and simultaneous revolutions: the jump from the Neolithic to the Iron Age, the advent of the European image, and therefore the representation of three-dimensional space, the adoption of a expression based on alphabetic writing, books and printing. The insertion of the kingdom in the intercontinental circulations maintained by Iberian globalization is not the least of these upheavals. Its consequences are incalculable.

To tell the truth, indigenous Mexico never passively receives impositions from outside. In any case, the Spanish administration would not have the means to reproduce in America the institutions and policies that it exports from the Iberian Peninsula. In Mexico, as elsewhere, colonial society was the often chaotic product of diktats, adjustments and compromises that changed according to local power relations and impulses from across the Atlantic.

What world does Diego live in? The battle of Lepanto in 1571, the revolt of the Netherlands in 1579, the assassination of William the Silent in 1584, the hostility of Elizabeth who deals with the rebels of the Netherlands: such is, in broad strokes, the European context from which neither Mexico City nor provincial cities like Tlaxcala escape. The coasts of New Spain are increasingly dreaded by the Dutch and English corsairs who threaten the region of Veracruz, while other heretics already infest the lonely shores of Central America. Recently, Catholic Europe confronted Protestant Europe in the New World. On the other hand, Islam remains a distant scarecrow: until then, Barbary and Ottoman ships have spared the West Indies. But who knows what the future holds for them [3]?

In the other hemisphere, the road to China unfolds its irresistible charms like the sirens of the *Odyssey* : "Their watchword was 'Leaving for China' and so many decided to leave, because they knew that it was very rich and that there they would make a **fortune**. But the South Sea – the Pacific of the Spaniards – swallows up many candidates for fame and wealth.

How to behave in environments traversed and often upset by so many such brutal forces? Where do you stand when you belong to several worlds at the same time – to indigenous Mexico, New Spain and Iberian Europe – and when you navigate by sight within a society that emerges on heterogeneous bases, in partly ruined and apparently irreducible? To belong to two worlds like Diego is to be the product of two societies that conquest and colonization brutally juxtaposed, then inextricably intertwined. In fact, at a time when mestizos are still only a tiny minority of the population, all the inhabitants who occupy Mexican territory, whatever their origin, are part of several worlds: the Spaniards, who in their vast majority have, by force of circumstances, broken moorings with their native land, as much as the Indians, who find themselves subject to lifestyles, ways of believing, obeying and working resulting from an evolution millennium in which they took no part since it was played out on the other side of the Great Ocean.

A provincial town

It was in Tlaxcala that Diego was given the task of answering the Crown's questionnaire [5]. This city commands the indigenous province of the same name which extends to the west of the Valley of Mexico. Today, the arid and dry landscape hardly does justice to what dominated before the Conquest. In the 16th century, the eruption of large herds of ruminants introduced by the Spaniards quickly had harmful consequences. Often left to their own devices, these new beasts trample the cornfields. Elsewhere, they ruin the vegetation cover. However, according to Diego, in 1580, it was still "the most fertile province, the richest in corn, in other foods and in legumes, that exists in all of New Spain [6]". He exaggerates, but his painting is undoubtedly closer to the landscape he has before his eyes than to that which the tourist discovers today. Far to the east, beyond the mountains, the paths descend towards the tropical lands of the plain of Veracruz, bathed in the warm waters of the Gulf of Mexico. To the west stretches the rich Valley of Mexico where sit the colonial authorities, Audience and Viceroy [7].

Because the city is on the road to Mexico City, Tlaxcala hosted the conquistadors even before Moctezuma lodged them in Mexico City-Tenochtitlan. After the first rather violent exchanges, the well-understood interests of the invaders and the Tlaxcaltecs dictate an alliance which will reserve for the latter a leading role in the crushing of Tenochtitlan and the conquest of Mexico. The nobles of Tlaxcala played the card of what we would today call collaboration, without anticipating the irreversible consequences of their engagement alongside the invaders. Once the dice have been cast and Mexico submitted to Spain, all that remains is for them to exploit this card which assigns them a unique status within of the American possessions of Castile. A status based on privileges which spared the province the tribute paid by the rest of the Amerindian world, which guaranteed it its own indigenous administration and which held more or less – and, over time, less and less – of the Spaniards and the Europeans at a distance respectful of the lands and resources of the region. Officially, Tlaxcala depends directly on the Crown, but it pays contributions to the Church, to the convents, and participates in particular in the construction of the first cathedral of Puebla.

16th century town is a recent creation. It dates back to an initiative of the Franciscans who founded a Spanish-style settlement along the Zahuatl River. According to Diego's calculations, the city has occupied its site for about forty-five years [8]. It was in the 1540s that the new town of Tlaxcala became the capital of the province and hosted a government entrusted to a necessarily indigenous governor and to representatives of the four main seigniories. Between the pre-Hispanic past and the 1580s, therefore, a first colonial past had already slipped in, which began to screen between the realities of the moment and the events of the Conquest. A timeline to keep in mind to understand Diego and the games of his memory.

Order reigns in Tlaxcala

As in the rest of the country, the indigenous population of Tlaxcala is not homogeneous. The common people rub shoulders with families of notables and clans of aristocrats. In 1541, when Diego was still a child, it is calculated that more than 3,000 *principals* – notables – lived in the province [9].

The Tlaxcaltec political system contrasts with that of other Mexican lordships. To the point of attracting the attention of European observers very early on and prompting descriptions as idealized than reductive. In the compilation he devotes to the geopolitics of the world, the Augustinian monk Jerónimo Román y Zamora proclaims his admiration for the pre-Hispanic city: "The Republic of Tlaxcala is not governed by a monarch, that is to say by a king, but by the aristocracy, it is a government of the good and the few. It was divided into four cantons or seigneuries [...]. From these four seigniories or from their families came those who ordinarily applied the laws and ordinances taken by the ancestors [10]. Note that the word "canton" also appears in Román's pen when he describes the Switzerland of his time. In Tlaxcala, conversion to the Christian faith only confirmed these good principles by adding a new practice: elections. These take place every first of the year in a recollected atmosphere: the day before, Vespers of the Holy Spirit are sung, "with strong vocal and instrumental music", and the next day the monks celebrate a solemn mass. The lucky ones are led to the church to the accents of the hymn of the Holy Spirit. For Román, before and after the Conquest, order and peace reign in Tlaxcala [11].

The old local elites – "the very noble lords, governor, *alcaldes* and *regidores* of this city [12]" – maintain solid positions. In principle, political power is concentrated in the hands of a town council, made up of natives who elect to positions of responsibility the candidates of their choice. During the 16th century, the elites reserved for themselves all the charges that the Crown introduced by imprinting their style on the structures that were imposed on them. In pre-Hispanic times, the territory was divided into at least four major sectors (*cabeceras*), each endowed with a local dynasty. Since the 1540s, as we have seen, the heads of these four houses monopolize the management positions within the municipality: these are the *regidores perpetuos* . The other members are elected. The title of governor rotates every two years between the representatives of these four *cabeceras* , during elections which mobilize an electorate of more than two hundred notables. Despite everything, the Castilian sovereign had the last word, in the person of his viceroy and his representative in the province, the *alcalde mayor* , who confirmed the lucky winner.

This form of tetrarchy was to last until the end of the century. She oversees an impressive number of civil servants, all of whom are also indigenous. Among these notables, many devote most of their time to politics and administration by being in turn *alcalde, regidor* , governor. We imagine them busy negotiating and deliberating in the great hall of the municipal chamber under the gaze of the Virgin and Saint John. They tame day by day this insidious manifestation of Westernization: the colonial bureaucracy. This one, fussy, has nothing to envy to its Castilian model: it was ground in the decades which precede the drafting of the geographical relationship. Notables are not children. Indian or not, a penny (*tomín*) is a penny. The slightest request from the *alcalde mayor* is examined with a magnifying glass, whether it concerns the hiring of a servant or a cook. Nothing gets done for nothing: this is what the indigenous authorities tirelessly plead, demanding from 1555 a salary, even modest, for the governor, the alcaldes, the four *representatives* of the seigniorial houses and all the *regidores* [13]. In exchange, everyone applies to follow the same code of conduct: there is no question, under penalty of a fine, of disclosing the content of the deliberations to the outside world. The duty of reserve is a golden rule. Nor is there any question of a woman claiming the title of *tlatoani* and leading a stately home (*teccali*). Cost what it may, the old order must be maintained [14].

Can we pierce what this European facade conceals? The king, the viceroy as the four representatives stately homes are given the title of *tlatoani* . A way of translating the Spanish word *señor* , still imbued with the resonances of pre-Hispanic power. *Tequitl* designates the charge, the office, exercised by both native officials and Spanish representatives of the Crown. Both *Tequitl and tlatoani* connote forms of social organization, work organization and responsibility inherited from the world before the Conquest [15]. Moreover, it is enough to observe the way in which bureaucracy and elections operate today in any Latin American country to understand that the Tlaxcaltec notables are anything but doubles of their Castilian counterparts.

Rules and principles do not prevent all sorts of infractions and irregularities which can, in extreme cases, lead to the dismissal of the native governor [16]. The city council nevertheless exercises considerable influence, even if necessary to oppose a decision by Madrid or Mexico City. It manages its own funds and keeps its assets in funds provided for this purpose, the most important of which is the safe with five keys shared by notables and *alcalde mayor* [17].

It was with this young bureaucracy, braced on its privileges but ready for many arrangements, that Diego shared quite a few years of his life. This circle of notables has representatives throughout the province and maintains daily relations with the colonial administration, the *alcalde mayor* , his notaries and his interpreters, including Diego. From 1567, Diego held this office at the court of the *alcalde mayor* [18] and attended the discussions that we have just mentioned, enough to learn about the games of local power and to see successive generations. But the municipality also cultivates close contacts with the capital of New Spain, where she is represented by a Spanish prosecutor and lawyers. Its members, moreover, do not hesitate to travel each time an important question has to be submitted to the viceroy. As Tlaxcala claims to depend only on the Crown, the trip to Spain is the last resort: it will be practiced several times during the century. All this is expensive, but the municipal council is not without means.

A world of notables

Who is Diego dealing with when he writes his relationship? In 1583, the native governor came from Ocutelulco, one of the four great stately houses. His name is Antonio Mocallio de Guevara and will be part of the delegation that will embark for Madrid with Diego the following year. In 1585, when the seat of governor returns to the *head* of Tizatlán, it is Pablo de Galicia who assumes the function, which he has already occupied before. Pablo is another veteran of local politics: more than twenty years earlier, he too had had the privilege of leading a Tlaxcaltec embassy to the court (1562).

This world of notables, about half a thousand people counting the wives, more with the offspring, still has beautiful properties, vassals, criados, servants *and* servants full of their households. All practice the race for privileges: carry a sword, prance on horseback or on the back of a donkey, dress in Spanish style. We don't just show off: we generally know how to read, write, we speak Castilian – the most curious know a little Latin – and, above all, we get along with the young colonial society. These nobles are of course the first to face the changes caused by the westernization of the country, but also the first to benefit from them. They did not wait for the Spaniards to engage in commercial activities: the lord of one of the four great houses, Maxixcatzin, bore the traditional title of "lord of the market" because he levied taxes (alcabalas *)* on everything that sells in the market established in front of his palace, "and other rents in accordance with their ancient privileges ."

Around the four great houses of Tlaxcala gravitates a mass of lesser nobles whose fate is highly variable. Some do better than others maintaining all sorts of relationships with Spaniards and mestizos. Witness Diego.

– *There are also ruined nobles who hardly survive?*

– Even if they are very poor, they reject manual trades as well as low and vile trades, they avoid at all costs carrying loads, digging the ground with a kind of hoe (coas) or *spades* ; they maintain that they are *hidalgos* , that they don't have to engage in these crude activities, that they can only serve in war and defend the borders, like hidalgos, *and* die fighting.

– *These families cling to the memory of their ancestors and to the services rendered to the Crown in the past...*

– They claim that they are *hidalgos* and knights from the beginning. They claim that they are even more so now that they have converted to the true God and become Christians and vassals of the Emperor Don Carlos, King of Castile.

– *On what do they base their claims?*

– They also helped [the emperor] to win and conquer the full extent and power of this New World; they brought him the rights they had over the Mexicas [20] so that he would become their universal king and lord. This is why they would be *hidalgos* and knights [21].

" *Is all this really serious?"*

– This virtuous madness, it lasts and persists until today. I'll spare you other bravado, other craziness, because they never stop wanting to show off [22].

" *Locura virtuosa* ": the expression and its context make one think of the delusions of the knight Don Quixote, even if Cervantés has not yet written his masterpiece. Perhaps we should see there the indirect and distant influence of Erasmus and his *Praise of Madness* which haunts many European writers, starting in Spain with that of the author of *Quixote* [23].

On these fallen nobles, Diego casts a look tinged with irony and sometimes condescension. Our man appreciates the native aristocracy when it is still rich and powerful. When she declines, her aspirations for him are reduced to pure boasting. But the setbacks of some are the happiness of others. Commoners present themselves for what they are not. The notables of the council must redouble their vigilance to prevent the rise of upstarts, of

Indian or European origin. Suspicious, they got into the habit of closely examining the pedigree of candidates for positions of responsibility [24].

The small people of macehuales

As everywhere, the native masses constituted the vast majority and suffered the upheavals of the Conquest, even if the privileged status of the province cushioned the harshest blows. The difficulties encountered by the nobility and the local aristocracy have repercussions on the much less protected working classes.

When in 1567 the viceroy demanded that the Tlaxcaltecs build churches and monasteries everywhere, the elites welcomed the government's order while warning that there was no question of them paying the workers themselves since these works are carried out for them and in their interest: will these arrangements not facilitate their access to the mass and the sacraments? In any case, the nobles are categorically opposed to the coffers of the "republic" – those for which they are responsible and from which some do not hesitate to dip – being put to use. Paternalistic and Christian, the council nevertheless took care not to overload the *macehuales with work* , and for good reason: they would risk neglecting the work in the fields, in which case the income of the authorities and the native nobles would suffer immediately. Nor is there any question of embarking on spectacular works – "the churches and monasteries will remain modest" – since there should not be more than two or three religious in places. These authorities, so reasonable, moreover hasten to take advantage of the new religious policy of regional planning to keep the plebs away from the elites: only the nobles will have the right to live in the vicinity of the monasteries and to benefit from a privileged relationship with the religious. If the *macehuales* decided to join them, the consequences would be disastrous: "They would abandon their nopals, their magueys and their fields, and then everything would become wasteland [25] . That is to say how well the elites get along in diverting or distorting the Christianization promoted by the Crown and by the Church.

The bulk of the indigenous population consists of *macehuales* , the "villains" for Diego. These environments are very composite. Farmers, craftsmen, locals, but also "foreigners", Indians emigrated from neighboring lands, from Mexico City, Cholula or Texcoco, rub shoulders there. The last native slaves were freed in 1537 [26]. They were the lowest layer. Between the nobility and the *macehuales* is inserted an intermediate category whose members claim a relationship with the noble families [27]. Little is known about the rights and obligations of these servants or *criados* . Finally, the heterogeneity is also ethnic: the province is mainly populated by Nahuas, related to the Mexicas, but areas are inhabited by Otomies and Mazahuas.

In the 1580s, the little people no longer held their own. Not that native society was more stable before the Conquest. The turbulent story told by Diego makes it impossible to idealize the pre-Hispanic reality, but the upheavals caused by the invasion shook the positions acquired everywhere. They have shaken individuals as much as communities. The image of the plebeian from all eternity attached to the earth and to his condition is crumbling. The luckiest, admittedly a minority, achieve relative ease and distance themselves from their former lords. Others simply abandon their village and their fields to go and earn their *tortillas* in nearby towns, Puebla or Tlaxcala. They prefer to sell their labor power in the proliferating workshops. In 1580, the Indian Lucas Suchitlame worked in the *obraje* of a Spaniard, Francisco Lopez, to repay a debt of 6 pesos in common gold. He signed up for six years, but at the end of the contract his boss refused to release him and to pay him the 100 pesos to which the salary accumulated over these years amounted. As for thousands of other natives, his job is to work the wool; this employment propelled him into the new colonial economy which dictated working conditions, freed the individual from his community obligations and often left him alone in the face of the demands, even the abuses, of the Spanish master. In Mexico, it happens that these workers of a new kind do not let themselves be taken. Some learn the tortuous ways of royal justice. Sometimes they win: Lucas obtains an order from the viceroy so that one examines its situation and that one returns to him justice [28].

The case is not isolated, as evidenced in this same year 1580 by disputes that broke out in Puebla, the Spanish city founded about thirty kilometers from

Tlaxcala [29]. In this new city, the *macehuales* managed to come out of their isolation and to organize themselves to protest to the authorities of Mexico against the abuses of which they were victims. These urban Indians no longer have any nobles on their backs. They now escaped their secular grip, but their young freedom exposed them to the forms of exploitation, often brutal, imposed by colonial capitalism [30].

Even in Tlaxcala, in a partially preserved indigenous setting, the plebs do not live out of time. She knows that there is a new world, that of salaried work, money, loans, sales to the highest bidder, a new contractual regime governed by habits, laws and privileges introduced by Europeans. .

The epidemics

This same plebs is hit hard by epidemics. Although not very reliable, the figures of the XVI E century reveal the extent of the demographic collapse which sweeps the region: 120,000 fires in 1519, half in 1538, more than 40,000 tributaries in 1569 and only 24,000 in 1583, the time of writing the report. Low water will be reached in 1626 with just under 9,000 fires [31]. In number of inhabitants, it is estimated that there were perhaps half a million Indians when the Spaniards arrived. The population then falls to 250,000 in the 1520s to remain more or less at this level for about fifty years. The decline in housing confirms the trend. It is calculated that between 1557 and 1623, 70% of the villages of the province were wiped off the map, but the decline certainly began immediately after the Conquest. In total, 90% of the Tlaxcaltec population would have disappeared between 1531 and 1648 [32].

The cruelty of the figures speaks for itself. In waves, epidemics of smallpox, measles and *matlazahuatl* (typhus) ravaged the indigenous populations. The most virulent frame the period of writing of the *Description of Tlaxcala* : one in 1576 and the other in 1586 and 1587. Diego writes between these two disasters which last several years. These epidemics seem so inevitable that they do not cause in him any particular emotion, except that the high mortality of the Indians becomes a characteristic feature of the local populations.

– *Why did the Indian population collapse?*

– The first is that because of the wars and the conquests there was a lack of many Indians and that they found themselves populating different provinces; the second is linked to the great epidemics which occurred after the arrival of the Spaniards.

– *Which were those which most affected New Spain?*

– The first is that of smallpox [33], brought and spread by the Negro of Pánfilo de Narváez, which contaminated all of New Spain. It happened in 1519. The natives say that ditches and ravines were littered with corpses. It was one of the biggest epidemics in the world. It is also for this reason that the war in Mexico ended earlier, as the epidemic struck the weak and the sick who had barely recovered. A second outbreak was the deadliest imaginable. It ruined and annihilated villages and hamlets which today are nothing but wasteland. It broke out in 1545. The third was that of 1576. I cannot say which was the most serious [34].

- *But still?*

– I say that the first must have been the most devastating, because there were more people; the second, too, was very important because the country was still intact. The last was not as strong as the first because, although many people died, many also escaped thanks to the remedies given to them by the Spaniards and the religious.

– *How can this relative decline in the disease be explained?*

– To the arrangements made by Don Martín Enríquez, the viceroy of this New Spain; he ordered judges to be sent throughout the country to look after the health of the Indians. Great care was therefore taken to care for them body and soul with fasts, prayers, processions and public penances until it pleased the Divine Majesty that such a great epidemic should cease, as it has ceased. , whom God sent to the world for our sins.

– *Do diseases alone explain these hecatombs?*

– This decrease has other causes, such as the multitude of slaves that they extracted from these lands to send them to work in the gold mines and in the islands. Let's add personal service, early abuse, and today's *coatequitles* .

– Coatequitles *, is that a word of indigenous origin?*

- So. In their world of yesteryear, the Indians did not leave their lands, they did not change temperature, they did not pass through other climatic zones: those from cold lands did not go to hot lands, nor those from hot in cold lands. And they maintained in good health by remaining in their natural environment. Now, in our days, this rule is no longer observed. The Indians are in constant contact with each other, and in order to go to distant lands they pass through all kinds of provinces, which is why there is a huge shortage of people. The population is in free fall, it is in sharp decline.

– *You mean that* coatequitl *designates a form of forced labor to which labor is forced out of its natural habitat.*

“Today, many people claim to be noble! »

The Indians fleeing the countryside did not only settle in the Spanish city of Puebla. The development of the city of Tlaxcala in the middle of the 16th century attracted natives from all over the province and even from further afield [35], such as the Valley of Mexico. However, from the middle of the century, another immigration was added to the previous one. Europeans do everything to settle in the province, despite the laws that exclude them. Many farmers, but also breeders, millers and carters. “They came to settle in convenient neighborhoods and in places that lend themselves to contact between people and to business with the Spaniards, merchants and traders [36] . »

How to stem these intrusions, ever more frequent and wilder? The common people are practically defenceless, but in the middle of the century the native municipality still possesses the legal means and the energy to oppose these invasions. She brandishes the privileges granted by the Crown in the face of newcomers who, for their part, mobilize support in the capital of the kingdom or distant Castile. Some Spaniards even were quick to establish their residence in the city of Tlaxcala [37].

The effects of the foreign presence are parasitizing the traditional organization of work and injecting the poison of money into all strata of the population. Nothing illustrates this better than the intensive production of a scarlet red dye from an insect, the cochineal.

The cochineal boom had a corrosive impact on the social order, strongly denounced by the indigenous authorities. Resellers (*regatones*) scour the markets and invest the houses of the peasants who collect the insects nested on the prickly pears. They enlist a female workforce to support them in their collections. These Indians are introduced more easily among farmers. Attracted by the proposed payment, the farmers develop their cochineal production to the detriment of their harvests of corn or peppers. It is as much lost for the nobles whose subsistence depends on the work of their vassals. The most active of these small entrepreneurs made a fortune, bought luxury foodstuffs – cocoa, wine imported from Castile – and, shockingly, slept on soft cotton mattresses. For the municipality of Tlaxcala, it's the end of the world: "Here everywhere there are lots of people claiming to be noble [38] ! Absolute horror for aristocrats who want things to change at all costs in order not to change. Not all poor people get richer, far from it, but money triggers the most irreversible of acculturations.

1. Yourcenar (1982), p. 519.

2. Serge Gruzinski, *The War of Images from Christopher Columbus to " Blade Runner ", 1492-2019* , Paris, Fayard, 1990.

3. Id., *what time is it there? America and Islam on the Edge of Modern Times* , Paris, Seuil, 2008.

4. Juan Suárez de Peralta, *Tratado del descubrimiento de las Indias y conquista* , Giorgio Perissinotto ed., Madrid, Alianza Editorial, 1990, p. 183.

5. Gibson (1950), p. 195-208.

6. D3r°.

7 . 7. The Audience of Mexico is a court made up of judges (or auditors) who rule the country on the sides of the viceroy.

8. D7v°.

9. Charles Gibson, *The West in the Sixteenth Century* , Stanford, Stanford University Press, 1952, p. 143.

10. Jerome Roman and Zamora, *Republics of the World* , Part III, Salamanca, Juan Fernandez, 1595, fol. 158r°.

11. *Ibid* ., fol. 158v°.

12. Eustaquio Celestine Solis *et al.* (ed.), *Acta de cabildo de Tlaxcala, 1547-1567* , Mexico, AGN et Tlaxcalteca Institute of Culture, 1985, p. 419.

13. *Ibid* ., p. 349.

14. *Ibid* ., p. 351.

15. *Ibid.* , p. 350, 352.

16. Gibson (1952), p. 105-106.

17. The system began to falter in the 1590s: Diego's son gave it the coup de grace by acceding to the functions of governor in 1608, although he was not a native (ibid., p. 107) .

18. Celestino Solís (1985), p. 419.

19. D7v°.

20. The Indians of Mexico-Tenochtitlan, in other words our "Aztecs".

21. Diego Muñoz Camargo, *History of Tlaxcala* , Alfredo Chavero ed., Mexico, 1947, p. 115-116, dorénavant C115-116 ; Gibson (1952), p. 143.

22. D126r°.

23. Francisco López-Muñoz *et al* ., «Crazy and insane in Cervantes literature: about Cervantes' medical sources on neuropsychiatric matters», *Revista de neurologia* , t. 46, 8, January 2008, https://www.researchgate.net/publication/237829597_Locos_y_dementes_en_la_literatura_cervantina_a_proposito_de_las_fuentes_medic [1]

24. Celestino Solís (1985), p. 26-34.

25. *Ibid* ., p. 421 422 .

26. Gibson (1952), p. 144 ; or somewhat later according to Celestino Solís (1985).

27. Celestine Solis (1985), p. 351 - 352 .

28. Silvio Zavala et Maria Costelo éd., *Sources for the History of Labor in New Spain* , t. II, Mexico, CEHSMO, 1960, p. 319-3

29. *Ibid* ., p. 198 , 368 ,

30. *Ibid* ., p. 290.

1. https://www.researchgate.net/publication/237829597_Locos_y_dementes_en_la_literatura_cervantina_a_proposito_de_las_fuentes_medicas_de_Cervantes_en_materia_neuropsiquiatrica

31 . Peter Gerhard, *A Guide to the Historical Geography of New Spain* , Cambridge, Cambridge University Press, 1972, p. 325.

32 . Wolfgang Trautmann, « Examination of the Depopulation Process in Tlaxcala during the Colonial Period », *Communications* , t. 7, Puebla, German Foundation for Scientific Research, 1973, p. 102.

33 . Diego spells " *smallpox* ", but it's hard to identify with certainty the pathologies ravaging the country.

34 . D35v°.

35 . Gibson (1952), p. 143.

36 . D5r°.

37 . David M. Szewczyk, "New Elements in the Society of Tlaxcala, 1519-1618," in Ida Altman and James Lockhart eds., *Provinces of Early Mexico: Variants of Spanish American Regional Evolution* , Los Angeles, UCLA, Latin American Center Publications, University of California Press, 1976, p. 139.

38 . Celestino Solís (1985), p. 339, no ˙ 492: "En todas partes de Tlaxcala muchas personas pretenden ser pilli. »

CHAPTER III

Who is Diego Muñoz Camargo?

"Each conversation is a way of adding to the model of the character. »

Marguerite Yourcenar, *Notebooks of "L'Œuvre au noir"* [1].

– *Do you like short-haired dogs?*

– I currently have some of this breed. They are really very weird. You have to see them [...]. By nature, they do not have any kind of hair. In the world of old, there were many of [them].

- But these dogs are not your favorite meat?

– Less than thirty years ago [= 1550], I remember, there were still butcheries of dogs: they were sacrificed and their hearts were removed from the left side as in the sacrifices. We notified the authorities and arranged for it to be terminated [3].

– *You are a meat lover and it is one of your only tastes that you mention.*

– Some believe that the meats of the Indies are not as firm or as tasty as those of Castile.

– *What should we think?*

– The meat of animals raised in hot lands has little flavor and less consistency, because it does not hold together not. But the meats that come from the Cold Land or the Chichimec region, beef or mutton, are as good and tasty as those eaten in Madrid, Valladolid or Medina del Campo.

– *How do you know?*

– I don't want to talk about it as someone who [like me] has seen and tried both. It is the lack of meat in Castile that prevents the appreciation of tastier flesh. We do not know the abundance of meat that is the rule in New Spain [4].

Diego's writings drop here and there information that one would seek in vain from other witnesses of the sixteenth century . Enough to get closer to the character's intimacy and illuminate his face for a moment, too little to go around and embrace "the whole man [5]".

Father's name

sixteenth - century Mexico , especially in the province of Tlaxcala. One of them belongs to the native aristocracy and holds the office of governor three times. Others are Spaniards or mestizos. Ours is the son of a conquistador, Diego Muñoz, therefore of a Spaniard.

Diego senior landed in Mexico following Gonzalo de Salazar whom Charles V named postman, that is to say tax collector for New Spain [6]. Diego senior took part in the conquest of the country by campaigning in Jalisco, Honduras (Higueras) and the Zapotec lands. It is claimed that he was involved in the poisoning of a high official whom the Crown had sent to investigate the conduct of Hernán Cortés: the *juez de residencia* Ponce de Léon. The conquistador's friends had every interest in eliminating this cumbersome character. It is very probably Diego senior who took charge of the dirty work and it is he who will be accused of having offered the creams and cheeses that got the better of the judge. If he does not grow it, this political past has undoubtedly served him.

The family's first ties with Tlaxcala are the affair of the father. Back from Honduras, the colonial authorities instructed him to repatriate the Tlaxcaltec auxiliaries who had fought alongside the conquistadors to their homes. This first contact with the Tlaxcaltec world did not prevent him from settling in Mexico City, in the shadow of power. Like any self-respecting Spaniard, he maintains liaisons with Indian women who give him at least two mixed-race children, our Diego and his brother Juan [7].

The young Diego is a mestizo, but the sources of the 16th century avoid presenting him as such. At the beginning of the following century, the Franciscan Juan de Torquemada, who must have known him, identified him as "a native of Tlaxcala", without a word more [8]. On the other hand, historians of the 18th and 20th centuries make him a native cacique. Let us remember that he was very probably born in Tlaxcala around 1529, that he was brought up in Mexico City, where he shared the games of his brothers, legitimate or not, and that the label of mestizo attributed to him generally does not go without saying.

– During your childhood, an adventure happened to you which reveals that, even in the capital of the country, in the middle of the 1530s, idolatry had not said its last word and that it could still show itself agressive.

– It happened in Mexico City, fourteen years after Cortés conquered the country. I crossed the native quarters with other Spanish children. Indians painted red ran after us, and out of six or seven of us, they captured one of our comrades and carried him off. We were never able to find **him**.

- What was his fate?

"Whether it was him or others, they kidnapped everyone they could to eat them or make them Indians.

– Ten years after the Conquest, Indians, probably priests since their bodies were painted, still practiced human sacrifices in the heart of New Spain.

– In the time of paganism, those who fasted wore black clothes and painted their own bodies black or red [10].

" *But stealing children to turn them into little Indians seems even more confusing. Could adults also be victims of these acts?*

– They killed the Spaniards who traveled alone and consumed them in secret without anyone ever being able to know anything about them again. Until we get it sorted [...]. So we took great care of ours. Wherever they went, their destination and place of residence were recorded. They were described as old as they were, whether they went on foot or on horseback, the clothes they wore and what color they were.

– A report before the letter... Two years later, in 1537, you are seven or eight years old, and you are entrusted with the religious education of a group of

Indians who arrived from Florida with Cabeza de Vaca and Andrés Dorantes 11 after their famous odyssey through what would become the southern United States of America

– Indians followed them out of friendship from the interior of the country. And they brought over thirty of them to Mexico City. It was from these Indians that I learned the catechism and the holy prayers so that they could be baptized, because I had received the charge of them, still a child, very young page that I was [13].

– *You took the opportunity to learn things about Florida and develop your theory on the Jewish origin of the Indians.*

– I often spoke with Cabeza de Vaca, with Castillo Maldonado, with the black Esteban, who was *ladino* [14] and a man of great common sense, and with Andrés Dorantes, about the things of this region and their peregrination. I learned, especially with Andrés Dorantes, how clearly and obviously they had found the name "Ruben [15]" in use in certain provinces.

When Diego catechized the Florida Indians, he was a page. The task supposes that he was attached to a superior, an ecclesiastic or a Spanish notable [16]. Like so many other young natives of good birth, Diego was taken in hand by the Franciscans of Mexico or Tlaxcala. The monks used to employ these teenagers in their evangelistic campaigns. In any case, the task entrusted to him reveals an astonishing precocity and personality for this age, even if he is only asked to escort neophytes to mass and make them recite their prayers, Pater Noster and *Ave* Maria . , before the baptism ceremony [17].

In his childhood or later, did Diego meet another celebrity from Tlaxcala, Diego Valadés, born like him in the 1530s, son like him of a conquistador (and perhaps also of an Indian) [18]? This other Diego passed through the Franciscan monasteries, but the order did not let him go and made him one of its own. His career benefited from the support of Pierre de Gand, a Flemish cleric related to Charles V, whose ascendancy over the Church of

New Spain was then considerable. Thanks to which the Franciscan Diego Valadés will experience a meteoric rise that will take him to Spain, France and Rome. Around 1565-1567, he stayed in Tlaxcala, where he could meet our Diego [19]. Tlaxcala leads to everything.

Diego's father invested himself in the construction of a country that arose from odds and ends on the rubble of pre-Hispanic Mexico. Like so many others, once the fighting was over, he turned to business and went into administration: the viceroy entrusted him with the management of the *haciendas reales* in the Puebla region and appointed him *corregidor* of Nopaluca, a town nestled today on the border of the states of Tlaxcala and Puebla. Breeding tempts him. Soon he is a breeder of herds around Tlaxcala; in the middle of the century, everything suggests that he shares the operation of his ranch with his son Diego. The ex-conquistador would have owned some 40,000 heads of sheep. Anxious to improve his livestock, he exploits his relations with the power in place. By crossing his sheep with merino cattle introduced to Mexico by the Viceroy Mendoza, he obtains a wool appreciated by his compatriots [20]. Her son is forming by her side.

Diego, "natural from Tlaxcala"

Years later, Diego settles in Tlaxcala, his hometown. There he married a noble Indian, Leonor Vázquez, who gave him a son and a daughter. In 1573, Leonor appeared with him in a real estate transaction, a sign that this woman, never mentioned by her husband, came from an influential and wealthy family [21].

The Spanish blood he inherited from his father barred his access to the functions of native governor, but not to the Castilian bureaucracy: he became lieutenant of the *alcalde mayor* , acted as official interpreter and tax collector. Thanks to his father, Diego is also a breeder who sells the meat and skins he produces. All this does not prevent him from engaging in various commercial activities, including the sale of real estate.

He adds a string to his bow: the food industry. In a country where consumer needs and habits are changing, this sector can only attract him. At the end of the century, the Crown grants him a concession in the north of the province of Tlaxcala, on the road which leads to Veracruz, to exploit saltworks, where he creates a company in San Juan Iztacmaxtitlan [22]. This requires workers to extract the salt, roads and carts to transport it, intermediaries to sell it on the markets. Salt, which allows the carcasses of animals to be preserved longer, is of major interest in a region which was deprived of it when it was subject to the blockade. imposed by the Mexicas at the time of their greatness. The common people had grown accustomed to doing without it. With the fall of Mexico City, the blockade was just a bad memory and many Tlaxcaltecs rediscovered the taste and benefits of salt [23]. By keeping an eye on the town's slaughterhouses – in 1576, his brother Juan was "butchery inspector [24]" – the Muñoz Camargo family dominated the chain that led from the large breeder to the consumer. For all these activities, Diego surrounds himself with an abundant workforce: black slaves are active in his service at the same time as teams of Indians whom he recruits by contract. Unquestionably,

Diego is one of the five or six big entrepreneurs in the province of Tlaxcala [25]
.

To which is added the organization of the Tlaxcaltec embassy which visits Philip II in the 1580s. His qualities as an interpreter and his interpersonal skills predispose him to this. Logically, the Indian government appoints him as its *procurador* . This trip to Spain does not sound the end of Diego's career, even if, in June 1589, the colonial authorities order that he be expelled from Tlaxcala, he, his brothers and other mestizos accused of exploiting the Indians [26]. But, to all appearances, the measure will never be applied.

In 1591, Diego was named "provider and general distributor of land in the colonization of northern New Spain" and founded San Miguel Mezquitic de la Nueva Tlaxcala Tepeticpac. A new role was assigned to him, that of exporter of Tlaxcaltec troops and manpower to the northern border. Viceroy Luis de Velasco entrusted him with the preparation of the expedition which brought together several hundred families. He will also take care of the distribution of land between Tlaxcaltecs and Chichimecs.

Diego died around 1600. He was about seventy years old, an advanced age for the time. He is probably buried in Tlaxcala in the Convent of San Francisco, where his relatives should eventually join him.

Diego has also worked for the future: his son (also named Diego, as if the first name were hereditary) will make a beautiful marriage by marrying the noblest heiress of the city, Francisca Pimentel Maxixcatzin. Francisca united in her person two prestigious houses, the Pimentel of Texcoco, one of the former capitals of the Triple Alliance [27], and the Maxixcatzin of Ocotelulco. The Maxixcatzin are one of the four great families of Tlaxcala. In 1608, Francisca's husband became governor of Tlaxcala, a title hitherto reserved for the native nobility. By receiving this charge from the viceroy, Diego junior reached the top of the provincial hierarchy, an irrefutable sign of the rise of new men and the irreversible decline of the old aristocracy [28]. His Métis origins should have barred his access. They are the ones who opened it to him. Unquestionably, a posthumous victory for the author of the *Description of Tlaxcala* .

Métis, Indian or Spaniard [29] ?

About the "ethnicity" of Diego, one evoked an "identity neither accepted nor assumed [30]". It remains to be seen if this "ethnicity" has any meaning in the sixteenth century and if identity is anything other than a question that we project centuries back because it haunts us today. In the name of what should Diego accept or assume his "ethnicity"?

First evidence: Diego never appears as half-breed. He always has a word in his mouth, "ours", to designate the Spanish camp. Why doesn't he have an interest in advancing his Métis origin? Because, in his world, the word has a negative connotation. From the years 1540-1550, the children of Spaniards and Indians, born in the horrors of the Conquest and the post-war period, reached adulthood, and a systematic mistrust developed against these new members of colonial society. In 1554, the country's highest authority, Viceroy Luis de Velasco, wrote worse than hanging half-breeds from the crown: Blacks have everything to fear [31]. Half-breeds are therefore no longer seen as children without a future, left to fend for themselves and "lost among the Indians " [32], but as potential criminals, of the ilk of blacks, who are most of the time slaves. These mestizos without family, without resources and without education are said to wallow in idleness. They pose a threat that worries the viceroys. Those who hang around in the native villages must be handed over to their parents so that they may be educated in "Spanish urbanity (*policía*)" and "take a love for the things of our homeland ." Despite this, in the middle of the 16th century , half-breeds as well as Indians were barred from entering the newly created university.

How can we be surprised that Diego was in no hurry to claim this quality? And that those who refer to him qualify him purely and simply as " *natural of Tlaxcala* "? It will be remembered that biological crossbreeding, for us obvious, can be erased when the crossbreed in question is, by his social position, very close to the best Castilian society. His network of relations, which now remains to be explored, made him a Spaniard in the eyes of all. He also knows that he could, by bad luck, have fallen over to the other side, like his little comrades who disappeared in the suburbs of Mexico City, caught up in the native environment, when they didn't end up in the stomachs of their kidnappers.

1. Yourcenar (1982), p. 858.

2. C167; D153v°.

3. C168.

4. C277.

5. Montaigne (1965), t. II, p. 55.

6. « House of Diego Muñoz, father of the Muñoses of Tlaxcala », Baltazar Dorrantes de Carranza, *Summary relation of things in New Spain* , Mexico, Jesus Medina ed., 1970, p. 278.

7. Dorantes de Carranza ne lui donne que deux fils métis sans dire un mot d'un quelconque mariage; Marilyn Miller, "Covert Mestizaje and the Strategy of Passing in Diego Munoz Camargo's *Historia de Tlaxcala* ," *Colonial Latin American Review* , vol. VI, 1, 1997, p. 41-57, https://www.tandfonline.com/doi/abs/10.1080/10609169708569907.[1]

8. Juan de Torquemada, *Monarquía indiana* , Mexico, UNAM, 1975, t. II, p. 247.

9. D217v°.

10. D77v°.

11. Alvar Núñez Cabeza de Vaca recounted their endless journey through the *Naufragios* (*Travel Relation* , Actes Sud, 1999).

12. Manuel Carrera Stampa, « Indigenous Historians and Novo-Hispanic Mestizos. Sixteenth and seventeenth centuries », *Spanish journal of American anthropology* , Madrid, vol. 6, 1971, p. 205-244, https://journals.ucm.en/index.php/REAA/article/view/REAA7171110205A [2]; Gabriel Cárdenas Z. Cano, *Chronological Essay for the General History of Florida* , 1829, Madrid, Sons of Doña Catalina Piñuela, p. 104 ; D82r°-82v°.

13. *Ibid.*

14. D'esprit vif and speaking Spanish.

---

1. https://www.tandfonline.com/doi/abs/10.1080/10609169708569907

2. https://revistas.ucm.es/index.php/REAA/article/view/REAA7171110205A

15. The tribe of Reuben is one of the twelve tribes of Israel.

16. The chronicler Suárez de Peralta recounts the tragic story of Arrutia, "a young mestizo so vile that he didn't even deserve to be a page" (1990, p. 213).

17. Andrea Martínez Baracs, *Un gobierno de indios: Tlaxcala, 1519-1750* , Mexico City, FCE, 2008, p. 116.

18. Esteban Palomera, *Fray Diego Valades, ofm Evangelizador Humanista de la Nueva España: El Hombre, Su Época y Su Obra* , Mexico, Universidad Iberoamericana Departamento de Historia, [1962] 1988; Boris Jeanne, *Mexico-Madrid-Rome. In the footsteps of Diego Valadés, a study of Roman environments oriented towards the New World during the Counter-Reformation period (1568-1594)* , doctoral thesis in history and civilizations, Paris, EHESS, 2011.

19. Penny C. Morrill, *The Casa del Dean, New World Imagery in a Sixteenth Century Mexican Mural Cycle* , Texas, Texas University Press, 2014, p. 86.

20. Enrique Florescano and Virginia García ed., *Technological mixing and cultural changes in Mexico* , Mexico, CIESAS, 2004, p. 223 ("Textiles under technological miscegenation").

21. Elle appartenait au *tlaxilacali* de Culhuacan dans l' *altepetl* de Ocotelulco : Emmanuel Rodríguez López, « Links with Cihuapipiltin Tlaxcaltecas of the 16th century: access to indigenous seigneurial power of the tlahtocayotl of Ocutelulco », p. 56, https://dialnet.unirioja.es/servlet/articulo?codigo=5156324.[3]

22. Gibson (1950), p. 202.

23. D9v°.

24. Gibson (1950) p. 154.

25. *Ibid* ., p. 203.

26. Magnus Mörner and Charles Gibson, "Diego Muñoz Camargo and the Segregation Policy of the Spanish Crown", *Hispanic American Historical Review* , vol. 42, 4, 1962, p. 558-568.

3. https://dialnet.unirioja.es/servlet/articulo?codigo=5156324

27. Before the Spanish conquest, this alliance between Mexico City, Tlacopan and Texcoco dominated what was called the Aztec Empire.

28 . His (eldest?) son Diego is also a large landowner, who devotes himself to the exploitation of salt and other mineral resources. Juan, his brother, would hold the salt monopoly of Ixtacmaxtitlan; Diego's widow, Leonor Vázquez, invests 500 pesos d' *oro común* in the saltworks of her son-in-law Gabriel Muñoz, husband of her daughter Isabella. Emmanuel Rodríguez Lopez, *Survival of a tlaxcalteca lineage. Los Maxixcatzin y su preponderancia como pipiltin, comerciantes, terratenientes y religiosos (1519-1634)* , master's thesis, Mexico City, CIESAS, 2014, p. 89, http://repositorio.ciesas.edu.mx/bitstream/handle/123456789/315/M622.pdf?sequence=1&isAllowed=y.[4]

29. Joanne Rappaport, *The Disappearing Mestizo. Configuring Difference in the Colonial New Kingdom of Granada* , Durham and London, Duke University Press, 2014 ; Pedro Carrasco, "Indian-Spanish Marriages in the First Century of the Colony," in Susan Schroeder, Stephanie Wood, and Robert Haskett eds., *Indian Women of Early Mexico* , Norman, University of Oklahoma Press, 1997, p. 87-104.

30 . Salvador Velasco, « Historiography and emergent ethnicity in colonial Mexico. Fernando de Alva Ixtlilxochitl, Diego Munoz Camargo and Hernando Alvarado Tezozomoc », *Mesoamerica* , vol. 38, December 1999, p. 14.

31. Magdalena Chocano Husband, *The Fortress* docta *Lettered elite and social domination in colonial Mexico (sixteenth-seventeenth centuries)* , Barcelona, Bellatera, 2000, p. 165.

32. *Ibid* ., p. 164.

33. The supplication (1556) concerns also the little Spaniards living in Indian villages : Fernando del Paso y Troncoso, *Epistolary of New Spain* , t. VIII, Mexico, Porn, 1940, p. 108.

---

4. http://repositorio.ciesas.edu.mx/bitstream/handle/123456789/315/M622.pdf?sequence=1&isAllowed=y

CHAPTER IV

A relationship essaim

Diego is far from being an isolated man. Throughout his testimony, references, anecdotes and hat-tricks constantly add names to the list of those who matter or have mattered to him. This frantic desire to show that he knows everything that weighs in the kingdom of New Spain makes you smile more than once. In sixteenth - century Mexico , as in the world today, a man without connections has no social existence, and therefore no future in the corridors of power, whatever that may be. You have to start with a name: even a bastard is entitled to it.

Families

His father's name connects him to Castile and to the circle of the conquistadors, to those invaders who fought to carve out a fortune on the backs of Mexico, which they subjugated and pillaged. His surname, Muñoz, the origin he claims – the "we" that constantly comes up in his remarks when he mentions the Castilians – identify him as Spanish. His bastardy did not prevent him from having a solid footing in the group of conquistadors and encomenderos *who* disputed power with the civil servants and the royal bureaucracy. He's somebody's son. And this someone, still alive in 1555, is in business with other conquerors reconverted like him in the breeding and exploitation of agricultural wealth of New Spain [1]. The relationships that Diego inherits are coupled with more personal ties: he admits that he himself knew and frequented the oldest conquistadors, who gladly served as informants to fill in his gaps [2]. Among his relatives, Diego can count on his brother Juan, half-caste like him, as active as he is, and on his nephews: they in turn married women of the native nobility 3 before following in his footsteps in the world of trading.

From his birth, his maternal origin plunged him into the indigenous environment. Diego understands his habits, his beliefs, his behaviors; he draws from it an intimate, physical and immediate knowledge; its flavors and smells are familiar to him. Whether it was his mother, the women of his maternal family or the crowd of servants who went about domestic chores in the conquistador's residences, Indian women surrounded him, carried him and nursed him in his early childhood. His first language was Nahuatl, and Mexican were all the foods that were put in his mouth. It does not matter that the maternal entourage was modest: as soon as he saw the light of day, Diego lived in symbiosis with indigenous Mexico.

Church people and letrados

His education opened other doors for him. In the *Description of Tlaxcala* , he mixes classical references and pious considerations: Plato, Végèce, Artaxerxès, the Bible. This formation reveals the influence of a third circle, as determining as the family entourage: that of the Franciscan missionaries who cherish these mestizos and these Indians whom they took in hand from their most tender age. Impossible to escape them in Tlaxcala. The order of Friars Minor settled there in 1524, five years after the arrival of Cortés. Tlaxcala is one of their first foundations and one of the major centers of evangelization in New Spain [4]. The province saw the passage of several eminent figures of the young Mexican Church: the Dominican Juan Garcés, first bishop of the new diocese; the Franciscan Toribio Benavente Motolinía, chronicler of Christianization and tireless evangelizer, proud to have baptized hundreds of thousands of Indians. But it was with Gerónimo de Mendieta, another prominent Franciscan, that Diego seems to have worked closely, especially in the 1580s, when distributing the natives over a territory depopulated by epidemics.

Does Diego know Latin? He does not rely on it. If he did not go through university, he attended doctoral defenses [5]. Its references to ancient authors do not make it a *letrado* of an exceptional level, but an educated man who had in his hands or who must have seen many books and even manuscripts, and not only those of the Friars Minor. . The culture of this lay person is in the image of that of the educated milieu which radiates from the Mexican capital. His contemporary, the Creole Suárez de Peralta, shares more or less the same reading: he too has access to major writings on the indigenous world, including those of the Dominicans Bartolomé de Las Casas and Diego Durán, confirmation if any is the notoriety of texts that were believed to be confined to the secrecy of monasteries [6].

The young capital of New Spain is already a hotbed of thought. Since the middle of the 16th century , Mexico City has housed a university intended to train theologians, jurists and doctors the new kingdom needs. The students animate an intellectual life there which overflows from the university cloisters and spreads in the city.

Not far from Mexico City, other homes are appearing. The rise of Puebla dates back to the second half of the 16th century . Tlaxcala remained an indigenous city, and the colonial authorities decided to build from scratch a few tens of kilometers away a city reserved for the Spaniards, the Puebla de los Angeles. In 1579, Diego made his debut as a commissioned writer by writing a pamphlet for the occasion: he describes the welcome given by Tlaxcala to the new bishop of Puebla-Tlaxcala, Diego Romano. And it is to a canon of the cathedral of Puebla, Anton García, that he dedicates his text. Two birds with one stone: Diego, so close to the Franciscans, this time targets the secular clergy, then on the rise.

Interpreters and Nahuatlatos

In New Spain, translators – or *Nahuatlatos* – constituted an indispensable cog in the administration and an essential link in bringing the worlds into contact. Diego is one of them. This environment has its entrances into colonial society. During the second half of the 16th century , the interpreters were often mestizos whose father had been a conquistador. At least four of them in the 1570s bear the high-sounding title of interpreters of the Audience. When they are of Spanish origin, these intermediaries sometimes married into the native aristocracy in Tlaxcala or Texcoco. In addition to their emoluments, they receive bonuses and, one suspects, kickbacks. The salary of interpreters employed by the Audience in Mexico City could exceed 300 pesos. To which is added in the case of Diego a charge of *teniente de corregidor* , welcome to round off his income.

Translation requires not only proficiency in Nahuatl and Castilian, but also as solid a knowledge of Iberian law as it does of indigenous customary traditions and their respective terminologies. Diego's role is all the more appreciable since the indigenous elites (and sometimes more popular circles) very early on grasped the benefit they could derive from Spanish laws and courts. The nobles are well aware that the monarch owes them aid and protection; they know that the Spanish judicial machine can work in their favor as it is able to give them access to the sovereign. It is up to them to familiarize themselves with these new rules and with the members of the bureaucracy responsible for applying them. In this game which contributes to reaffirming the omnipotence of the king while offering a protective screen to the litigants – a balance that is always unstable – the interpreter plays a key role. Better than anyone, he realizes to what extent royal justice invariably opens up a field of negotiation: the king is all-powerful, but written law enjoys an even higher authority. In principle, the prince is sovereign, but he is also extraordinarily distant and his decisions are liable to be modified, put on the back burner or short-circuited in a thousand ways [8]. *Deus ex machina* , the prince can also intervene to cancel measures deemed iniquitous.

This elasticity sheds light on an essential facet of Iberian globalization. By creating a uniform framework of references and practices, the exchanges, pleas, orders and counter-orders that cross the oceans share the same rules and the same values with groups living thousands of leagues from each other and belonging to different worlds.

Finally, the quality of interpreter interests us for a precise reason. Our *Nahuatlato* is not a translator of novels or history books. Diego, for example, did not translate Old and New Testament books into Nahuatl, whereas Indians and monks did at that time. He devotes his time to "interpreting" royal orders, to translating questions and answers. The exercise familiarized him with interrogation situations and his ear quickly learned to dissect a question to render it in the other language, and therefore to imagine its background and what was not said. Listening to the answer, he engages in the same work. The interpreter is one of those who build the language common to Indian elites and colonial elites. Better than anyone, even if he remains invisible, he is aware of what passes and what does not pass, whether it concerns the limits of what can be said within the framework of a court of law or what is understandable between two at first sight irreducible traditions. While brilliantly cultivating the art of smoothing things over, he has a panoramic view of the worlds between which he circulates.

Listening to Indians is not just about collecting and analyzing oral testimony. It is, most of the time, to confront them with the information contained in the paintings brought by the natives. In Mexico, the skill of the interpreter depends as much on his ability to decipher the pictographic codices – " *declarar las pinturas* " – as on his understanding of the local language. This must necessarily be based on a new art: an intellectual dexterity able to play on languages that belong to two systems of thought and perception of reality that are radically foreign to each other.

Besides these qualities, Diego possesses over us – and over all the historians who will succeed him – the indisputable superiority of knowing infinitely more about New Spain. He will obviously lack knowledge of our 21st century, of the expectations, prejudices and shortcomings of our time, in other words of everything that would enable him to interpret our questions.

A budding intelligentsia

Beyond the university and the convents loom circles mixing all those who are interested in literature, history, science, "things of the Indies" and the debates of the time. Diego is one of them. He could have taken on board this admission of Suárez de Peralta: "I know very little Latin, but I am an avid reader of stories and always eager to meet scholars [9]. As today in the provincial towns of Latin America, small groups of enthusiasts share books and manuscripts that circulate from hand to hand. Always worried about missing the novelties of Spain and ready to face the visits of the Inquisition, they knew how to be discreet. Mexico City is a city where even a tailor can possess books suspect in the eyes of the [Church]. We would like to know better this population of clerks, bachelors, priests, minor bureaucrats and schoolmasters, but also of doctors, apothecaries, merchants and craftsmen whom the Inquisition regularly accuses of possessing books forbidden and, of course, to dive into it. Let us add a few daring readers, also deemed worthy of appearing on the lists of the Holy Office.

Despite the distance from Europe, the spies of the Inquisition teach us that the inhabitants of New Spain are fond of Petrarch, Boccaccio, Ovid, Virgil, that they read the Portuguese Camoens, that they buy books of history and devour novels of chivalry or the best-sellers of the time like the *Orlando furioso* [11]. Booksellers and printers are responsible for supplying this clientele who are not without means and who sometimes live very far in the interior of the country. Diego, now settled in Tlaxcala, has hardly a long way to go to unearth what suits him, unless he simply goes to the library of the Franciscans.

Diego consulted a treatise on air and earth (a manuscript now lost) and a great epic poem, *Nuevo Mundo y Conquista* . These two books are the work of Francisco de Terrazas. Born a few years before Diego (around 1525), Francisco is also the son of a conquistador, and not least since he was the butler of Hernán Cortés. He is above all one of the great Mexican poets of the 16th century . Diego admits to being one of the fervent admirers of "Terrazas, who in such a sublime way chronicles this New World [12]". To have had these manuscripts in your hands, you must have been one of Francisco's relatives and therefore have frequented him before his death, around 1580 [13] .

Diego's links with Francisco de Terrazas may have brought him into contact with a Petrarchist circle, influenced by the Italian Renaissance. The famous sonnet " *Dejad las hebras de oro ensortijado* " ("Leave the golden hair curled") appears in all anthologies of Mexican [poetry]. Was he interested in the poetry that is written in this milieu? We don't know. Or to other authors that this group practices, such as Plutarch [15] and Erasmus, several titles of which circulate in the Mexican capital [16]? Did Francisco lend Diego his Plutarch, which was the object of the attentions of the Inquisition? In 1573, the Holy Office conducted an investigation into the holders of banned books in Mexico City. A track leads to Francisco de Terraces. The poet, who is not at his first hitch with the Inquisition [17], is accused of having a copy of Plutarch's *Moral Works* [18]. In the 16th century , the Latin translation of this work is associated with the hated name of Erasmus, because the great humanist accompanied his translation with personal comments: this version published in Basel was supposed to introduce his ideas in contraband [19] . The Europe of the Counter-Reformation had condemned the thought of the humanist of Rotterdam, Rome had put it on the Index and, since the middle of the century, in all the Iberian lands it had been the target of the inquisitorial thunderbolts. Didn't Erasmus maintain that the historian of Chaeronea (Plutarch) was "the holiest author after the Holy Scriptures" since he taught a more effective morality than all theological discourses?

In the prologue to his *Description* , Diego relates the story of the peasant who, having nothing of value to offer Artaxerxes, draws water from a river and holds out his palms filled with the refreshing liquid to the great king. The anecdote is famous in the 16th century and is attributed to Plutarch. In fact, if Diego seems to have read this Greek historian, the episode as he relates it comes from a rarer and less compromising version, that of Claude Elien, a Latin historian from the beginning of the third century [20]. Diego didn't do like most of his contemporaries. When he only had to open Plutarch or a medley of references, with countless reissues, the *Silva de varia lección* [21], which was hard on him, he may have prudently preferred Aelian to his illustrious predecessor.

We have no factual data on Diego's relationship with the circles of the capital, the cloisters or the university. However, it is undeniable that he consulted all the great missionary chronicles of his time, from Motolinía to Mendieta passing through Sahagún. The extent of his reading demonstrates his flair as well as his interest in the past, the Spanish conquest and the Christianization of New Spain. On the other hand, when he evokes figures of the stature of Bartolomé de Las Casas, Vasco de Quiroga, Juan Garcés, bishop of Tlaxcala, or Juan de Zumárraga, archbishop of Mexico, we remain skeptical. He has undoubtedly crossed these characters, but his young age excludes any serious exchange. The lists of names he includes in his *History of Tlaxcala* confirm that he knows who's who in New Spain. But this display perhaps says more about the character's vanity than about his own relationships. And I want to add to these names that of Juan Bautista Pomar, a mestizo to whom we also owe a remarkable geographical relationship, the *Texcoco Relation* . Pomar is not only the Diego of this great Indian city, he is the cousin of Francisco Pimentel, the father of the Indian daughter-in-law of Diego [22]. Like Diego, he frequented the doctor and antiquarian Francisco Hernández whom Philip II had sent to Mexico to investigate the fauna and flora. The world is already small!

A man of all knowledge

Diego's technical knowledge is no less negligible: it touches on issues as diverse as indigenous units of measurement – what is a league for the Indians? –, mountains, trips across the Pacific, therefore long-distance navigation, or earthquakes.

– *Can you describe a Mexican earthquake?*

– We could talk about the earthquake that took place in the province of Avalos in 1577 [23]. The land has opened up for more than fifteen leagues across plains and mountains. The fault engulfed a man on horseback: everything went through it, the man with the horse, and a small village of Indians sank to a depth of more than three stadia 24 without any house collapsing, except a few unimportant ones, and the people inside lost their lives.

– *Have we deplored other destructions?*

– Elsewhere, churches and monasteries have collapsed. In this village, today, we go out by climbing ladders. It is submerged, but few people remain there; they left to settle elsewhere. In some places, springs and rivers suddenly gushed out, and new waterholes and fountains sprang up. In the rift that opened up, giant bones were found in some places.

– *How did the animals react to this earthquake?*

– During the earthquake and the tremors, the roosters were crowing, the dogs were barking and howling, the horses were neighing. Everyone felt them very strongly.

– *Were effects also observed on the hydrographic network?*

– A river called the Amecarro River, very powerful, stopped flowing for three whole days, then it resumed its old course.

– In May 1582, an earthquake struck the province of Tlaxcala?

– The earthquake was so violent and so fast that the bells rang by themselves and oscillated from side to side [...]. In all the churches and all the chapels, bells fell from the steeples. The earthquake happened at five o'clock in the afternoon, just at the time of the full moon, according to Chaves.

– Jerónimo de Chaves is a Sevillian cosmographer who was interested in natural phenomena. Did this earthquake cause significant destruction?

– At that hour, the sanctuary of Tepapayeca [25] collapsed, except for the tabernacle where the most holy sacrament was. The whole monastery collapsed without causing any casualties. A tower lost its balance as well as a campanile of the village of Topoyanco which almost collapsed on the ground [26].

Diego knows the geographer Ptolemy as well as his scholarly contemporaries. He is interested in the climate, the wind regime, temperature changes, the passage of the seasons, their impact on habitat and land use. In November and December, he observes, “in the sun, it's summer, and in the shade, it's winter”. The movement of the sun from one pole to another and from one tropic to another holds no secrets for him [27]. No more than the cosmographer and pilot Jerónimo de Chaves, author of a *Repertorio de los tiempos* which won enormous success in the Iberian world: twelve editions in forty years for a work released in 1548 [28].

It is with Chaves that Diego learns to recognize the "signs of earthquakes", harbingers of disasters. It is also from him – and, through him, from Sacrobosco (1195-1256?) – that Diego borrows the idea of “machine of the world” which he applies to the New World [29]. With Alonso de Santa Cruz, his eldest, and other cosmographers, Chaves was part of the Sevillian circles that evolved around the Casa de la Contratación [30], designed, measured and represented the continents that the Iberians approached. Diego knows the importance of these contacts. When he mentions the expeditions launched across the Pacific, he twice gives the name of the pilot who informs him, and does not hesitate to associate him with Magellan and the first circumnavigation of the globe [31].

But our friend is even more involved in the scientific history of New Spain than it seems. He is credited with, in addition to his historical writings, a report on the cochineal (the *grana cochinilla*) that Philip II's physician Francisco Hernández mentions in his *Natural History* [32]. Diego would have written it at the request of the Spanish scientist whom the king had dispatched to Mexico to carry out a vast investigation on the fauna and the flora of the country. Elsewhere, his observations on the elasticity of latex (*uli*) are premonitory: "If we made shoe soles in this *uli* (ours give it another name, *batey* , borrowed from the Indians of our island of Hispaniola), it seems to me that, wherever it would go , the Indian who would wear them would move by jumping without wanting to [33]. »

On the side of Guermantes

Although he frequented ecclesiastics, scholars and scientists, Diego appears above all fascinated by the local aristocracy. It is she who in his eyes embodies the memory of things, the heroic past, military grandeur and noble values.

The great seigniorial families of Tlaxcala kept codices or *pinturas* and recited *cantares* through which the memory of the elders and their prowess passed to new generations. A large *linen cloth* , or painted canvas, like that of Tlaxcala bears witness to the importance that the elites still granted to painters (*tlacuilos*) in the middle of the 16th century and to the interest they had in a traditional mode of expression. , but which, by dint of interbreeding, had managed to dialogue with the styles and techniques introduced by the invaders.

Reading the paintings was a subtle operation. It demanded the mastery of conventions, processes, shortcuts that usually escaped the Spaniards. The indigenous orality that unfolded in the *cantares* was hardly more transparent. The stories and memories of indigenous elites often had the darkness of what emanates from another world. All these obstacles, however, did not discourage Diego. When one has the art of deciphering speech in a court of law, one has a trained ear. The songs accompanying the celebrations regularly organized by the Tlaxcaltec aristocracy distil valuable information on pre-Hispanic times, and Diego knows this well. But the Nahuatl of the singers is not that of the courts. It conceals messages that Diego qualifies *enigmas* [34], using the term employed by exegetical literature when it comments on the Song of Songs [35]. In the medieval West, every parable is also an enigma, like everything that comes from an allegorical reading. It is the assurance of a difficult reading, but which always conceals its own keys: any enigma, Diego knows, calls for decryption.

To take up the challenge, Diego frequented the families where the shadows of the past survive and he was able to gain their trust. His discretion, put to the test by the meetings of the municipal council which impose a duty of reserve on everyone, opened the doors of memories and local archives to him. The relationships of friendship and complicity established throughout these interminable investigations made things easier. Not all lords were fans of the historical compilation. But some were interested in things of the past and even had to devote their leisure time to them. Diego remains silent about his contacts. Admittedly, his silence guarantees his impartiality, but could sometimes not be disinterested. Spanish colonization is far from having put an end to the rivalries between the seigniorial houses or to the conflicts which divide each of them. Controlling memories is always a mark of power.

Besides, in Tlaxcala, our columnist is not a pioneer. The local nobility has already given historians to the province. Apart from a few Franciscans, it was the natives, and not the Spaniards, who were the first to interpret the local past [36]. Among Diego's predecessors stands out the name of Tadeo de Niza, author of a text (circa 1548) whose authenticity would have been sanctioned by some thirty notables in the city. Although his work is now lost, there is reason to believe that part of it was preserved by the Métis historian Alva Ixtlilxochitl [37]. The latter, a goldsmith in the field, exalts the story of Tadeo, according to him "the most certain and the most truthful of all those that have been written [38]". In addition to oral traditions and pictographic paintings, local historiography erected safeguards that Diego had to take into account [39].

These same large families do not live locked in an indigenous bubble. They are also beginning to get to know what constitutes their “new world” for them, the Iberian Peninsula. They are the ones who provide the Tlaxcaltec envoys to whom devolves the insignia and costly privilege of going to Spain to kiss the hands of their monarch. One can imagine that these embassies to the Spanish sovereign each time carried an official version of local history [40]. All carried out information campaigns to defend Tlaxcaltec privileges at court. It was the members of one of these deputations, who returned to the fold in 1541, who would have served as informants for Bartolomé de Las Casas [41]. The Dominican would have exploited their testimonies and perhaps even their writings to compose the passages of his *Brief Apologetic History* concerning Tlaxcala. In the 1550s, it was the *Histoire de Tadeo de Niza* and the *Lienzo de Tlaxcala* , a veritable "tapestry" painted two meters by five, which took to Spain in support of native claims [42].

Finally, in Tlaxcala, the past is also present in images. The construction of the *Casas Reales* dates back to 1545. In the large assembly hall, one never tired of admiring frescoes relating scenes from the conquest of Mexico and the conversion of Tlaxcala. Diego had plenty of time to be explained and re-explained the exploits of those who had collaborated in the triumph of Cortés and the Christian faith. And it wasn't just about Tlaxcala. The painting depicting Christopher Columbus at the feet of Charles V, the one introducing Pizarro and the conquest of Peru suggest that the Tlaxcaltec elites saw far and that they were not unaware of which world they now belonged to.

A precious man

So, if the most illustrious family of Tlaxcala, the Maxixcatzins, represents the side of Guermantes, is Diego their Charles Swann, fascinated as he is by this noble circle straddling genealogies, the Who's who and the *respect* of sources, and who always keeps one eye on Mexico City and the other on Madrid? Importance of margins: Diego is mixed-race, and Swann Jewish. Diego's intelligence, his taste for worldliness, his erudition, his passion for chivalry – Swann also never ceased to complete a study on the Knights of Malta – suggest looking to Proust for the key to his attachment to the big world. Much of what is at stake between Swann and the Faubourg – and which escapes the researcher – could help to imagine the nature of the links which unite Diego to the old families. In the end, the same joint destiny of worlds originally irreconcilable: Swann's daughter will marry the nephew of the Duke of Guermantes, and Diego's son the granddaughter of Juan Maxixcatzin.

His Christian upbringing, his knowledge of Nahuatl, his intelligence – but what would they be without his personal connections? – make Diego a perfect intermediary in all kinds of situations. We discovered him writing Tlaxcala's answers to the *Geographical Relations questionnaire* . But an interpreter is called upon to intervene in a number of legal cases which are often family matters. He is used to the workings of Spanish justice, imbued with the forms of Castilian law, close to these swarms of judges, notaries, prosecutors and paper pushers who abound under Spanish domination and who all profit from the chaos of the aftermath. -conquest and colonial effervescence to prosper and impose their services.

For their part, the representatives of the Crown have every reason to call on this fine connoisseur of the native nobility and local lineages. His historical works never lose the opportunity to specify a genealogy. Diego is able to greet the survivors of a fallen family by recalling the greatness of his origins, people "poor even if they are great lords, still esteemed and held for such

43 "–. Or to defend the reputation of the powerful of the moment. Do malicious rumors surround the origins of the illustrious Maxixcatzin family which reigns over Ocotelulco at the time of the Spanish invasion, "because some regard them as intruders and of mediocre lineage"? Our Diego takes his finest pen – "what happens in this case is that..." – to explain that the ancestors of this family, "endowed with all the qualities and very well regarded44 "–, first established in the venerable city of Cholula before joining the province of Tlaxcala. Yes, the Maxixcatzin are people from elsewhere and upstarts (*advenedizos*), but these are *advenedizos* "of great lineage [45]". By the way, hello!

As for the Tlaxcaltec aristocrats, how could they do without this man who knows so well who they are, where they come from, and for whom the colonial administration and the "developers" of all stripes, colonists, encomenderos, Spanish *traders* and half-breeds have attentions? Diego, on the other hand, cultivates the art of taking advantage of the situation in a changing society where the indigenous elites are losing ground just as much as the sons and grandsons of the conquistadors. Lowered by the new masters of the country, weakened by the progress of Spanish power and the rise of the colonial system, the Tlaxcaltec nobles had to face popular strata increasingly reluctant to their ancestral demands. The proliferation of trials opposing natives to each other or natives to the Spanish sector struck and annoyed contemporaries. To soften the blow, the large families – "the most upscale in this province " [46]– needed these intermediaries who were as familiar with the workings of the colonial bureaucracy as with the old structures of power. Diego has everything to please: a clear idea of the economic, social and political geography before the Conquest and an address book in the administration and the Spanish circles that dominate the country: landowners, merchants, men of the Church , *alcaldes mayores* and *corregidore* s, without counting the *letrados* and the chroniclers.

Little is known of the innumerable small and great services rendered by his well-rehearsed memory to the sons and daughters of the Tlaxcaltec nobility. With probably elevator referrals. His defense and illustration of the

Maxixcatzin family is there to remind us that he will succeed in marrying his son into this illustrious lineage. All these helping hands come at a high price: the grateful indigenous town council has donated land to the versatile interpreter taken from communal property and shares with him the revenue from a tax raised to finance the sending of ambassadors natives in Madrid. Predictably, the tax continued to be collected years after the envoys returned. The Indians did not fail to complain about it, and the Crown was moved enough to call for an investigation, but the latter, should we be surprised, got bogged down fairly quickly.

Deals

The scholar, the intermediary, the servant of the king does not circulate only in the patios of the native palaces and the offices of the colonial bureaucracy. He's not just a cabinet man. In Tlaxcala, he and his brother Juan were considered to be the "caciques du commerce [47]". Diego knows how to take advantage of tax exemptions and jump on the opportunities offered by a booming colonial economy. Thanks to his Spanish, Métis or Indian partners, he captures the metamorphoses of a society where Tlaxcala and New Spain have become inseparable from the Iberian Peninsula and the worlds of the Catholic Monarchy.

Diego is the image of this expanding society – "the land that remains to be taken and conquered48 "– where wealth seems within reach. Even Spaniards who indulge in begging are candidates for fortune, like this individual whose name Juan Suárez de Peralta withheld from his name so that the shame would not fall on his descendants, and who had returned to Spain with enough savings to found a surcharge of 300,000 pesos. In the Mexico of the young Diego and Suárez de Peralta, "there are no poor people", among the Europeans of course. It is a land where only silver currency prevails, where all copper currency is banned, first by the Indians, a land where colossal and dazzling fortunes are built like that of Alonso de Villaseca, the 'King of Cocoa', which everyone knows began by retailing cocoa in markets [49].

"We are all hidalgos "

How does Diego perceive the society in which he lives? We get a glimpse of it in an anecdote where he depicts noble natives who insult the Spaniards:

"Let an evil Spaniard mistreat them, and they tell him that he is a bad Christian, that he is neither *hidalgo* nor knight, because if he were one, his behavior and his words would remain modest, like those of a knight; that it must be a villain, a Moor, a Jew or a Basque, and in the end, when they have no more words to insult him, they hurl at him: "In the end, you are Portuguese", in thinking he had done her the greatest affront. »

At the top of the ideal society that the Indian nobility has in mind, the nobles and the knights; below, first the villains, that is to say the populace, then two groups of non-Christians, the Moors and the Jews, followed by one of the nations of the Peninsula, the Basques, who ordinary is noticed and sometimes detested by its particularisms; finally, at the foot of the ladder, the enemy brothers, the Portuguese, yet united in the same empire since 1580. There is every reason to think that Diego adheres to these clichés, even if he makes fun in passing of the claims of the nobles ruins.

To be *hidalgo* or not to be! In Diego's taxonomy, there is no trace of the categories of Indian or mestizo (the one which, in principle, primarily concerns him). Not a word of mulattoes, blacks and slaves, populations nevertheless more numerous than the Basques. The most valued status corresponds to that of *hidalgo* : one must be born "son of someone" without "ethnic origin" entering into it for anything. The term has a particular resonance for the Indians of Tlaxcala. When, at the beginning of the 1590s, there was talk of sending Tlaxcaltec families to populate the *Gran Chichimeca* in northern Mexico, the Indian memorial stated straight out: "All Tlaxcaltecs are *hidalgos* [50]. " And the capitulations promulgated by the viceroy will confirm to them their privileges of *hidalguía* "which belonged to them by reason of the royal charters and ordinances". These documents will extend to all Indians a status hitherto reserved for the *principals* of Tlaxcala. The equation *hidalgo* = Tlaxcaltec says a lot about the local attachment to a social distinction that transcends ethnicity. For the nobles of Tlaxcala, Diego explains it to us, descending from the Chichimecs is like in Spain descending from the Goths, the illustrious founders of the Christian monarchy on the Peninsula [51]. This is one of the few times he alludes to the history of Spain, probably from a reading of Gonzalo de Illescas' *Pontifical History , published some time earlier and often exported to the West Indies* [52].

Diego does not seek to explain Mexican society to us. It echoes and assumes a point of view, the idea that, regardless of whether one is Indian, Spanish or in-between, therefore mixed-race, it is not ethnic origin that counts, but birth. And this requires a purity of blood to which neither the Moor, nor the Jew, nor the Portuguese – generally considered to be of Jewish origin – could claim. What's the use of being Spanish if it's to be badly born? What's the point of having been born on the other side of the ocean if it's to be Portuguese? European extraction is nothing without birth and purity of blood. The Inquisition is there to remind it and put it in order. Morality: nothing prevents you from being both Indian and *hidalgo* . Diego's position also reflects the obsession, which he shares with many Creoles, of belonging through his father to a nobility consecrated by the great deeds accomplished during the Conquest, even though the majority of the conquistadors were of obscure origin. The chronicle of the Conquest that Francisco de Terrazas had written in verse idealized the exploits of the founders of New Spain, and Diego had it before his eyes.

Does this vision explain his political conformism? Diego is careful not to question the colonial power or to deplore the condition imposed on the indigenous masses. Is this an understandable diplomatic silence in a document addressed to the sovereign? Or is it simply an expression of his love of order? In his geographical account, written in Texcoco and at the same time, the mestizo Juan Bautista Pomar does not hesitate to issue criticisms (more or less veiled) against colonial domination. This proves that this type of inquiry and the situation it created could open the way to discordant views [53]. But, with Diego, loyalty is flawless.

And the Indians who do not belong to the nobility?

"There are Indians so simple and whose understanding is so limited that they can be compared to beasts devoid of reason.

– *How to behave with them?*

– These Indians – that's the majority of Indians – they have to be treated like children according to their abilities and abilities, as one treats a child from Spain aged eight or ten.

– *Concretely, what do you mean?*

– For their well-being, we must encourage them, show them a lot of love, but chastise their weaknesses by punishing and correcting them like children, using threats like their elders did. They must thus understand that they must receive a punishment.

- *Are they all like that?*

– [Let's leave aside] some who grew up more or less freely with Spaniards. They just do what they want. They are naughty rascals focused on wickedness and devoid of any virtue.

- *And the others?*

– They are very weak, they have vile thoughts, they are unable to take care of a serious thing when they are in charge of it. As for the Spaniards, who want to react to their anger and their fury in the same way, they are as stupid as the Indians. These are so fragile and so pitiful that the slightest disturbance, the slightest threat finish them off. Wanting to pull them out of their state and their natural baseness in order to bring them up to the level of the talent that God has given to the Spaniards is an aberration.

– *So your assessment is negative?*

"They lack honor and reason. Left to themselves, they are pusillanimous to an extreme point. But if they feel supported, then they become bold and daring [...]. They do not protect themselves against contagious diseases and, when they fall ill, they let themselves go and die like beasts. They eat very little and feed on very light things. But those who eat well and take care of themselves are perfectly capable and very skilful: they learn well everything that is taught to them, for they grasp things quickly [54].

1. Gregorio de Villalobos like Diego senior are conquistadors and encomenderos *converted* into herders: Peter Gerhard, *Síntesis e índice de los mandamientos virreinales 1548-1553* , Mexico, UNAM, 1992, p. 219.

2. C233-234.

3. Gibson (1950), p. 197.

4. Martinez Baracs (2008), p. 214. The strong bond with the order of Saint Francis was maintained throughout the sixteenth century and, when 400 Tlaxcaltec families left to found colonies in the north of New Spain, in the remote *Gran Chichimeca* , the native authorities obtained that Franciscans from the province of Tlaxcala take charge of it instead of the anticipated Jesuits.

5. D104v°.

6. Suarez of Peralta (1990), p. 24, 71.

7. 7. Caroline Cunill, « A mosaic of languages: the interpreters of Mexico's audience in the sixteenth century », *Mexican History* , vol. LXVIII, 1 (269), July-September 2018, p. 7-48 ; id., « The Interpreters of Yucatán : private negotiations and initiatives in the fragua of the Iberian empire, sixteenth century », *Colonial Latin American Historical Review* , Second Series, 1, 4, 2013, p. 361 - 380 ; Alonso Iciar, Jesús Baigorrí et Gertrudis Payàs, « Nahuatlatos and Families of Interpreters in Colonial Mexico », *Journal of the History of Translation. A Journal of Translation History* , no . 1-12.

8. Brian Philip Owenski, *Empire of Law and Indian Justice in Colonial Mexico* , Stanford, Stanford University Press, 2008.

9. Suárez de Peralta (1990), p. 24.

10. Francisco Fernandez del Castillo, *Books and booksellers in the sixteenth century* , Mexico, FCE, 1982, p. 477.

11. *Ibid* ., p. 510. The masterpiece of the Arioste was accomplished in 1532.

12 . D13r°. Sur Terrazas, Juan Carlos Cabrera Pons, « *The New World and Conquest* of Francisco de Terrazas in the Construction of a Creole History of New Spain », *Scaffolding* , Mexico, UNAM, vol. 12, 29, September-December 2015, p. 141-160.

13 . Georges Baudot, «Lupercio Leonardo de Argensola continuer of Francisco de Terrazas. New data and documents », *New Magazine of Hispanic Philology* , t. 36, 2, 1988, p. 1083-1091.

14 . *New Spanish poets* , Alfonso Méndez Plancarte ed., Mexico, UNAM, 1964, p. 29.

15 . Fernández del Castillo (1982), p. 470 (*Lives*) ; p. 483, 476 (*Morales*).

16 . Les *Adages* d'Érasme est l'un des titres fréquemment recherchés par l'Inquisition (Fernández del Castillo [1982], p. 476, 477, 482, 484, 486, 491).

17 . Roberto Ramon Reyes-Mazzoni, "Francisco of Terraces, Novo-Hispanic Creole," *Archipelago* , UNAM, p. 17, 66, 2009, http://www.journals.unam.mx/index.php/archivelago/article/view/20169.[1]

18 . Fernandez of the Castle (1982), p. 472, 476 ; C268. On Erasmus and Plutarch, see Louis Lobbes, "Erasmus the Editor of Plutarch: the *Apophthegms* ," *The Scribe Editor* , Adirel, t. XIV, 2001, p. 139-148 ; Alicia Morales Ortiz, *Plutarch in Spain : Translations of Moralia in the Sixteenth Century* , Murcie, University of Murcia, 2000.

19 . *Apophthegmatum from the best writers of both languages by Desiderius Erasmus of Rotterdam collected book 8* , Basel, 1545, np, https://www.cairn.info/revue-litteratures-classiques1 [2]-2014-2-page-63.htm#

20 . The episode appears in Plutarch in the *Moral Works* (*Moralia*), "Apothegmes of Famous Kings and Captains", D. Richard trans., http://remacle.org/bloodwolf/historians/Plutarch/apophtegmesgeneraux.htm, [3]and under a distinct form in the *Life of Artaxerxes* . Plutarch gives neither the name of Persia nor that of the river. According to Claude Aelian (175-235) – a historian later than Plutarch – the river is the Cyrus and the Persian has the name Sinetes: Thomas Stanley trans., Claudius *Aelianus: His Various History* , London, Thomas

1. http://www.revistas.unam.mx/index.php/archipielago/article/view/20169

2. https://www.cairn.info/revue-litteratures-classiques1

3. http://remacle.org/bloodwolf/historiens/Plutarque/apopthtegmesgeneraux.htm

Drink, 1665, l . I, ch. 23, http://penelope.uchicago.edu/aelian/varhist1.xhtml. [4]Frequently reported, the anecdote appears in the *Orationes sapientiae* of the Portuguese Antonio Pinto (*Oratio academica* , Coimbra, 1555), in the prologue of *Eastern Ethiopia* by João dos Santos (Lisbon, 1609) or even in Juan de Castellanos, *Elegias de varones ilustres de Castilla* (Madrid, 1589), which gives the name of the river (Ciro) and of Persia (Sinetis).

21 . Published by Pedro Mexía (1497-1551) in Seville in 1540.

22 . Gruzinski (2017), p. 265-292.

23 . D233 v. In the current state of Jaliso.

24 . About 500 meters.

25 . In the current state of Puebla, not far from Izucar de Matamoros.

26 . D234r°.

27 . D6r°.

28 . Mariano Cuesta Domingo, «Alonso de Santa Cruz, cartographer and manufacturer of nautical instruments», *Complutense Magazine of American History* , vol. 30, 2004, p. 7-40. René Acuña identifies le Chaves de Diego with Alonso de Chaves, author of a *Mirror of navigators* , resté manuscript, et de *Examenes de pilotos, de maestros de la carrera de Indias* (Séville, 1561). Cosmographer, cartographer, Alonso de Chaves collaborates in the elaboration of the *royal register* , manufactures the maps and navigation instruments, but does not seem to be the author that Diego cites.

29 . Jerónimo de Chaves, *Tractado de la Sfera composed by doctor Joannes de Sacrobosco* , Séville, Juan de León, 1545.

30 . The Casa de Contratación is a Spanish institution, created in Seville on January 20, 1503, at the dawn of the colonization of the New World. She controlled trade with this continent.

---

4. http://penelope.uchicago.edu/aelian/varhist1.xhtml

31 . In 1583, a Portuguese, Nuño de Silva, pilot of Drake for fifteen months, was condemned in Mexico City by the Inquisition: José Toribio Medina, *Historia del tribunal del santo oficio de la Inquisición en México* , Mexico, Ediciones Fuentes Cultural, 1952, p. 77.

32 . Carrera Stampa (1971). On the probable relations between Doctor Hernández and Diego, D218r°.

33 . D220r°-v°. Hispaniola is the island of Santo Domingo or Haiti.

34 . C227. Tesoro *de la lengua castellana o española* by Sebastián de Covarrubias (Seville, 1611, p. 353) gives the meaning of " *obscura alegoría* ", "an obscure allegory".

35 . Origen, *Comentario al cantar de los cantares* , Madrid, Ciudad Nueva, 2007, p. 55.

36 . Even if, in the early times, the Franciscan Motolinía served as a guide in writing a European-style history; see Gruzinski (2017), p. 75-109.

37 . In his *Historia chichimeca* , Gibson (1952), p. 259.

38 . Fernando de Alva Ixtlilxóchitl, *Complete works* , Edmundo O'Gorman ed., Mexico, UNAM, t. II, 1977, p. 213; João Luiz Fukunaga, *Mexican Chronicle by Hernando Alvarado Tezozómoc and the networks of intelligibility of memory (1538-1598)* , mémoire de maîtrise en histoire sociale, São Paulo, Pontifícia Universidade Católica, 2008, p. 161.

39 . Pour une introduction au *Lienzo de Tlaxcala* , http://www.latinamericanstudies.org/tlaxcala-lienzo.htm.[5]

40 . Anna Díaz Serrano, *The political model of the Hispanic monarchy from a comparative perspective. The republics of Murcia and Tlaxcala in the 16th century* , thèse de doctorat, Murcie, University of Murcia, 2010 ; id., "Otherness and alliance: consolidation and representation of the power group in the republic of Tlaxcala in the 16th century", *Nuevo Mundo, Mundos Nuevos* , 04/28/2008, https://journals.openedition.org/nuevomundo/31083?lang=en.[6]

41 . Gibson (1952), p. 13.

---

5. http://www.latinamericanstudies.org/tlaxcala-lienzo.htm

6. https://journals.openedition.org/nuevomundo/31083?lang=es

42 . *Ibid.* , p. 165. Une vision générale dans Saliha Belmessous (dir.), *Native Claims, Indigenous Law Against Empire* , Oxford, Oxford University Press, 2014.

43 . C88.

44 . C89.

45 . C91.

46 . C88.

47 . Rodriguez Lopez (2014), p. 137 , 138 ,

48 . D98r°.

49 . Suárez de Peralta (1990), p. 166 167 .

50 . Andrea Martinez Baracs, "Tlaxcalte Colonizations," *Mexican History* , vol. 43 , 2 , 1992 , p. 195-250 (particularly pp. 209, 206, note 22, p. 210); the memorial is published in Carlos Sempat Assadourian and Andrea Martinez Baracs, *Tlaxcala. Texts of their history. General History of Tlaxcala* , Mexico, Tlaxcala, Conaculta, 1991, vol. 6, chap. ix, p. 532 and

51 . D55v°.

52 . Nejma Kermele, "Theory and Practice of World History in the *Historia pontifical y canonica* de Gonzalo de Illescas", *E-Spania* , June 30, 2018, https://journals.openedition.org/e-spania/27783.[7]

53 . Gruzinski (2017), p. 280-283.

54 . D37r°.

7. https://journals.openedition.org/e-spania/27783

CHAPTER V

History for what?

When he prepares to answer the Crown questionnaire, Diego is over fifty. He never wrote a history book. The passion he puts into writing is all the more surprising since he is not a man of the pen and even less, at this age, a budding historian. Moreover, the colonial administration did not ask him to become one.

In New Spain, the historians are not plethora. Some belong to a regular order – Franciscan, Dominican or Augustinian – they have in mind writing models inspired by ecclesiastical history [1]. Others are Crown officials brought up in the cult of Castilian law and royal power. Originally, Diego is none of these. He writes simply to respond to an outside request, as he related a few years earlier, in a commissioned text, the reception given to the bishop of Tlaxcala.

All about Tlaxcala

In the eyes of the Spaniards, Diego is not the first to approach the history of Tlaxcala. Before him, in Mexico, monks like Motolinía and Las Casas, humanists like Cervantes de Salazar [2] carried out their investigations. These writings have remained in manuscript, with the exception of the *Historia de las Indias* , by Lȯpez de Gȯmara (1552). In the 1580s, in New Spain as in Peru circulates a synthetic description of Tlaxcala inserted in a treatise on the geopolitics of the globe ambitiously entitled *Republics of the world* . This Renaissance Wikipedia appeared for the first time in Salamanca in 1575. The Augustinian Jerónimo Román y Zamora is the author [3]. Many copies cross the ocean and are available from booksellers in Mexico City and Lima. Like so many others, Diego was able to discover the pages devoted to the Republic of Tlaxcala.

The book touches on the pre-Hispanic world [4] and its survivals [5]. The section devoted to political organization is more comprehensive, as we mentioned above [6]. Román especially insists on the autonomy of Tlaxcala: "These people of Tlascala [*sic*], before and after, governed their republic from their side. From him, we will remember the laudatory description of a native administration which survived the Conquest and which constitutes an exceptional case of political continuity in the Indies of the sixteenth century . In fact, this Tlaxcala, which looks like an exemplary aristocratic republic, owes a lot to Bartolomé de Las Casas and his *brief Histoire apologétique* [7]. Flattering considerations, therefore, that Diego and Tlaxcaltec readers had to share. But has Diego read Román? We don't know. His reference to the writings of Las Casas perhaps passes through the chapters of the *Republics of the world* which plunder the Dominican.

In any case, the brevity of Román on Tlaxcala – relative in a work that covers almost the whole world – does not could only encourage him to go deeper into the subject. The sources and networks at his disposal are his best assets.

An indigenous tropism?

To which is added an attraction that is more difficult to detect, a tropism that inclines him irresistibly towards the native side. He could have married a woman from Castile or a rich mestizo. Or introduce his son into a Spanish house in Mexico. Instead of reinforcing his Hispanicity by slipping into a European family and encouraging his offspring to follow this path, he chose the opposite option: alliance with the nobility of pre-Hispanic origin. His son, half-breed like him but who had to spend more time with his indigenous family, will marry the heiress, also Indian, of two prestigious Altiplano lineages. Years later, this ennoblement by alliance will facilitate his access to the functions of governor of Tlaxcala, hitherto reserved for the nobles of the region.

In fact, between a Hispanicity tainted by an illegitimate origin and communities of interest and matrimonial ties with circles that capitalize on an undisputed antiquity and legitimacy, Diego does not hesitate. He chooses the indigenous side which guarantees his local establishment. Better for the Muñoz to blend in with the Tlaxcaltec aristocracy than to be the third or fourth cutthroat among the Spaniards in the Mexican capital.

Unless we are on the wrong track and the dilemma (Indian or Spanish?) that we spontaneously think of did not exist in Diego's head. If we remember that in his eyes the key value is the quality of *hidalgo* , only one option was imposed on him, that of native marriages for lack of being able to rally the Castilian nobility, a species still rare in New Spain . Diego would therefore not have played the Indian card against the European card, but that of the nobility against commoners.

Proximity, personal strategy and empathy could encourage him to go beyond the space usually reserved for the answers expected by the Crown. But from there to blowing up the frame habitual of the geographical relationship! What devil pushes him to dive deep into local memories and to mobilize all of his knowledge to transform the elements he brings together into a real story?

The effort of reflection, interpretation and formatting, the intellectual energy and erudition that run through all its pages cannot be explained solely by the zeal of a faithful collaborator of the Philippine bureaucracy in symbiosis with the Indian nobility. More was needed to satisfy the demands of the colonial power while flattering local chauvinism. Still passes for the Spanish administration, which has other things to do than to search the past natives. But to convince his native interlocutors that his interpretation is in conformity with the interests of the city (and, above all, of the groups that support him) and that he, Diego Muñoz, has a vocation to become the informed and exclusive spokesperson of Tlaxcala and its past, that's another matter. He will succeed nevertheless, to the point that his compilation will survive him and that it will be taken up in the great stories of the New World. Royal chronicler Antonio de Herrera's Decades of the New World and Juan de *Torquemada* 's *Indian Monarchy*[8] **rescued it from oblivion before** nineteenth- and twentieth - century scholars recirculated its *history* in modern Mexico .

Our exchanges with him may tell us more.

1. For example, Eusebius of Caesarea, in Gruzinski (2017), p. 45.

2. D226v°.

3. Under inquisitorial censorship, the redacted work was republished twenty years later in 1595.

4. Roman (1595), fol. 141v°, focuses on the practice of sacrifice and self-sacrifice, whose refined cruelties manifest the hand of the devil.

5. *Ibid* ., fol. 142.

6. *Ibid* ., fol. 158.

7. Diego does not refer explicitly to the pages of Román. In revenge, he cites a cohort of auteurs souvent majeurs who are penchés south Tlaxcala: Andres de Olmos, Motolinía, Mendieta, Sahagún, Alonso de Santiago (C169).

8. Antonio de Herrera, *The general history of the events of the Castilians in the Islands and Mainland of the Ocean Sea that they call the West Indies* , Madrid, 1601-1615; Juan de Torquemada, *Indian Monarchy* , Seville, 1615.

9. Dans l'édition d'Alfredo Chavero en 1892, Mexico, Secretaría de Fomento.

CHAPTER VI

These people from elsewhere

Let's start our conversation with Diego with the origins. The seigniory of Tlaxcala, of which he is the spokesperson and the chronicler, has not existed for all eternity. It is the culmination of several centuries of history populated by invaders who came to roam the entire extent of ancient Mexico.

The controversy over origins

– Why do we have so few sources on the indigenous past?

– So the first Spaniards and the first religious who arrived at the beginning burned and destroyed them, because they thought they were idolatrous writings. The Indians themselves buried and hid other texts so that all the writings were lost.

– With what consequences?

– It was a huge loss for all of us! If we had these writings, we would understand important matters and secrets of their ancient times, but time has consumed them and sunk them into oblivion for eternity.

" Which means that there is no longer any trace of the past?"

– We manage to understand certain things transcribed with the signs that the Indians used.

– But how?

– We need people who can comment on them.

– What sources do you have in mind?

– To make their prowess eternal, the Indians sang them in public and thus they remained engraved in their memories. They also used statues that they placed in the temples [2].

– Were there other kinds of oral information?

– In their ancient times, the Indians used adages, proverbs, questions in the form of riddles and riddles, and all of this in a very elaborate language [3].

– What do you mean?

– Their language was abstruse [...] and the Indians are great storytellers [...]. If one does not have a clear knowledge of these codes and these metaphors, one hardly understands them [4].

– Your information also comes from witnesses who survived the Conquest and agreed to share experiences that they could have kept secret.

"Yes, one of them had been a priest of the demon and he told me that when he tore the heart from the entrails and from the side of the wretch being sacrificed, the heart beat and throbbed with such force that it could pick it up and lift it three or four times before it cooled [5].

In the 16th century , many were interested in the origins of the Indians of Mexico. On the Spanish side, this quest responds to very diverse strategies [6]. For the missionaries, it is crucial to identify the origin of the Native American populations of America. Did they descend from Jews deported by the Assyrians and mysteriously disappeared? According to eschatological beliefs, as soon as these tribes are found, the Judgment last would be imminent. But others are radically opposed to this belief.

"Knowing and discovering the origin, the coming, the root and the trunk" of the ancient Indians takes on a whole new meaning when the Crown demands it from Viceroy Antonio de Mendoza or from the conquistador Hernán Cortés. Nothing to do with a missionary's obsession or a historian's curiosity. Rumor has it that the distant northern lands from which the ancestors of the Nahuas came would be extremely wealthy and abundantly populated, if only the splendours discovered in the Valley of Mexico were projected onto the north of the continent [7]. By going back to the geographical origins of the inhabitants of the Altiplano, concretely by exploring these unknown lands, one imagines discovering a new hen laying golden eggs, even more prodigious than all the treasures of Mexico-Tenochtitlan.

– How do you explain the origin of the Indians? You are not tender with some of your contemporaries.

– They want us to believe with specious arguments that these people came from the Eastern countries [8]. [...] I searched and investigated for a long time, with a lot of curiosity and attention, the arrival of these naturals, among the ancients as among the moderns. I wanted to know their origin and provenance. But there is such a diversity of opinions and the contradictions are so strong and so dissonant between these authors themselves that in my opinion very few give truthful information [9].

– You rule out the possibility of an accidental landing of sailors from the Canary Islands, Santo Domingo and Cuba, or even Newfoundland and even Ireland. But what are the Irish doing here?

– The reason given for making them Irish is that they scarified their faces like the people here, that they ate human flesh and that they were near Newfoundland.

– You also reject the theory that identifies the Indians with the descendants of the Jews that the Emperor Titus would have exiled from Jerusalem and deported on ships launched in the middle of the Atlantic. The idea that these populations would come from Spaniards who were victims of the Arab conquest of Spain or of a particularly deadly drought seems to appeal to you even less [11].

– All these reasonings have no real foundation that could shed light on our initial argument [12].

– Some claim that the ancestors of the indigenous populations would be Carthaginians stranded on the American shores at the time when they were at war against the Romans [13]*?*

– For me, all these explanations contradict each other and do not answer what we are looking for. I will therefore not follow any of these opinions because these people know that they come from the Ponant region [14].

– So you opt for the hypothesis of a Jewish origin of the Indians with two arguments: the use among the Indians of northern Mexico of Hebrew names,

such as Reuben and Benjamin, and the presence of a particular ritual ornament [15].

– These people used the woven feather to adorn their tabernacles. Now God commanded that the Tabernacle be decorated with embroidered curtains, woven with feathers, as we see in Holy Scripture. We know that so far no nation in the world has known or applied this technique; none knew how to implement it because of its difficulty, with the exception of the Mexican Indians. From which I conclude that they are really [Jews].

– *Still advancing towards the east, these migrant peoples must have ended up reaching the Caribbean Sea?*

– From this mainland, they occupied the islands of Cuba and Santo Domingo, as well as the other neighboring islands. Indeed, all these peoples eat bread and ears of corn, fruits, vegetables, roots, plants, the same species of hen; they have in common tobacco, games, dances and entertainment, musical instruments, chile, *ají* [17], cassava, clothing and feather ornaments. All seem cut on the same model [18].

Diego insists on the community of origin and the traits - "customs and ways of life" - that the Indians of New Spain share with the other inhabitants of this part of the world, presenting the notion of Mesoamerica, developed over centuries later. Nothing, on the other hand, would bring these populations closer to the Romans or the Carthaginians, "our ancient world". The plants, the fauna, everything is singular in this America. Could it have been the object of another creation? Thesis that he immediately sweeps away – Inquisition obliges – because contrary to the Bible, by invoking the bones of giants found underground, reassuring proof of an antediluvian settlement common to all humanity.

– *What other manifestation of the Deluge can we observe in New Spain?*

– There are several kinds of soil in the great ravines of the sierras and mountains: some are made of sand at the height of a stadium and more 19 , others [of] gravel and pebbles, still others of rocks of different kinds, mixed with saltpeter, to which nature has given this form over the centuries. We can clearly see that they are the product of an enormous storm and hurricane, similar to the Deluge [20].

– *Your interest in the nature of the soil is not surprising in a country where prospecting and exploitation of mines occupy an essential place* [21].

A Detroit Story

– *Where do these populations come from?*

– All with one voice affirm that they came from the direction of the west. Almost all Indians, old and old alike, agree on [this].

– *How were they dressed?*

– Most of them went naked and without clothes. And those who managed to get some wore very strange clothes and finery, very different from one province to another, which allowed them to get to know each other and to distinguish themselves.

- *By what route did they arrive?*

– It is said that they crossed an arm of the sea using tree trunks [23].

– *What should be understood by "tree trunks"?*

– It was a way of talking to them to keep track of such an important thing [24]. It must be understood that these are badly squared canoes or rafts, sorts of crude and rudimentary boats. It is on this that they crossed this narrow passage, this strait [25].

– *What type of strait is it?*

– All came from an identical path, road, path, region. And they crossed this strait – or a mighty river – although some say it's the Rio de Toluca or another [26].

The Franciscan chronicler Mendieta writes that, "at the time of their arrival, they would have passed an arm of the sea which could be the third strait [27]". *Estrecho* , "strait": in 1580, the word carries multiple resonances for an informed ear. While at that time, in South America, the Viceroy of Peru sent Sarmiento de Gamboa to reconnoitre and occupy the Strait of Magellan [28], another passage, that of North-West America towards China, excited the curiosity and greed of the Spaniards in Mexico, fueling a torrent of speculation, dreams and vain hopes. It is the "third strait" mentioned by Mendieta, the second probably being that of Labrador, between America and Greenland.

– *How was this crossing?*

– In those days, it was considered that crossing the sea was a feat requiring a lot of daring, *especially* among peoples who had never known navigation, for lack of boats and instruments essential for such an occasion and at such a crossing.

– *Which Indians acted as scouts?*

– To our knowledge, [the Tarascans] were the first to cross the strait which must be on the western side of us [29].

– *How did the Tarascans do it?*

– At the time of crossing, they looked for a way to cross and they used tree trunks, rafts and other things according to the circumstances. Thus, they had to make ropes and large lanyards (*maromas): to do this, they removed the bands and the maxtles* panties (this is the name given to them in the Mexican language) [...] around their waists to tie their rafts and pieces of wood [...] until they were transported to the other side with women and children. That must have been a lot of people [30].

– *How is it that the Indians have kept such a vivid vision of this event?*

– Never again did the Tarascans put bands around their waists (*bragueros*), never again will they stop wearing the *huipil* of their women, while the latter will never wear them again in remembrance, in memory of this peregrination and this passage [31].

– One of your contemporaries, the Dominican Diego Durán, offers another interpretation of this detail of clothing. He explains that the Mexica, seeing the Tarascans bathing, would have taken the opportunity to steal their clothes and prevent them from following them on their way [32]*. Your story ends, not without a touch of humour, on the origin of the name "Tarasque".*

– The Mexica called the inhabitants of the province of Michoacan "Tarasques" because their genitals dangled between their thighs and they made them squirm, especially when they ran [33].

– Spanish chroniclers are always intrigued by Indians who "show off" their penises [34]*. But who was at the head of these invaders "coming by the west road"?*

– When it was a question of very important personages and of great talent, they made them their gods, in particular Camaxtli, Quetzalcoatl, Tezcatlipoca and all the other idols.

– This is the explanation by euhemerism popularized by authors of Antiquity such as Diodorus of Sicily. The gods of the Greeks and Romans would have been deified human beings for their exceptional gifts. Were Camaxtli, Tezcatlipoca and Quetzalcoatl, as with us, founding heroes or kings who wanted their memory to be perpetuated?

– These beings of whom they made gods must have been magicians, sorcerers, enchanters or necromancers, or else they must have made a pact or be in league with the demon [...]. Or else they were men born of incubi, so strong was the demon over them [35].

The Seven Caves

– *Where did the migrants settle after crossing?*

– They eventually came to land where they found the Seven Caverns. They lived there for a long time, then they left the Seven Caves and walked through great deserts feeding on game, fruits and roots of the fields [36].

– *How long did this first occupation of the country last?*

– They have spent more than two thousand years doing [this].

– *The troglodyte life constitutes a transitional stage between the landing on the coasts of Mexico and the dispersion throughout the country. The place of the Seven Caves is often described as the original matrix of the Nahua peoples of the Altiplano. For you, on the contrary, it's a space of transition and a stage in a secularized story where the events are linked together naturally and are explained in relation to each other. THE ancestral peoples would therefore not be more indigenous than the European invaders [38]. What did they look like?*

– These nations were mostly made up of people who were naked or in rags [...]. Most of them could not find clothes to cover themselves with, except for a few nations who wore leather and animal skins [...]. Either they didn't know the techniques to produce them, or they didn't have the tools to work with cotton or wool, or they didn't have everything they needed to dress [39].

– *Nothing to do with the nudity-innocence that Montaigne, your contemporary, fantasizes about, or the nudity of a world still immersed in childhood imagined by Christopher Columbus [40]. Could the migration have obeyed climatic factors?*

– They came in search of the most temperate lands they could find to more easily preserve their nudity and their way of life [41].

The long walk of the founders

At that time, a veritable human tidal wave swept over the Altiplano. Diego speaks of it as a "very long, itinerant and unheard-of peregrination [42]". A peregrination, in the language of Rabelais, is a trip to a foreign and distant country, on the roads of the world.

– *What do we know about the ancestors of the Tlaxcaltecs and the Nahua Indians of New Spain, those whom you call the "true Chichimecs"?*

– The true Chichimecs are those who came from the Seven Caves [43] [...]. The Chichimecs were the last and ultimate inhabitants of this province of Tlaxcala [44]. [...] "Chichimeca" proper means "wild men" [...] in fact, the origin of this name derives from a group of men who ate raw meats, drank and sucked the blood of the animals they killed . Indeed, in the Mexican language, *chichiliztli* means to give the breast, *chichiualiztli* means the thing that one sucks, and *chichimeca* is the breast or the udder [45]. Where does their name "suckers" come from?

– *When did the irruption of these Chichimecs date back to?*

– There are probably about three hundred years since they arrived with armies formed to seek and populate lands where to live as the other peoples who had settled before them had done [46].

– *How was their progress?*

– These people came out of the caves in search of those who had gone before them; they followed their trail, trying to establish themselves in various parts of the world. During their pilgrimage, they had to cross great deserts, impenetrable and wild regions, cordilleras and great steep mountains [...]. They went in search of the Culhuas, the Tepanecas, the Aculhuaques, the Chalmecas, the Ulmecas and the Xilancas, their allies and their relatives, since they all belonged to the same lineage. They had the same language, the same way of speaking .

– *Why the same language?*

– The Mexican language is their mother tongue [...], even if in each province they had different ways to express themselves, but only in the consonances or the tone they wanted to give it to mark their difference. Everything else was the same.

– *How to describe this language?*

– It is the one that is used in this New Spain and in most of the New World [...]. It is the most copious and richest language that exists after Latin; she is at the same time serious, gentle and suave; it is a noble language, full of confidence, which says a lot in few words, accessible and which lends itself to everything. The language of Mexico and that of Texcoco pass for being the most elegant and the most refined.

– *Is there a hierarchy between the languages?*

– Apart from these, all the other languages are considered coarse and clumsy [49] [...]. [They] pass for barbarians and foreigners.

– *Back to the great migration. How to explain this chase through Mexico?*

– As I have just said, the Chichimecs came after their allies and their relatives. They passed from country to country and from province to province, and they found the greater part of the country already occupied and peopled by their own allies. When they learned that the most important populations were even further away, they wanted to continue, which they did. And so it was that from place to place, and from country to country, they arrived in the province of Xilotepeque and Hueypuchtlan, then in Tepotzotlan and Quauhtitlan, where they settled for some time.

" *Why didn't they settle there?*"

– When they saw the multitude of Chichimecs who had already arrived there and the exiguity of the land, they resumed their journey to the province of Texcoco [50].

– *So it is in this country that they would have settled for a time?*

– Today, the natives of Tlaxcala claim to have rights to these lands, because the lords and kings of Texcoco have indeed donated them [51].

The look of the antique dealer

- Let's go back in time. What do we know about populations established before the Chichimecs, Ulmecas and Xicalancas?

– Nowadays, there are impressive traces of their arrival: very large buildings, even if they collapsed and fell into ruins, which they built and occupied as they progressed and s were establishing. These agglomerations, with their constructions and their imposing buildings, are today in deserted and depopulated places [52].

– Who are these Ulmecas [53]?

"As we know, these first occupants came in three legions from the Seven Caverns. Both had the same language, the same aptitudes, they were of the same race. [...] We can consider that they were the first occupants of the province of Tlaxcala, which they populated without encountering any resistance, because they found the lands uninhabited and empty [54].

Ulmecas and Xicalancas would have settled on the mountain of Xochitecatl and Tenayacac. Even today, in several places in the region, one can visit the remains of an occupation dating back to the pre-classic period and which conceals traces of Olmec presence. With its ceremonial area and its fortifications, ditches and great earthen walls, Cacaxtla, which developed from 650 after the decline of Teotihuacan, seems to be the origin of Diego's descriptions.

– The Ulmecas settled where the village called Santa María de la Natividad is located and in Huapalcalco. [...] It is there, in this place, that the Ulmecas mainly settled to inhabit the place, as the ruins of their buildings reveal to us today. From what we see of them, they were large and fortified. And the fortifications, the barbicans, the wells, the ditches and the bastions suggest that it was the best fortified place in the world, that it was built by a colossal and very numerous labor force, that of the people who came to settle [55].

– *The prologue of the* Description of Tlaxcala *invokes Végèce, a name that among your contemporaries is linked to his treatise on war* , De re militari . *It is widely read in medieval Europe and Castile* [56]. *The fourth chapter of* De re militari *describes the fortifications, towers, portcullises and ditches. We imagine that this reading is familiar to you. What does* Cerro *des Ulmecas look like?*

– Their main establishment and their fortress are on a mountain or a rock which is about two leagues in circumference. Around this rock, on the side of the accesses and the climbs, before reaching its summit, there are five wells and as many moats and pits twenty paces wide. The earth extracted from these pits was used to build a bastion or a wall to solidly fortify an embankment [57].

– *How deep?*

– The depth of these moats must have been considerable because, even if they have been in ruins for quite some time, they are still more than a pike high [58]

.

– *How do you achieve this degree of precision?*

– Because I entered several of these moats on horseback and decided to measure them: a man on horseback with his lance fails to reach the top in quite a few places, even though more than three hundred and sixty years later, with time and floods, they have filled with earth.

– *What was the place like when you visited?*

– Today, many Indians have settled on the rock, which in places was carved into the living rock. They took advantage of the many caves to live on this mountain. It is at the very top in this stronghold as ancient as it is impregnable [...] that women and children withdrew and took shelter when Captain Hernán Cortés and his companions came to conquer this land and entered by the province of Tlaxcala until they are given assurances of peace.

– *Do you know of the existence of other remains?*

– In addition to this ancient agglomeration, there were others [...] in different places in this province. Their constructions are known, but they are only ruins [59].

– *You also mention, outside the province of Tlaxcala, the achievements of the Zapotecs of Oaxaca.*

– It is said that these peoples built the superb Roman buildings of Mictlan (which means "hell" in Mexican). Undoubtedly, it is a set to see, because those who raised it would have been men of rare intelligence, gifted for a thousand things [60].

Told by Diego, the indigenous past covers a turbulent history, made up of landings, chases and invasions that follow one another. But Diego is not only interested in events. He also studies the " *antigüedades índicas* [61]", when in the 16th century , throughout Europe, a growing passion for the vestiges of Antiquity spreads. These scholars of a new kind, the ancestors of our archaeologists, are then called antiquarians. Born in Italy with Petrarch, this curiosity developed during the 15th century in the wake of the humanist Flavio Biondo before invading the rest of Europe, without sparing the Iberian Peninsula [62]. From now on, history is no longer just a matter of compiling archives and chronicles: it also feeds on the research of antique dealers. In the 1570s, the collection of ancient inscriptions and coins, the exploration of ruins, the criticism of material sources became common practices in Spain while, everywhere, hypotheses on the first settlements and the original languages proliferated. New Spain and Peru were no exception: the "antiquaries fever " [63] gripped many Spaniards, mestizos and even natives who set out in search of Amerindian pasts. In Texcoco, she trains a mestizo like Juan Bautista Pomar, while in Tlaxcala she mobilizes Diego's curiosity.

Antiquarianism is not just a scholarly pastime, a mere auxiliary technique of history. From the outset, this interest is embodied in powerful personalities who know how to share their enthusiasm. Philip II sent to New Spain a scholar of exceptional stature, Doctor Francisco Hernández [64]. Diego was lucky to have his manuscripts in his hands and he probably even rubbed shoulders with him. Not only did Hernández become the unequaled specialist in Mexican plants and animals, but he was also the author of a pioneering study of Mexican antiquities, in which he describes ancient customs and pre-Hispanic ruins. Hernández's influence on Diego manifests itself in multiple ways, in words borrowed from the ancient lexicon (*teatros*), in comparisons – the "swimming pool" of Mexico and that of Jerusalem [65] – or in digressions – he takes up the description of the ruins of Texcoco that the Spanish scholar had explored. It is also no coincidence that his pen reverts to the qualifier "Roman" to describe the buildings of Mictlan attributed to migrants gifted in the arts and techniques, or the Mayan ruins "so strong and so remarkable" which cover the Yucatán. This attention to material culture has earned us observations on the use of weapons, on pre-Hispanic musical instruments – drums, trumpets and whelks (*caracoles*) – and the sounds they produce and which are accompanied, in combat, of the deafening echo of the blows of the sword struck on the shields [66]. Or even on finds which, without being anything spectacular, reveal phases of settlement and occupation and confirm dating.

– *You are describing an incorruptible wood, which the Spaniards call sabine.*

– This incorruptible wood [...] can be kept underground for more than three hundred years without corrupting or rotting. It was while digging a well in the valley of Atzompan, in the middle of the plain, that a sabine wood more than six furlongs long was found. Apparently, this excavation had been used in the past. It had been dug exactly at this place and many broken tiles and shards were found there.

– *What explanation do the Indians give for the well?*

– They say that this well served for a long time their Chichimec ancestors and those who were the Ulmecas when they came there defeated, defeated and fleeing the Teochichimecs of Tlaxcala.

– *How long ago?*

– More than three hundred years, according to their ancient documents and their calendar [67].

Like the antique dealers of Spain, Diego is as sensitive to old woods and old stones as he is fond of etymologies. But he moves away from it when he adds to the classic methods of investigation the systematic collection of oral testimony, impossible or difficult to collect around the Roman remains that dot the Iberian Peninsula.

Chichimecs

– Why distinguish two kinds of Chichimecs: the historical Chichimecs, whose irruption and settlement on Mexican soil in distant times we have just seen, and those of the 16th century who jeopardized the colonization of northern New -Spain?

– We hold in great esteem those who descend from these Chichimecs by direct line [...]. They are the real ones, the ancient Chichimecs [68] [...]. Today, this name of Chichimec has remained so deeply rooted that this is the name given to all those who live like savages, who feed on game, who attack and massacre the pacified Indians. Likewise, those who revolt with their bows and arrows and behave like Arabs are considered and called Chichimecs. Especially nowadays, they are the most cruel and appalling ones ever seen. [...] Today, they kill men, pillage the roads and indulge in great carnage and unheard-of cruelty against the Spaniards, against their haciendas and their ranches [69].

– Over time, has the term Chichimec lost its prestigious connotations?

– In fact, the name Chichimec, which was the noblest there was among the Indians, ended up taking on another meaning. By "Chichimecs", today, we must understand brigands and highwaymen [70].

– However, you are severe for the Chichimecs of old who invade the region of Tlaxcala.

– The Chichimecs arrived [...] when the local populations felt calm and safe. They were seditious people, cruel and devoured by ambition. They were the last occupants and the last conquerors of the province of Tlaxcala [71].

– "Seditious, cruel and devoured by ambition": this description could apply word for word to the Spanish conquistadors...

– Why did the Indians who lived in the Valley of Mexico want to get rid of the Chichimecs of Poyauhtlan, who had settled in the province of Texcoco?

– Because the Chichimecs began to behave like bad neighbors and mistreat them, because they wanted to grow and expand [72].

– Did the battle that took place on the edge of the lagoon leave any memorable traces?

– The ancient stories tell that [...] all the mudflat which occupies the edges of the lagoon was only corpses and streams of blood. So that all along the shore the water looked not like water, but like pure blood and a lagoon of blood; she was entirely converted to blood.

– What memories do the Indians have of this massacre?

– In memory of such a bloody battle, the Indians there eat a kind of crustacean that lives in this lagoon. It is called *izcahuitli* and is found in abundance. It has the color of blackened, tawny blood, it is like a sort of red-colored mud that is collected in large quantities and exploited by the local fishermen [73].

– What is the relationship between the battle and this crustacean?

– The Indians mean by this that the spilled blood turned into mud and gave the crustacean that color.

– This story is therefore the story of a metamorphosis, that of spilled blood transformed into a mollusk.

- It's a fable. [...] Because "blood" in Mexican is called *eztli* , and as the word has become corrupted, we call this mud *izcahuitli* [74].

– By fable, you mean "fabricated story" (" narración artificiosa [75] *").*

The Wonders of Creation

– *After this war, our Chichimecs decide to abandon the Valley of Mexico. For what reasons ?*

– To go forward in search of larger and more extensive territories where they would feel more at ease [...] and because their god Camaxtli also told them to break camp, it was there that they were to settle, they were to advance further to where "the sun would rise and set". A way of telling them that there they would become absolute lords and would know peace and quiet [76].

– *Once again, the god Camaxtli resembles the Moses who leads Israel to the Promised Land. But you see the story differently...*

– These lands of New Spain, so ample and extensive [...], it was God who had reserved them for the Indians to live there [77].

– *The Chichimecs therefore set off again in the direction of the east and the sea* [78]. *Guides lead them to the summit of the Mount Tlaloc which offers them, at more than four thousand meters, a striking view.*

– These are very high mountains and shady sierras where I have been. I have seen them and I can say that from up there you can see two hemispheres at once, because they are the most imposing and highest peaks in New Spain. I cannot find words to exalt the beauty of these trees and these exceptionally high reliefs, cedars, cypresses and pines which seem to touch the sky at nature's command [79].

– *Breathtaking splendour?*

– Indeed, I have no words to explain the ideas that this show inspires in me. I rely here on the understanding and intelligence of the reader [80].

– For the ancients, the mountains were inhabited by the divinity, they were the pillars of a sacred geography of the Altiplano and its two cordilleras. The Tlalocan was the "mountain of Tlaloc", the god of rain and fertility. How do you view this mountain?

– Apart from the Sierra Nevada and the Volcano [Popocatepetl], which are higher than these mountains, the Artisan of the world [81] placed here one of the major ornaments of his Creation. From there, on one side we discovered the kingdom of the Mexica Tepanecs with their immense lagoon, and on the other the kingdom and the province of Tlaxcala, Cholula, Huejotzingo [...] as well as other provinces populated by innumerable nations [82].

– What lesson can we learn from this?

– To see these two panoramas, we give infinite thanks to the Universal Artisan of all Creation, especially today.

– Why "especially today"?

– The reversal of things which the true God has wrought through his own fills us with immense gratitude and we overflow with praise at the thought that what was entirely in the hands of the devil is now subject to the true God and his Church Militant.

- We understand you...

– Who would tire of crying for pure joy? Who is not filled with enormous joy in the face of these miracles so well known and so manifest, seeing that after so many thousands of years it has pleased Our Lord to make his holy faith known to so many peoples and countless nations? Let us praise and give thanks to His Divine Majesty for all the benefits that She grants every day to her creatures of [reason]!

– Didn't the Indians attribute a particular aura to these mountains?

– For them, the Sierra Nevada de Huejotzingo and the Volcano were divinities. They claimed Volcano and Sierra Nevada were husband and wife.

The Volcano, they called it Popocatepetl, and the Sierra Nevada Ixtacihuatl [84].

– *On the Tlalocan stood one of the great sanctuaries of pre-Hispanic times, but it was also a kind of astronomical observatory* [85]. *What do the Chichimecs discover from these peaks?*

– Plains, with their rivers and springs, like a kind of New World and New Hemisphere [86].

– *Your story suggests a parallel between the discovery of the Promised Land by the Hebrews, that of the "new world" by the Spaniards and that of the province of Tlaxcala by the founders. But once the Chichimecs have contemplated their promised land, like Moses on Mount Nebo, is it not the God of the Christians who comes into action?*

The promised land

– The Chichimecs celebrated great festivals in honor of their idol Camaxtli [...]. It is reported that while talking with them he told them to start moving, that this land over there was the one they were to occupy and where they would remain the masters [87].

– *Is it important to give us in detail the names of the* caudillos *who led these men and women?*

– It is because today there are many notables who descend from these people [...]. It will be noted that at that time the Chichimecs had only one wife, and today those who are still rebellious have no more than one. They greatly appreciate the sons they bear and hate the daughters [88].

– *In their progression towards Tlaxcala, do the chichimec groups modify their eating habits? I ask the question to the breeder and the lover of good meat.*

– From then on, they began to eat cooked, stewed or grilled meats. Before, they ate them raw or badly prepared on a grill; moreover, they were more raw than grilled.

– *What did they cook their food in?*

– Over there, they were offered terracotta pots for them to eat [89].

– *The region of Tlaxcala, as we know, was populated before the arrival of the Chichimecs. How did they behave with the local populations?*

– Once established in Tepeticpac, they finished expelling from there all the Ulmecas and Zacatecas who lived in these lands of Tlaxcala and Xocoyucan, when they were there the owners. Tepeticpac is near the pueblo of San Felipe of this city [of Tlaxcala] [90].

– *What was the fate of these first occupants?*

– They let them go and they went towards Mitlmani and Cuyametepec [...]. And, as in these regions they found no caves in which to shelter, they suffered greatly because a light rain fell on them for more than twenty days. And there old people and children cried very loudly for the lands they had lost. This is why this valley is now called Huehueychocayan ("where the elders wept").

Civil war

– But the occupation of the region results in a split within the invaders. What reason could have pushed some of the migrants to rebel against those you call the "old Chichimecs"?

– Because, from there, they were going to submit them and make them their vassals. It was perfectly unjustified, because all were equal in lineage. And, as all had come to settle, each had to be content with what he had acquired and earned for himself, his parents and all his descendants [...]. No question of being subject to a governor, a king or a single captain [91].

– To qualify these conflicts, you use an expression that one encounters in the historians of Antiquity and in particular in Plutarch, you speak of "civil wars".

– Ambition and greed were so strong that civil wars broke out between them [92]. They began to conspire against their principal captains, lords and chiefs, against those who had brought and guided them from such distant lands at the cost of exhausting peregrinations [93] [...]. They ended up fight the fiercest and bloodiest civil war the world has ever known, slaughtering each other like cruel enemies and rabid dogs, fighting brother against brother, father against son, son against father, mingling the blood shed by themselves and by [members of] their own homeland. The unthinkable cruelties that have been perpetrated and produced in this war, there are no words to explain and too much cannot be said

– What are the opposing groups?

– In the name of freedom, boundless ambition mobilized most of the plebs. They ran and marched against the most important of their Chichimec captains.

– So it's a revolt of the plebs against its leaders.

– They did all this to emancipate themselves and become masters of what they had won and occupied with their people [96]. [...] All the common people, the plebs and the other bands called for the extermination of the Chichimecs [97].

– Finally, after an episode to which we will return, the siege of the Chichimec fortress of Texcalticpac fails and the insurgents are crushed.

– Those who were able to escape brought back such stories that they would have had enough to tell of the defeat for an eternity [98].

– This battle, we know it through an Indian source.

– This story keeps the memory of two battles among the most famous, the most cruel and the most lamentable that the world has known: that of Poyauhtlan, on the edges of the lagoon between Cohuatlichan and Chimalhuacan, and the second and last, that of Texcalticpac [99].

– You attribute this story to Tequanitzin.

– Tequanitzin transmitted to us the memory of these two battles. He was a man of good faith and worthy of credit. His stories have remained famous, because they immortalize the fame of their ancestors and perpetuate their memory among the living in the past, present and future centuries [100].

– This war is followed by an era of peace. After the storm, the thinning...

– The Chichimecs wanted to make friends with all their neighbors and never provoke their wrath again. [...] They remained at peace for a very long time with all these peoples, these provinces, these nations, without experiencing any clashes. All had peaceful relations and they traded with each other in friendship [101].

– How did this stabilization phase translate?

– They established themselves by marking the limits and borders that each province had to have. To this end, they designated the rivers, sierras and cordilleras of the great mountains and delimited their sector according to what each legion or captaincy deserved or had obtained by fate [102].

– *An era of "universal concord" then sets in between the Tlaxcaltecs and the other Nahua peoples?*

"A lot of things happened then. To avoid prolixity and to be brief, I will not talk about it [103].

We will conclude that the Tlaxcaltecs are not natives, Diego repeated it in all tones. Their ancestors came from elsewhere, like the ancestors of the Romans and like the conquistadors, the latest invaders. In describing these invasions of Mexico, the successes of these waves of conquerors, their violent establishment at the expense of the indigenous populations and their unchallenged hegemony, Diego undoubtedly has in mind the birth of New Spain: people who came from no one knows where, warlike and greedy conquerors, of new kingdoms. Recent history echoed ancient history without reproducing it term by term, more like a resonance than a repetition. Is this mirror effect deliberate? Does it respond to the desire to trivialize the Spanish domination which would be, after all, only the last wave breaking over the Altiplano?

This concern is not incompatible with the persistence of the old indigenous logics: for the ancient Mexicans, only those facts that recurred made sense – and therefore constituted events. If our hypothesis is correct, Diego's story had precedents. In the early 1540s, the perspective of ancient history and contemporary history undoubtedly inspired indigenous painters in the neighboring province of Texcoco. They compared the irruption of the Spaniards to the invasions which had preceded the Conquest, which in fact then lost its incomprehensible monstrosity and its absolute novelty. In Tlaxcala, long before Diego, indigenous scholars were able to engage in the same parallel by combining opportunism, the search for meaning and local tradition. Two birds with one stone: the old way of seeing things trivialized and, in a sense, legitimized the Spanish conquest at the same time as it justified collaboration with the occupier [104].

1. D69r°.

2. C171.

3. C172.

4. D156r° and 73r°.

5. C17 ; D156v°.

6. Gregorio García, *Origin of the Indians* of *the New World and West Indies* , Madrid, CISIC, [1607] 2005.

7. Baltazar de Obregón, *History of ancient and modern discoveries of New Spain* , Mexico, Editorial Porrúa, 1988, p. 10.

8. D69r°.

9. D68v°.

10. D84v°.

11. D69v°.

12. D70r°.

13. D69v°.

14. D70r°.

15. D82v°.

16. D83v°.

17. Taino term for a pepper.

18. D70v°.

19. D71v°: between 185 and 200 meters.

20. *Ibid.*

21 . In Europe, the first research on rocks and fossils was published in the 1540s (Agricola) and 1560s (Conrad Gesner); in 1569, *De re metallica* by Pérez de Vargas tackled the question of metals in Spain. See Jean Gaudant and Geneviève Bouillet, "Paléontologie de la Renaissance", *Works of the French Committee for the History of Geology* , French Committee for the History of Geology, 2005, 3 rd series (t. 19), p. 35-50, https://hal.archives-ouvertes.fr/hal-00872119.[1]

22 . D70r°.

23 . D72v°.

24 . D74r°.

25 . D89v°.

26 . C26.

27 . Mendieta (1997), XXXII, p. 268.

28 . Pedro Sarmiento de Gamboa, *Course to the Strait of Magellan* , J. Batista ed., Madrid, History 16, 1987; *Trips to the Strait of Magellan* , Maria Justina Sarabia Old ed., Madrid, Alianza Editorial, 1988.

29 . C26.

30 . D90r°.

31 . D90v°. The *huipil* is a sort of chasuble.

32 . C26, note 3.

33 . C27.

34 . Fray Pedro de Aguado on the Indians of the province of Mérida, *Recopilación historial de Venezuela* , Caracas, Biblioteca de la Academia nacional de la historia, 1987, p. 455-457.

35 . C53.

---

1. https://hal.archives-ouvertes.fr/hal-00872119

36. D72v°; C22-23.

37. D74v°.

38. This interpretation of the "Place of the seven caves", *Chicomoztoc* in Nahuatl, agrees with that given by other pictographic manuscripts such as the *Lienzo de la peregrinación* or the *Codex Boturini* .

39. C23-24.

40. Frank Lestringant, *The Huguenot and the Savage. America and the colonial controversy in France during the Wars of Religion* , Paris, Klincksieck distribution, 1990.

41. C24; D89r°.

42. C53.

43. D73v°.

44. D95r°.

45. C43; D97r°-97v°.

46. D95v°; less than four hundred years for the *Culhuaques Mexicanos* (D74v°).

47. C40; D95v°.

48. D95r°.

49. *Ibid.*

50. C41-42.

51. *Ibid.*

52. D70r°.

53. Adopted by archaeologists, the name "Olmec" refers to the civilization that developed on the Gulf of Mexico between - 2500 and - 500.

54. C39.

55. C37.

56. María Elvira Roca Barea, "El "Libro de la Guerra" y la traducción de Vegecio por Fray Alfonso de San Cristóbal", *Anuario de estudios medievales* , vol. 37-1, January-June 2007, p. 284.

57. C37.

58. C38.

59. C37-39.

60. D85r°. Diego refers to Mitla in the state of Oaxaca.

61. D64v°.

62. Frédérique Lemerle, *The Renaissance and the antiquities of Gaul: Gallo-Roman architecture as seen by architects, antique dealers and travellers, from the Italian wars to the Fronde,* Turnhout, Brepols, 2005; Andrew Hui, *The Poetics of Ruins in Renaissance Literature: Studies in Poetics* , New York, Fordham University Press, 2016.

63. Richard Cooper, *Roman Antiquities in Renaissance France 1515-1565* , London, Ashgate, 2013.

64. Patrick Lesbre, " *De Antiquitatibus Novae Hispaniae* : Francisco Hernández and his *Antiquities of New Spain* ", *E-Spania* , February 2017, https://journals.openedition.org/e-spania/26472.[2]

65. D82r°.

66. D155r°.

67. C298.

68. D97v°.

69. C43; D97v°-98r°.

---

2. https://journals.openedition.org/e-spania/26472

70. C43.

71. D95r°.

72. C46.

73. D99r°.

74. C47.

75. Covarrubias (1611), 393v°. In the sixteenth century , the fable can be a story invented for fun, aimed at evoking things that are not true and without foundation. But it also serves to describe physical phenomena, in particular the "transformations which are called metamorphoses and which are due to the corruption of certain things and the generation of others".

76. C47; D101r°.

77. D74r°.

78. C48.

79. C49; D100v°. On one of the first descriptions of Mexican nature, Toribio de Benavente says Motolinía, *Historia de los Indios de la Nueva España* , Madrid, Centro para la edición de los clásicos españoles, 2014, p. 199-223.

80_ C49.

81. Dieu comme *artifex Mundi* dans Isidore de Séville, *Opera emendeda* , Madrid, at the Monastery of Conception Hieronynianae, 1778, t. I, "On the nature of things", chap. xxiii, p. 99.

82. C49; D100v°.

83. D100v°-101r°.

84. C143.

85 . Stanislaw Iwaniszewski, "Archaeology and Archaeoastronomy of Mount Tlaloc, Mexico: A Reconsideration", *Latin American Antiquity* , vol. 5, 2, June 1994, p. 158-176.

86 . C49.

87 . C50

88 . C54-55.

89 . C62.

90 . C63.

91 . C64-65; D108r°-v°.

92 . *Ibid.*

93 . C65.

94 . C66.

95 . D108v°.

96 . C66.

97 . C72.

98 . D114v°.

99 . *Ibid.*

100 . C77.

101 . C79; D115v°

102 . C80.

103 . D116v°.

104 . Gruzinski (2017), p. 113-193.

CHAPTER VII

Does Diego believe what he says?

"The reductionism of fabulation has been done in several ways which have in common that they are egocentric, because each era takes itself for the center of culture. »

Paul Veyne, *Did the Greeks believe in their myths* [1]*?*

Does Diego believe the stories he has reported and, if so, to what extent? Sometimes he opposes his truths to the nonsense of these "barbarians", but he often gives the impression of adhering to the stories and even the myths of the Indians. Or, at least, not to say. The game is subtle, as is subtle in this mixed-race society the boundary between, on the one hand, positive truth, gospel truth, authenticity of tradition and what the elders say, and, on the other, diabolical imposture, error of the mind, ignorance and drift of the imagination.

God according to Diego and the Indians

– *What idea did the Indians have of divinity?*

– They had knowledge of one God and one cause, when they said that he was the substance and the principle of all things [...]. Everything had its god and they concluded by saying: “Oh! God in whom are all things”, which is said in *Tloquenahuaque* [2], as if we said today “this person in whom all things are present”, “this cause of all things together”, which is only an “essence” [3].

'The principle of all things', 'the cause of all things together', 'nothing but an essence': would the god of the Indians therefore be only a primary essence? Saint Augustine is not so far from it when he maintains that "there exist three entirely distinct persons: the Father, the Son and the Holy Spirit, but only one essence or divine nature [4]". As for the God “in whom are all things”, he appears word for word in the *Soliloquies* of the Father of the Church, who qualifies God as “principle, cause and source of all that is good and beautiful ”.

– Would *the indigenous elites, who informed you, have reviewed their old beliefs in the light of the writings of the Father of the Church? Where is this your own reading? Your own God, how do you define him?*

– The Artisan of the world [...]. The Universal Artisan of all that has been created [6]; the supreme Craftsman and Creator of all things [7].

The conversation stumbles on this thorny topic. Diego does not come forward. In the climate of religious repression which prevailed at the end of the 16th century, any response deviating from orthodoxy could be used against him, especially since, not being a cleric, he had no vocation to meddle in theological issues. The poet Francisco de Terrazas, whose work as a historian he praises, knows something about it. Inappropriate remarks reported to the court of the Inquisition made him have a very bad time.

The expression "Universal Artisan of all created things " [8] dates back to the beginning of Christian literature, and even earlier still: it refers to Plato's demiurge. This demiurge, whom the *Timaeus* presents as the Worker of the world [9], is the creator of all natural things [10]. Diego knows of Plato's existence and quotes him in the prologue to the *Description* , giving him the epithet "divine" reserved for him by Renaissance humanists. This would link it to a Platonic tradition of Christianity, taken up by Saint Augustine and by the whole Church [11]. However, it is unlikely that he had direct contact with the philosopher's writings or with Neoplatonic thinkers. With the exception, perhaps, of the king's first physician, Doctor Francisco Hernández, whom he no doubt met in Mexico City or Tlaxcala. The scholar appreciates Plato and reads Leo the Hebrew, the author of the Neoplatonic-inspired *Dialogues of Love* [12].

Nevertheless, certain pages of Diego conceal other intriguing resonances. Like those where he evokes the nine skies above which the goddess Xochiquetzal lives, a strange mixture of native cosmology and celestial geography again of Platonic ancestry [13].

Let's move on to firmer ground. In the 1580s, Métis and indigenous circles wondered about the nature of the supreme deity and agreed to demonstrate the existence of a pre-Hispanic monotheism. At the same time, a contemporary and almost a neighbor of Diego, the mestizo author of the *Relation of Texcoco* , Juan Bautista Pomar, developed speculations in this direction, no doubt with the same ulterior motive: how to reconcile, or at least establish a bridge between a pagan past and a Christian past, if not by attenuating what idolatry harbors most scandalous and by drawing native traditions towards Christian doxa? There was nothing here to offend a Christian since it was a question of taking up the very widespread hypothesis of an original monotheism. But, in the context of the Counter-Reformation and from the perspective of the construction of the indigenous past, the position took an undeniably political turn. It attenuated the paganism of the Indians [14].

What did the Tlaxcaltec believe?

Diego addresses the beliefs of the Tlaxcaltecs in two separate chapters, after examining the origins of Tlaxcala. The shadow of the tribunal of the Inquisition and the ongoing extirpation of idolatry imposed on him a kind of jargon as on all his contemporaries. It is also true that we are not dealing with a free thinker, but with a convinced Christian, for whom Christian belief and knowledge of the truth meet and even merge.

– You take care to distinguish between the arsenal of knowledge available to the Indians [15] *and what comes from their adherence, "they believed in it as if it were an act of faith* [16]*". As if you blamed them less for their disbelief than for their shortcomings, a lack of knowledge or an erroneous knowledge, blinded by lies.*

– They never knew nor perceived the lie in which they lived until they were baptized and became Christians [17].

– Do you mean that they knew nothing about God? But you explained that they were summoning Tloquenahuaque.

– It was the clue they had of the existence of a single God, placed above the gods.

– Do you see any other signs of an acquaintance that would bring them closer to Christians?

– In the same way, they had in their antiquity a vague idea of eternity [...]. Just as they were aware of the existence of nine heavens which they called *Chicuhnauhnepaniuhcan Ilhuicac* [18], where the pleasure was perpetual [...]. They were also convinced that there was pain and glory, reward for the good and punishment for the [wicked].

Diego probably draws things too quickly towards Christianity. The Franciscan Gerónimo de Mendieta provides a less "contaminated" version when he explains that "those of Tlaxcala believed that the souls of lords and principals were transformed into mist and clouds, into birds with rich plumage of all kinds and into *precious* stones of great value [20]".

– *How did the Indians interpret natural phenomena?*

– [They were convinced] that the rainwater did not come from the clouds, but from the sky, and that the gods of the sky poured it out in due time to water the earth of the world [21]. They attributed lightning, lightning, thunder [to the gods of the air] and, when these were angry with men, they sent them great earthquakes, rains and hailstones [22].

– *How did they explain the earthquakes?*

– Earthquakes and seisms [...], they attributed them to the gods who carried the world: they got tired and then began to move, this was the cause of the earthquakes [23].

– *Does the landscape have a history? Can a lake be an ancient volcano?*

– In the plains of Perote are the lagoons of Tlachac, Atlchichica and Quecholac, and people say that in other times there were mountains and volcanoes there. Time consumed them and they collapsed and became **lagoons**.

– *Was the world created? Do the Tlaxcaltecs have a creation myth?*

– What they understood was that the world had not been created, but had happened by chance, and they gave the name of *Tlaltecuhtli* to the god of the world and the earth. Likewise, for them the heavens were not created; they had never had a **beginning**.

– *How did they represent the world, what form did they give it?*

– They didn't understand that the world is spherical and round. They thought it flat. For them it ended and ended on the shores of the sea. And the sea and the sky were one. They were made of the same material, but the sea was more consistent.

– *What did they think of the four elements?*

– They had no knowledge of the four elements nor of the movements of the sky.

" *What did they know of heaven?"*

– They did not understand that there was more than one sky, and that this one [the celestial vault] was fixed and motionless. They only thought that the sun and the moon were moving, that they were moving. This is why they ignored the effects of the stars, the signs of the zodiac and the planets [27].

"Yet you told us they believed in nine heavens. How did they designate the things around them?

– There was no proper word in their language for the things they didn't have. And so, with the arrival of the Spaniards, they created many specific terms, but still understandable. As for the things they knew, they gave them a perfectly appropriate, self-evident name .

"What did they know of the sun?"

– [The Indians] were also wrong when they said that when the sun sets and night falls, he slept and rested from the task he had endured during the day [...]. They are convinced that when the sun was created, it did not move until the fourth day. The fable tells that the sun was a very despised god, because he was leprous and covered with pustules, so that he could neither walk nor show himself [29].

– Fable, we would say myth, is a word you rarely use. It has explanatory virtues when it accounts for the creation of the sun: the gods throw the leper into a kind of lime kiln and this becomes "light and they called it the sun".

– This is how, according to them, the sun was born, and this is how they took him for god and lord of the day.

– *When the moon was the goddess of the night. What influence did the sun and the moon exert on the firmament?*

– They say that the stars obeyed these two planets.

– *Renaissance Europeans interpreted the appearance of comets as bad omens. What about Indians?*

– Comets in the sky were believed to be ominous signs. They announced deaths, wars, famines on earth as well as other tests and other calamities [30].

– *Is the presence of pre-Hispanic deities still perceptible?*

– To be remembered forever, the gods and goddesses left their names to well-known mountains, [...] and today many mountains and sierras bear these names [31].

– *You talk about it as if all these divinities had existed, with the same familiarity as a European evoking the gods of Antiquity. For example, who was Quetzalcoatl for them?*

– He was a very important character [...] and later worshiped by the Choultecs and taken for god [32].

Reliable sources?

Diego's sources, we know them now, but what degree of credibility does he give them? Like Pausanias and the historians of antiquity long before him, Diego attributes considerable weight to oral tradition. This is what distinguishes him from Spanish or European authors, his contemporaries. Its information depends on a medium in which the speech remains the obligatory reference which continues to be authoritative. Orality is the gateway par excellence to the indigenous past and Diego makes us understand this on several occasions. It concerns the memories and traditions entrusted to it verbally by the Tlaxcaltec nobles, as it is expressed through the chanted messages contained in the *cantares* [33], these texts that the heirs of the native nobility sang and danced during great festivities. Proverbs also convey the memory of ancient events, such as the one which recommended: "Beware of the one who impregnated the women of Xicotencatl and keep an eye on your women: if they use both sexes, beware of them , that they do not fatten them up for you [34]. We will discover later the meaning of this riddle.

Diego has got into the habit of favoring the story of eyewitnesses as transmitted by their descendants. In the 1580s, despite their advanced age, some protagonists of the Conquest were still able to bear witness [35]. Diego knows this and he investigates tirelessly. When he returns empty-handed, he does not hesitate to admit it [36]. Each engulfed memory turns into an irreparable gap.

His sources are reliable insofar as they come from his social and family circle. The continuous frequentation of his interlocutors and the multiple interests that he shares with them are worth all the checks and cross-checks in the world. The social and political prestige of the aristocracy confers truth value on the information it provides, that is to say, ultimately, on the representation it intends to give of itself.

Diego, however, does not seek to appear as a specialist in the past who would diagnose the facts, authenticate them or reject them as false. Not just out of respect for his native informants or out of calculation. Its criteria are not ours. Indeed, in the sixteenth century , the "fable" is not the false in the sense that we understand it today. The origin myths elaborated by European Renaissance historians to flatter monarchs are all fables as well. But justifiable and justified fables. They serve the prestige of the crowned recipient and the pretensions of his dynasty. They are real political tools that belong to another program of truth [37].

The fable therefore deserves to be taken seriously and, as it usually belongs to pre-Christian worlds in Europe, observers from the New World quite naturally applied the same reasoning to the Amerindian world. The fable always conceals a share of historical truth or edifying testimony, therefore recoverable. Even if from time to time, in Diego's eyes, improbability crosses the line: he points this out by using the word *fábula* again , but this time in the sense of fabulous. Thus, the transformation into molluscs of human blood poured into Lake Texcoco during a terrible battle is in his eyes only "a fable", but this fable functions as a mnemonic device which allows the Indians to remember this war [38].

For the rest, Diego historicizes all the stories, whatever they may be, whether they reach his ears or his hands, and some of which would seem to us to belong to the register of mythology. But what is the meaning of "historicizing"? Restore a historical truth of the time or anachronize the information by interpreting it as one would have done a contemporary event? Or even humanize it: to explain the origin of the native deities, Diego, as we have seen, is part of a thousand-year-old tradition, euhemerism, which the chroniclers of New Spain and their informants have made their honey. natives [39]. In this sense, he also imagines himself producing truth.

The truth according to Diego

Does Diego believe everything he says? No need to ask him. Apart from what he explicitly identifies as a fable, his answer would necessarily be in the affirmative. To tell the truth, Diego is caught between two fires: the noble natives and the administration. Officially, his relationship is for Philip II and his entourage. The accusation of idolatry did not represent a risk for him at that time - he was not Indian, but "Spanish" - even so he had no interest in stirring up matters on which the sovereign imposed silence. In 1577, Philip II placed an embargo on anything that could awaken the memory of idolatry [40]. In his description of Tlaxcaltec beliefs, Diego must never imply that he lends them the slightest grain of truth. He blurs the tracks, mixes the registers, the mythological fund coexisting with geographical information, and even playful, when he evokes the ancient pastimes of the Indians. Caution remains in order: "These barbarian people had many good customs, but also many bad, tyrannical and irrational ones [41]. » To spare himself any reproach, the antiques suit suits him perfectly... and the happy medium.

Faced with the Tlaxcaltec nobles, his approach is different. Diego cannot reduce their past to a grotesque and diabolical farce. Impossible, however, to evade idolatry: it would not be credible, because it would tear essential threads from the weft of the story told by the elders. But he is quick to make cannibalism and idol worship a recent [phenomenon]. On this account, paganism is reduced to a demonic skid of the veneration that the Indians devoted to the statues of great men and cannibalism is no more than the effect of overflowing passions and hatreds. Everything becomes more presentable.

By historicizing the Tlaxcaltec past as much as possible, that is to say by bringing out earthly and human motives, by disguising or evading divine interventions whenever he can, Diego spares both the Crown and the aristocracy. Indian. Leaves, from time to time, to bring out the hand of the devil, for lack of being able to proceed otherwise. Without ever denying the Indians the use of reason, even if it is a question, as he observes, of "another order43 ", of a different rationality.

All these efforts are all the better understood since he is not a neutral intermediary, caught between his informants and the Philippine bureaucracy, torn between two regimes of truth. He has set himself a priority task which he endeavors to fulfill to the end, that of offering the eyes of the Spanish power the most decent image of Tlaxcala in order to preserve the privileges acquired during the Spanish conquest.

The magic vase

In May 2019, commenting on the last episode of the famous HBO series, *Game of Thrones* , the *New York Times* detected in it the expression of a disenchanted world which, while no longer believing in the marvelous, nevertheless fails to pass. The story that Diego develops shares traits of *Game of Thrones* : insane violence and political intrigues ending in lakes of blood or episodes of extraordinary sex. Like George RR Martin and the screenwriters of the series, Diego can't resist the urge to tell a prodigy, coming from a marvelous officially past, but still etched in the memories [44].

– *The people of the plebs had revolted against their Chichimec lords. A few days before the battle of Tepeticpac, which you date to the year 9-Flint, the Chichimec chiefs went to the sanctuary of the god Camaxtli, where they resorted to a "superstitious enchantment 45" to ensure their* defense.

– It happened like this: to prepare this diabolical prayer, they looked for a very beautiful young girl with one breast larger than the other, then they brought her to the temple of Camaxtli. There they made her drink a medicinal drink, thanks to which the breast gives milk. They squeezed her breast, but not more than a drop came out. This drop, they poured it into a vase which they called the "vase of god".

" *What did this vase look like?"*

– It was made like this: the base was round, cylindrical in shape, and the upper part, which formed the cup, was like a chalice, one elbow high; this part was of precious, black wood, the color of ebony; but others say it was of very finely worked black stone, intensely black and shiny. It is found in this region and the Indians call it *teotetl* , which means "stone of god".

– *What have we done with the vase?*

– The milk which they had extracted and poured into the vase, the reed stalks, the toothed harpoons and the fire-hardened spears, the points and sinews of deer, they laid all on the altar and the tabernacle of Camaxtli , then they covered the whole thing with laurel branches.

– Three days pass and no miracles happen.

– On the contrary, the drop of milk had almost dried up; it was withered and had shrunk.

– But, on the eve of the battle, signs appear .

– The high priest came to see the vase, the reed stalks, the pointed staffs, the tendons and the fire-hardened spearheads with their six hooks. He found that the arrows and harpoons were already fully mounted, that the tips hardened with fire were on their poles, with their hooks and their feathers. The vase was full of a froth that looked like a stream of saliva, and the foaming milk overflowed out of the vase and spilled all over the altar.

– It was then that a prisoner was sacrificed to the god Camaxtli and the miracle took place.

– [The priest] took the vase which contained the foaming milk and poured it on the one who had put on the skin of the prisoner who had been flayed. He immediately took one of the devilishly crafted arrows and shot it with a crooked, coarse, malformed bow against their enemies: instantly the other arrows began to move and sway. rush furiously against opponents.

– So what?

– As the arrows began to hit them, a thick dark fog suddenly lifted. [The enemies] no longer saw each other, they killed each other without knowing who they were fighting against. Become blind, mortally broken, exposed to all dangers, they threw themselves from the top of the cliffs, they fled looking behind them without knowing where they were going, they were seized with terror. [...] The ravines and defiles were strewn with corpses.

– It is the signal of the rout for the adversaries of the Chichimecs .

– After this demonic event, no one escaped death or captivity [46].

– *The miracle took place on the altar of Camaxtli, which you liken to a tabernacle. The transformation of the drop of milk is the effect of what you call an "enchantment".*

Plutarch does not like prodigies [47]. Diego, on the other hand, does not hesitate to report them in great detail and to believe them. He needs it here to describe the momentarily suspended outcome of the Battle of Tepeticpac. His gaze on the past is ambivalent: if the intervention of the god Camaxtli can only be demonic – *este endemoniado hecho* –, it is at the same time very real. In principle, after this long half-century, the evangelization of Mexico has expelled this diabolical force from the historical scene. But is the disenchantment total and final? And the Christian re-enchantment, effective? The Conquest is too recent, Christianization far from complete, and the old divine forces are not yet dormant.

The prism of the ancient

The manner of saying things is sometimes as determining as the substance of what one affirms. In the 16th century, the best way to "concrete" a subject was to offer it an antique setting. With Diego, the color is given from the prologue. A cocktail of three references – a dash of Plato, a bit of Végèce and a dose of Claude Élien, a 2nd century historian – is enough to set the stage for the antique, a prestigious and unmissable horizon at the end of the century. It resurfaces from time to time in the course of the text: such an evocation of the Greeks and the Trojans in connection with a question of armament refers to the Homeric epic [48]. The anecdote that features King Artaxerxes takes us into the Persian Wars. Artaxerxes received good press in the 16th century : Montaigne, a contemporary of Diego, also quotes him in his *Essays* [49], but he relies more classically on Plutarch while Diego favors the version of Claude Elien [50].

Are these references only a rhetorical dressing or a display of erudition? We think not. Diego resolved to put before the eyes of the sovereign an Indian antiquity, in the manner of Bartolomé de Las Casas in his *Summary Apologetic History* . To be convincing and even to seduce, it is better to give the indigenous past the luster of the great stories antiques by applying or adapting categories borrowed from illustrious predecessors [51] and endowing it with an epic and grandiose atmosphere. This closeness built from scratch makes it easier to understand the story when too many novelties and unknown names are confusing. This sprinkling feeds a genuine exoticism that never undermines, quite the contrary, the respect that Diego professes for the Tlaxcaltec past. Finally, what does not spoil anything, the connection to the antique adds an accent of truth.

But which antique? Plutarch triumphs in sixteenth - century Europe . In France, Amyot completed his translation of the *Parallel Lives* in 1572: the French volumes began to appear in 1559 – while Henri Estienne published the complete works in Greek, together with a Latin version. Montaigne swears only by Plutarch. The English followed suit and Shakespeare was inspired by it in several of his plays. In Spain, one devours as much the historian as the moralist, either in Latin translations of the *Parallel lives* , or in versions in Castilian of which the first go up at the end of the XV E century [52]. In Antwerp too, there was interest in Plutarch: two translations of *Moralia* (Moral Works) published in 1549 were inspired by the version given by Erasmus in 1531 and were viewed with suspicion by the Holy Office. Many authors interested in the Indies draw abundantly from Plutarch, whether they are called Gonzalo Fernández de Oviedo or Bartolomé de Las Casas [53].

Why dwell on the Greek historian? The realism and drama with which Diego describes the great battles of the pre-Hispanic era are too reminiscent of the pages of Plutarch (and Xenophon) not to be inspired by them. In the *Life of Marius* , the battle which opposes Romans and Ligurians to the Barbarians ends in a bloodbath: "The Barbarians, by rushing on each other, were killed on the banks of the river, whose bed overflowed soon blood and death [54]. " Diego, we remember, has this talent: "From the site of Cohuatlichan to Chimalhuacan, all the mudflat which occupies the edges of the lagoon was nothing but corpses and streams of blood [55]. »

As if he had observed them with his own eyes, in the manner of Xenophon, Diego plunges us into the heart of the clashes: "Over there, the whirlwind of arrows and spears hardened with fire that the only arms of the combatants threw at each other, and the darts obscured the light of day; like thick clouds of dust, they made the crystal of the diaphanous air opaque, and so mingled with each other in their velocity and unleashed fury that they obstructed the passage of the sun's rays -»

It is undoubtedly from Plutarch that he borrows the idea of qualifying as “civil wars” the conflicts which oppose the ancient Chichimecs to the “plebs”. As a result, he takes them out of their local context to hoist them onto a prestigious horizon [57]. Other borrowings from the prose of Antiquity: he speaks of "tyrant" and "tyranny" each time he intends to denounce regimes of oppression; the *macehuales* adorn themselves with the clothes of the "plebs" and the " *voz de libertad* " designates the emancipatory momentum of popular revolts [58].

The idea of "freedom" gives the Tlaxcaltec past an ancient color, dignity and gravity. According to him, from the most remote origins, freedom would have characterized the condition of the people of Tlaxcala: Tlaxcala would never have known any vassalage and never, since the release of the Seven Caves, would she have accepted the slightest authority. "of no prince in the world" above her, "because the Tlaxcaltecs have always preserved their freedom ." The "patrician blood" – which Diego always regrets that it flows too much – covers with an ancient purple machinations and sordid assassinations while marking the social hierarchies which are dear to him [60].

This antique patina is therefore anything but decorative. It is also more than a humanist framework responding to the expectations of the educated reader. Diego also draws from it an argument of prestige for his city: by endeavoring to explain the flow of past history by ideals and causes inspired by Antiquity, he erases all provincialism and gives the history of Tlaxcala a universal and timeless accent. The antique considered as the expression of a common past often appears in the sixteenth century as a marker of the universal in the same way as the biblical past [61].

The eye of the geographer

Diego is a man of the field. We imagine him as an amateur archaeologist riding in the hills and mountains of Tlaxcala. Perched on his mount, he measures the height of the remains he encounters, spends whole days under a tropical sun browsing the ruins, questions the peasants and local notables about the origin of the constructions he discovers. He knows his Tlaxcaltec province inside out. Diego geographer takes advantage of the experience of an earthquake to observe the dust darkening the skies, the mountains collapsing and the men panicking “at the approach of the end[62]”. Diego geographer is concerned with giving physical landmarks by linking the adventures of the past to a colonial landscape now marked out by evangelization: "the countryside and the mountains of Xoloteopan" are close to the "district of Saint-Nicolas[63]", Totollan is occupied today by the church of Saint-Jean, the chapel of the Purification stands where the “district of Teotlalpan” was. On the Christianized geography pass the shadows of an ancient epic.

When the Chichimec scouts reach the top of the mountains overlooking the province of Tlaxcala, to describe the landscape that emerges before their eyes and stretches as far as the eye can see, Diego uses two formulas: *otro nuevo mundo* and *nuevo hemisferio* . Both are borrowed from the vocabulary of Castilian geographers. As for the sea, it interested him as much as the mountains, judging by his interest in voyages of exploration across the Pacific and by his contacts with one of the seasoned pilots of the South Seas.

Diego doesn't just give geography lessons. His gaze is nourished by his experience in the field. A physical experience: he sees things as much as he feels them. He watched the fog thicken over Mexico Lake in the cool of the morning. He climbed the mountains of which he speaks, abandoning his horse on the too steep peaks to explore ruins invaded by brushwood. Eyewitness testimony reinforces the truth of his account. From the summit of Tlalocan, he cannot help but share his emotion. And the magic happens.

By putting himself in the place of the Chichimecs, he introduces us to the skin of the invaders who suddenly come to life before our eyes. This resuscitated moment of the pre-Hispanic past acquires a resonance that we are not about to forget.

As Diego is not Chateaubriand, his wonder is expressed in a religious and agreed language [64]. The beauty of nature reflects the perfection of divine creation . We are however far from the topos which, since Christopher Columbus and Amerigo Vespucci, associates America with a heavenly land. Facing the mouth of the Orinoco, Columbus thought he could guess the proximity of paradise on earth. Nature according to Diego is not confused either with this paradise or with the *locus amoenus* of the poets. It reaches spectacular and majestic dimensions that rather evoke the visions of the painter Albrecht Altdorfer (1480-1538). In Diego, the landscape expands to the gigantic size of a hemisphere, even a new world [66]. The geographer is sensitive to the shape of the globe, as was the painter of the *Battle of Alexander* (1529) where seas and peaks draw a line of the horizon whose curvature the setting sun accentuates [67].

Diego's eye plays on at least three registers. The Treaty of Tordesillas (1494) had divided the world into two hemispheres, one assigned to Castile and the other to Portugal. His all-encompassing vision projects this division of ecumenism onto the Mexican landscape. But this geometric and cosmographic canvas is not enough for him. His subjectivity is moved by the sight of a land that is his own. What he sees goes beyond him and inspires him with a metaphysical peroration that makes the terrestrial world the reflection of the celestial world. His gaze on the great battles of the pre-Hispanic era and his descriptions carry the same emotion and radically distinguish him from a chronicler who would only see in them an exotic object. On several occasions, words fail him. A rare admission in the colonial literature of the time: Diego is the antithesis of a courtier poet like Bernardo de Balbuena who, by dint of embroidering ancient clichés on his painting of the Valley of Mexico, makes him unrecognizable and transforms New Spain in a New Greece [68].

Diego's passionate eye irresistibly evokes another who preceded him by thirty years. In the middle of the 16th century , the Tlaxcaltec authorities decided to offer Charles V a huge painted canvas, or *lienzo* , celebrating the prowess of the Indians during the Conquest and magnifying their obedience and loyalty to the emperor [69]. The *Lienzo of Tlaxcala* (June 1552?) has been compared to a "giant gaze fixed on us", capable of hypnotizing the spectator's attention and drawing him into its depths. The *Lienzo* would also hold up a kind of gigantic mirror which would allow us to read the past and the future, to contemplate well what is distant in space than in time [70]. What the *Description of Tlaxcala still claims to be* thirty years later, but this time favoring writing over painting. More than a generation has passed, and the art of the ancient *tlacuilos* , hit hard by time and epidemics, is crumbling, although a gallery of drawings still accompanies Diego's text.

1. Paul Veyne, *Did the Greeks believe in their myths?* , Paris, Threshold, 1983, p. 132.

2. Alonso de Molina's Nahuatl-Spanish dictionary (*Vocabulario en lengua castellana y mexicana* , Mexico, 1571, fol. 148r°) gives for *Tloque Nauaque* "He on whom the existence of all things depends, who preserves and maintains them", in Miguel León-Portilla, *La Filosofía nahuatl estudiada en sus fuentes* , Mexico City, UNAM, 2014, p. 217.

3. C141/142.

4. Au début du xvii e siècle, le métis Alva Ixtlilxóchitl traduit *Teotloque nahuaque* par «the universal god of all things, creator of them», dans Alva Ixtlilxóchitl (1977), t. II, p. 7 (*History of the Chichimeca nation*).

5. *Soliloques* , l. I, chap. i, pair. 2 et 3, http://laportelatine.org/bibliotheque/docteurs/Augustin/les_soliloques.pdf.[1]

6. C49.

7. D33v°.

8. Leonardo Antonio de la Cuesta, *Sacred, chronological, genealogical and universal State of the world* , Madrid, Manuel Martín, 1766, p. 47.

9. Leon Robin, *Plato* , Paris, University Presses of France, 1968, p. 179.

10. Giovanni Reale, *For a New Interpretation of Plato* , São Paulo, Loyola Publishing House, 2004, p. 399.

11. José L. Montesinos Sirera, "Nature, Modernity and New Spain", in *Science and Culture between Two Worlds. Documentary Sources and Their Various Interpretations* , José L. Montesinos Sirera et Sergio Toledo Prats (dir.), La Orotava, Orotava Canary Foundation for the History of Science, 2010, p. 63-94.

12. In 1590, another Métis, Inca Garcilaso de la Vega, published a Spanish version.

13. D153r°.

---

1. http://laportelatine.org/bibliotheque/docteurs/Augustin/les_soliloques.pdf

14. Gruzinski (2017), p. 277-302.

15. C141, 142, 165.

16. C165.

17. C142.

18. The ninth heaven or the nine superimposed heavens.

19. *Ibid.*

20. Mendieta (1997), t. I, p. 209 (l. II, chap. xiii).

21. D140r°-140v°.

22. C142.

23. C143.

24. C300.

25. C162.

26. C143.

27. D16r°.

28. *Ibid.*

29. C143.

30. C144.

31. C167; D153v°.

32. D85r°.

33. C76.

34. C164.

35. C239.

36. C72.

37. Veyne (1983), p. 31.

38. C47.

39. C153.

40. Georges Baudot, *Utopia and History in Mexico. The first chroniclers of Mexican civilization (1520-1569)*, Toulouse, Privat, 1977, p. 477-487.

41. C150.

42. C153.

43. D76r°, 112r°.

44. On the importance given to spiers in Tlaxcala, Francisco Hernández, *Obras completas. Antigüedades de la Nueva España*, Joaquin García Pimentel trans., Mexico, UNAM, 1984, chap. xx, "De las razones para hacer guerra y manera de hacerla", http://www.franciscohernandez.unam.mx/tomos/06_TOMO/tomo006_004/tomo006_004_020.html.[2]

45. D111r°.

46. D114v°.

47. Paul Veyne, "Prodigies, divinations and fear of the gods in Plutarch", *Revue de l'histoire des religions*, t. 216, 4, 1999, p. 387-442.

48. C44.

49. On the application of laws in the Persian Empire, Montaigne (1965), t. II, ch. xi, p. 60.

50. See footnote 4, p. 61.

---

2. http://www.franciscohernandez.unam.mx/tomos/06_TOMO/tomo006_004/tomo006_004_020.html

51 . Probably Plutarch and Livy. The *Lives* are translated into Castilian by Alonso Fernández de Palencia (Seville, 1491), then by Francisco de Encinas (Strasbourg, 1551); Alicia Morales Ortiz, *Plutarco en España: Traducciones de Moralia en el siglo xvi* , Murcia, Universidad de Murcia, 2000. Diego Gracián published his Spanish version of the *Apopthegmas* in 1533 in Alcalá de Henares; the translation of the *Moralia* into Castilian by the same author is later (Salamanca, 1570 and 1571). See Vicente Salvá y Pérez, *Catálogo de libros antiguos o escasos* , Paris, Imprenta de Bacquenois, 1836, and Alexander S. Wilkinson ed., *Iberian Books: Books published in Spanish and Portuguese or in the Iberian Peninsula before 1601* , Leiden, Brill, 2010.

52 . Morales Ortiz (2000), p. 88.

53 . David A. Lupher, *Romans in a New World: Classical Models in Sixteenth-Century Spanish America* , Ann Arbor, University of Michigan Press, 2006.

54 . Plutarch, Life *of Marius* , 20, http://remacle.org/bloodwolf/historians/Plutarch/marius.htm.[3]

55 . C47.

56 . C75.

57 . C66.

58 . C84; D117r°.

59 . C122. The humanist Cervantes de Salazar describes the relationship between Tlaxcala and Mexico City by applying the notions of freedom and tyranny, in Martínez Baracs (2008), p. 47.

60 . C107. To be compared with a page of Livy: "The decemvirs [...] warn the senators to protect them against public hatred, so that their torture does not accustom this people to seeing the blood of the patricians spilled", in Tite- *Live* . Live, *Ab urbe condita (Roman History)* , l. III, ch. lii, 10, http://remacle.org/bloodwolf/historians/Tite/livre3.htm.[4]

---

3. http://remacle.org/bloodwolf/historiens/Plutarque/marius.htm

4. http://remacle.org/bloodwolf/historiens/Tite/livre3.htm

61. What the Portuguese painter Francisco de Holanda has in mind when he reflects on the artistic history of the world. See Alessandra Russo, *A New Antiquity (1400-1600). Art and Humanity as Universal* , in preparation.

62. C302.

63. C72.

64. Yves Giraud, *The Landscape at the Renaissance* , Association for Studies on Humanism, the Reform and the Renaissance, Fribourg, University Editions, 1988, p. 107.

65. Music can also be a symbol of the perfection of the universe, as in Fray Luis de León, http://blocs.xtec.cat/pcarrascliteratura/ascetica-y-mistica/ [5]; Frank Lesstringant, "Chorography and landscape in the Renaissance", in Giraud (1988), p. 9-21.

66. Giraud (1988), *passive* .

67. Christopher S. Wood, *Albrecht Altdorfer and the Origins of Landscape* , Chicago, University of Chicago Press, 1993.

68. Bernardo de Balbuena, *The Mexican Greatness* , Mexico, Porrúa, 1971.

69. Le *Lienzo de Tlaxcala* is a command of the municipal council of Tlaxcala (vers 1552-1564). A first version (verse 1548) constitutes the *Fragment of Texas* . Les peintures de la relation géographique dating back to 1568-1583, see Gordon Brotherston and Ana Gallegos, « The *Lienzo de Tlaxcala* and the Glasgow Manuscript (Hunter 242) », *Estudios de cultura náhuatl* , vol. 20, 1990, p. 117-140 ; Andrea Martínez Baracs, « The paintings of the Glasgow Manuscript and the *Lienzo de Tlaxcala* », *Nahuatl Culture Studies* , vol. 20, 1990, p. 142-162.

70. A shiny surface is called *ixtli* in Nahuatl. Represented by the design of an eye, *ixtli* , it is made to capture the eye that contemplates it. But the coat of arms that sits in its center could represent a gigantic shield intended to shelter the Tlaxcaltecs behind their memory of the Conquest. The entire *Lienzo* then appears as a coat of arms that coexists with that of Charles V placed in the center of the painting. Two heraldic geographies dialogue through the grace of the native *tlacuilos* . The cartographic grid of the kingdoms of the emperor, figured on his

5. http://blocs.xtec.cat/pcarrascliteratura/ascetica-y-mistica

coat of arms, would correspond to that of the *Lienzo* which draws up a map of indigenous Mexico, http://www.latinamericanstudies.org./tlaxcala-lienzo.htm.[6]

6. http://www.latinamericanstudies.org./tlaxcala-lienzo.htm

CHAPTER VIII

Birth of a global world

What do the six decades of colonial domination that had passed when he took up his pen represent for Diego? While he explores the pre-Hispanic past with the empathy of an antiques dealer and historical tourist – the ascent of the Tlalocan, the visit of the ruins – the time of New Spain has for him completely different resonances. If only first of all because it touches him personally: it is the time of "our people", that of his father and his father's friends, but also that of his childhood and his adolescence, on which he pinpoints two personal memories as precious to us as what he brings back to us from the pre-Hispanic world.

In its successive forms, this colonial past is measured by the yardstick of this linear, oriented and multi-millennial flow that Christians call time. Colonization introduced much more than a change of calendar or chronology, it imposed this singular notion without real equivalence for the Indians, time, which societies before the Conquest perceived only in association with space. [1].

These poor fools

Diego's memory – at least the one he intends to share with Philip II – is first of all that of Christianization. It is the memory of an upheaval. The Church of the missionaries established itself very early in Tlaxcala (1524), and throughout the century the city remained one of the great centers of Franciscan evangelization.

– *How to describe the success of evangelization at the end of the century?*

– The whole land of Tlaxcala was dotted with churches [2].

– *Were there too many churches?*

– No more churches should be built in the province, on the contrary the number should be reduced. For so many have been built or begun that they cannot survive without great cost to the poor. And many of them, the Indians will never finish them, they will serve no purpose but to attract favor and attention.

– *How did the indigenous elites who helped Cortés conquer Mexico respond to evangelism?*

– Among the famous captains who were present throughout the war, [...] there was one called Don Antonio Calmecahua [...]. He found himself with Cortés whenever he could. Today, he is still alive and, it is said, he would be one hundred and thirty years old [...]. He considers himself happy to have been baptized and to be a Christian; he laments the time when he was an idolater and repents of the error in which he and his ancestors lived. The same thing is said about a captain who has distinguished himself a lot, Antonio Temazahuitzin [4].

– *Apart from these two exceptional cases, how were the Franciscans received in Tlaxcala?*

– When they preached, the caciques lords said: “What's the matter with these wretches? See if they are hungry, and if they need anything, feed them. There were others who said, "These poor people must be sick or mad, so let those wretches roar, evil madness took hold of them [...]. They are certainly seriously affected, for they are fools who do not seek pleasure and contentment, but sadness and **loneliness**. »

– *How did the monks behave?*

– Since they didn't know the language, they pointed to the lower part of the earth with their hands to say that in hell there was fire, toads and serpents. After that, they looked up to heaven saying that one God is above, pointing their hand in the same way [6].

– *Where did they preach?*

– Always in the markets and where people gathered and gathered.

– *The children of the caciques played a decisive role in evangelization. In your childhood, you catechized the newly arrived Indians from Florida, so you lived this experience yourself. You also told us about your outings in the indigenous neighborhoods of Mexico City and the disappearance or kidnapping of one of your comrades who may have ended up being sacrificed by clandestine priests* [7]. *Was it risky for teenagers to get involved in evangelism?*

– A cacique by the name of Don Cristóbal Acxotecatl, principal of the *pueblo* of Atlihuetza, which depends on Tlaxcala, martyred one of his sons, also named Cristóbal. As he was a very young child, the monks called him Cristobalico, and his common name became Cristobalico as a token of **affection**.

– *Why did the cacique kill Cristobalico?*

– Because he was his son and he loved him so much, Cristobalico urged him to abandon the idols, to convert and to serve God.

– *How did the father react?*

– Don Cristóbal Acxotecatl became madly angry and terribly wrathful against his son Cristobalico, and one day [...] he came to blows and beat him with a wooden club he had. He tore his head to pieces and killed [him].

– Has Spanish justice intervened in this family affair?

– Don Martín de Calahorra, who conducted the trial, condemned him to death and had him hanged by order of Hernando Cortés [10].

– You could have told us the story of these young neophyte Indians who, carried away by their evangelizing fury, attacked a priest of the idols and stoned him to death. Are these incidents indicative of the troubled times that missionaries and conquerors had to face in this region and in the rest of the country?

– This lasted for many years until the whole earth was pacified and the villages and places where the Spaniards lived became populated, just like the villages of the Indians that the wars had decimated [11].

– The Franciscans multiplied mass baptisms. Not without causing some confusion?

"One day, the men were baptized, and they were called Juan; another, women were baptized, they were called Ana; another day, it was the Pedros' turn; yet another, Marias [...]. We gave them a piece of paper on which we wrote the baptismal name so that they would not forget it.

– The Franciscans have been reproached for these mass baptisms. The Dominicans, Las Casas in the lead, did not spare their criticisms.

– Many forgot their name and they came to look for it on the baptismal register. I saw the same thing in another province [12].

– But, cautious as usual, you avoid discussing the method [13]*. Did the Indians change morally after the Conquest and their Christianization?*

– In ancient times, they attached great importance to the truth, which was particularly true for their lords and even more so for their chiefs; they observed the commitments they made among themselves and never broke them, even at the risk of their lives.

– *And today?*

– With the freedom they enjoy now, they are first rate liars and crooks, but you can find everything [15].

– *Who are you targeting in particular? Do you think of the natives with whom you have been in business?*

– Many of them who are traders are honest and trustworthy people [16].

– *What is the main fault of the Indians?*

"One of their greatest evils is idleness, the mother of all vices. And even if it is true that sending them to work on the estates of others would be unfair, it would at least be absolutely just and deserved to occupy them with work which suits them, as, for example, the construction of comfortable houses where they themselves, their children and their grandchildren could live and live in a civilized way.

– *Were the Indians of Tlaxcala Hispanicized or "Spanishized", according to an expression of Juan Suárez de Peralta, your contemporary?*

"They borrowed a lot of things from us. For them, selling or renting houses, asking for a loan, was degrading. In their ancient times this was not practiced; they did not know what the debts were. They kept their promises and promptly fulfilled their commitments.

– *The change must have affected other areas. How did a monetary system, unknown to the populations, spread in New Spain?*

– We started by discovering many deposits of gold, silver, iron and copper [...], and we started coining money because before, to trade, Spaniards and Indians only used bars, gold nuggets and powdered gold. But it was less practical than currency, and barter for gold and silver gave rise to fraudulent transactions.

– With the minting and circulation of silver money, the Indians were less often ripped off by the Spaniards. But why didn't they want copper money?

– This currency began to circulate between the Spaniards and the Indians. The natives took it so badly that they laughed at this vile currency. They denied it any value, for them it was intolerable because, they said, it was a sign of great misery. They refused to receive it and to use it [18].

– Did they end up complying with the royal decision?

– Despite the rigor of justice and the obligation to use it, in a year or a little more, they collected more than 100,000 pesos of small copper change which they threw into the lagoon of Mexico City so that no trace remains.

– The strength of this protest movement, its organized nature, are surprising. Suárez de Peralta remembers that the operation was carried out in the greatest secrecy and attributes it to "the rusticity of the country [19]"!

– The Indians recovered all this currency and drove it out of the world, or at least from their land, so detestable and odious was it to them. Since that time, no other currency has circulated, except silver money, in pieces of eight and even in half- *reales* . It is a very good currency, entirely in silver.

– Let us return to the transformations brought about by the Spanish domination. Do you have other examples?

– The woolen trade boomed, as the Indians began to dress in woolen blankets and to wear other woolen garments as well [20].

– Are there any customs or expressions from the time of the Conquest that have continued over the past sixty years?

– All those who today are in the service of the Spaniards, they call them *tlamacazque* . This is because at first the Spaniards were taken for gods, so that all the people who were in their service received the name of *tlamacazque* , because this is how those who served in the temples of the gods were called. . And so this name has remained so entrenched until today that the servants of the Spaniards are called *tlamacazque* [21].

The "pacification" of Mexico

The conquest of Mexico does not end with the taking of Mexico City. The troubled situation of the first years can also be explained by the military campaigns which reduced the populations of the Altiplano and advanced as far as Guatemala and the lands of Central America.

– *How was this immense territory occupied?*

– Once the country was at peace and once its inhabitants were reassured, efforts were made to pacify the whole kingdom and we restored, or rebuilt, then repopulated [...] Mexico City [22].

– *You do not speak of "conquest", but of "pacification", in accordance with the royal decrees of 1573, as if words softened the facts* [23]. *Who organized the reconstruction of Mexico City?*

– Cortés has taken the best measures possible. He had houses and streets built our way by applying principles and standards that have allowed the growth and prosperity of the city until today.

– *Mexico was therefore promoted to the capital of New Spain. It was from Mexico that a series of military campaigns started, including the one that invaded Michoacan?*

– Nuño de Guzmán came as governor of the provinces of Pánuco, Mexico City and New Galicia. Passing through the kingdom of Michoacan, he had King Catzontzin executed by subjecting him to cruel tortures until death ensued.

– *What to think of the expeditious methods of this "peacemaker"?*

– [He perpetrated] outrageous and tyrannical actions. He committed cruelties against the Indians of this region and that is why the Emperor Charles V [...] ordered that he be taken prisoner back to the kingdoms of

Castile. But, before his departure, he remained locked up for a long time in the public prison of Mexico City.

– *You could add that he literally enslaved the good thousand Tlaxcaltec auxiliaries who accompanied him and that only about twenty of them would have returned home alive*[24].

Paradoxically, during the conquest of Mexico, new fields of action opened up to the Tlaxcaltec warriors since they escorted the Spanish troops in Huasteca, Guatemala and Central America, or even in the Mexican North-West. In principle, the Tlaxcaltecs considered everywhere as conquerors in their own right, and never as simple native auxiliaries at the mercy of the Castilians. This is the interpretation that the *Lienzo de Tlaxcala* exalts in the middle of the century , even if the realities on the ground are far from corresponding to the Tlaxcaltec claims. This is also what the drawings that accompany the *Description of Tlaxcala repeat* .

Heading for spices and China

The fate of New Spain is now being played out on a transoceanic chessboard. Decisions concerning it can be taken both from Central America (Cortés) and from Valladolid or Madrid. For centuries, the country will depend on continental and intercontinental geopolitics. Diego is already aware of this situation. A crisis erupts in Mexico City as Cortés fights in Honduras (1526). His hasty return from Central America narrowly succeeded in calming people's minds, but he had to return to Castile to justify himself to the emperor and fight "the venomous poison of his opponents"

– *Did Cortés obtain satisfaction at court?*

– His Majesty [...] showered him with graces and favours. She gave him the title of Marquis. She married him to doña Juana de Zuñiga, the daughter of the Count of Aguilar, and brought him back to our New Spain [...] with great advantages, exceptional prerogatives and privileges.

– *Cortés also received the title of Admiral of the South Sea, in other words the command of the Spanish fleet in the Pacific, even if it does not yet exist. What did he devote himself to after his return to New Spain?*

– He organized a first, the voyage and the South Sea expedition, in search of the islands of Solomon – as they were then called – and those of Tarshish and California.

– *Contemporaries believed that the islands from which King Solomon had extracted his wealth and that of Tarsus could be found in the Pacific Ocean – this will remain the name given to the Solomon Islands. Cortés set sail in April 1535 for Baja California, where he discovered large numbers of Indians, pearls, fish, but, it seems, the rest of the expedition did not follow.*

– Everything went wrong for Cortés and turned into a disaster. Almost all the ships were wrecked and he himself remained lost for more than a year in the region of the great Tyzón River and California. He endured all sorts of hardships and eventually believed he was going to perish along with all his people.

– *The Tyz ó n is today the Rio Colorado, which flows into the Gulf of California. But your memory is deceiving you: it was not Cortés, but Francisco de Ulloa who reached the mouth of the Colorado in 1539. What was the Californian coast like?*

– On the coast that Cortés traveled, there were many Indians and villages. But they are the most naked and barbaric people there is. These Indians live like Arabs; they are very miserable, they know neither gold nor silver.

– *You confirm what Díaz del Castillo writes about the savagery of the natives and the absence of corn* [27]*. Despite these setbacks, how did Cortés react?*

– Unable to continue further, for lack of ships and in the face of so many hardships, he decided to return. He had suffered considerable losses in men and money, but these reversals of fortune did not discourage him [...]. He then wanted to embark on the route of the Grocery Islands. This is the name given at that time to the Moluccas and the mainland of Greater China.

– *Are you thinking perhaps of the expedition of Hernando de Grijalva, which left Acapulco in 1536 and which also ended in disaster?*

– It was Alvaro de Saavedra Cerón who commanded this fleet.

– *Here, your memory still leads you astray: Saavedra Cerón, who is Cortés' cousin, left nine years earlier, in October 1527, long before Cortés' expedition to California, and he reached Mindanao. What do you know of his traveling companions?*

"The fleet had as quartermaster and pilot a man called Maestro Corzo, one of those who crossed with Magellan the strait which today bears that name.

– *Was this expedition important?*

– It was the first maritime expedition carried out from [Mexico] towards the islands now called the Philippines, and the second expedition launched on the South Sea in the time of Hernán Cortés.

– Indeed, the first transpacific expedition mounted after the Conquest was that of García Jofre de Loaisa. She sailed in August 1525. Was Saavedra Cerón's enterprise more successful than the previous one?

– The fleet disappeared and some of our people ended up reappearing in the great India of Portugal [28].

– You mean that the survivors returned by the Asian route, the one opened by Vasco da Gama, and therefore by the port of Goa, capital of Portuguese India. According to López de Gómara, of the eighteen survivors who languished for two years in Malacca in Portuguese jails, only eight managed to return to Spain. Did these expeditions resume after the arrival of the first viceroy, Antonio de Mendoza?

– It was during the time of this Christian prince who governed New Spain that the second Epicerie expedition set off.

– From New Spain then. Who funded the trip? The Viceroy?

– This fleet was mounted at his expense and in his name, in concert with Don Pedro de Alvarado. And it was Captain Ruy López, a native of Villalobos [29], who was in command.

– Who told you about this expedition which took place in 1542-1543, when you were still only a child?

– For the second time, [the fleet] had as pilot Maestro Corzo [...] whom I knew very well.

– How did the expedition go?

– The voyage and the crossing were lamentable, they were catastrophic to the point that the fleet was lost body and goods. All of this was for naught because, with everyone dead, there was no one left to bring the ships back to New Spain [30].

What does Diego remember from the 1530s and 1540s? It is above all the maritime expansion that marks the memory of this landsman. It doesn't matter if his memories are sometimes jumbled, as ours often are. We are struck by the echo left by this unfortunate epic. The movement that is gripping New Spain and propelling it beyond its natural borders is mobilizing frontline players like Cortés and Mendoza, consuming massive amounts of capital, and attracting crowds of adventurers and seafaring experts. Among these, a pilot, the Maestro Corzo.

Originally from Corsica, the Corzos were plentiful on the seas in the 16th century . Is it the Pedro Corzo who explored the surroundings of Panama in 1527, in particular the Rio de los Lagartos "from the point closest to Panama until arriving at the North Sea 31 "? Or of Antón Pablo Corzo, who crossed the Strait of Magellan in 1581 in the company of Pedro de Sarmiento [32] ? Neither. In contrast, a pilot by the name of Antonio Corzo sailed in the 1540s on the galleon *San Cristóbal* , in Ruy López's fleet of Villalobos [33]. All that we know of him is that he was Corsican and that he would have seen docking in Seville, according to him in 1524, the *Victoria* , the only ship to survive Magellan's expedition, responsible for cloves brought back from the Moluccas. He would have taken the opportunity to question the pilots of his acquaintance about the crossing of the strait and its perils [34], but he would have only collected stories without having participated in the circumnavigation of the globe. In 1527, he embarked with Saavedra Cerón, the cousin of Cortés. In 1538, justice consulted a forty-year-old Antonio Corzo, who claimed to be an excellent connoisseur of the South Seas: "On these seas, anyone who wants to can sail, provided that they are not put obstacle [35]. This Maestro Corzo is therefore not just anyone. Surviving these two transpacific voyages, he is one of the first Europeans to have circumnavigated the globe twice. Finally, it seems that it is the same man who escaped a shipwreck off Florida in 1554 [36]. Diego can congratulate himself on counting him among his informants.

– *What conclusion can be drawn from Ruy López de Villalobos' expedition?*

– The undue idea was drawn from it that because of the great currents and contrary winds the ships could not return to New Spain. This error persisted for many years. It was also said that one could not pass under the equinoctial line and other such nonsense that is not worth remembering.

– *Why not talk about it?*

– Because we now know the latitudes and maritime routes on all the seas of the world. The intelligence of men is so exceptional and so lively that they are capable of understanding everything and grasping everything with the understanding that God has kindly given them. Everything becomes easy and comprehensible to them [37].

– *We have the feeling that you are repeating word for word the words spoken by Maestro Corzo in front of the judges. Ruy López de Villalobos' expedition left Mexico in 1542. They were unable to return to Mexico, but they reached the Philippines anyway. Not all men have disappeared. Survivors, you tell us, even managed to return to Europe. How did they get there?*

– Among the survivors of this expedition, several ended up landing in India from Portugal [38], where they were held prisoner: García de Escalante, Guido de Labezares and Fray Antonio de Urdaneta [...]. They brought ginger from India and the credit goes to Guido de Labezares [39], who smuggled it out with great cunning and skill and transported it to Castile and from there to New Spain, where it was sown at Cuernavaca, in the *huerta* of Bernardino del Castillo. This is where the large quantities of ginger produced today in the islands of Santo Domingo come from, and which are loaded in Barlovento on ships leaving for Spain [40].

Diego is attentive to the unprecedented transfers that are beginning to proliferate across the globe. For his generation, it has become accessible in its entirety. The world of Diego is open to "all the seas" of the planet. Pierce here the modernity of a spirit convinced that men are capable of understanding everything. The "men" in question are of course the Europeans, starting with the Iberians, but also those who, like Diego, were born in the New World.

This humanism is nourished by field knowledge acquired from sailors. It is expressed in anecdotes and memories such as the journey of ginger. Enough to justify the efforts that the very young New Spain is multiplying to master the Pacific routes and project itself on the shores of Asia. The acuity of the gaze reflects a dynamic vision of the globe, sensitive to all the circulations that traverse it. As before him with the chronicler Oviedo, scientific curiosity develops hand in hand with flair, a sense of contact and business. Diego is curious about this Asian product, its origin, the methods of its transplantation, the care it requires, without however hiding the fraudulent nature of the operation carried out between Portuguese India, Mexico and the Caribbean. In his eyes, the skill of entrepreneurs excuses their lack of scruples. In Iberian globalization, all shots are allowed as the movement of people, things and plants around the globe is about to become routine.

– *After the departure of Viceroy Antonio de Mendoza for Peru, did New Spain persist in sending fleets to the Spice Islands?*

– We then launched the third expedition to L'Épicerie and the Ponant Islands, known as the Philippines. This was done at the persuasive entreaties of an Augustinian, Fray Andrés de Urdaneta, García de Escalante and Guido de Labezares, people who had seen this region and who had been there[41].

– *What was the result of the expedition?*

– It was such a success that it will be forever [remembered] because it initiated the biggest and best business relationship that has existed in the world, especially in these regions of Ponant.

Diego does not believe so well. Not only did the expedition lay the foundations for the colonization of the Philippines, but the Augustinian Urdaneta, who was taken from his monastic cell for the occasion, discovered the route back to America across the North Pacific. This time, the connection is definitively established. Exchanges across the Pacific will weigh on the history of the world and of the West. The silver bars sent to China and the purchases in return of luxury products, porcelain, silks, furniture and lacquered objects, will stimulate transactions with transoceanic spin-offs: "the best trade in the world". Avid of the precious metal that it prefers to gold, China will absorb a good part of the silver production of Mexico and Peru while the American elites will take a liking to Asian luxury and the delights of transpacific contraband [42].

– *Isn't the Philippine archipelago just an outpost facing China?*

– From this settlement great discoveries have been made in the kingdoms and provinces of Greater China, Japan, Tartary and other hitherto unknown nations. And many of them are beginning to know or have an idea of our holy Catholic faith.

– *You have probably not heard of the Jesuit Mateo Ricci and his mission in China. But perhaps you attended the* Coloquio in 1566 *that the poet Fernán González de Eslava, a relative of the Francisco de Terrazas you know, gave in Puebla, since this city is only a few leagues from Tlaxcala. The play celebrates the elation and enthusiasm that China arouses in the population:*

" What is happening ? What are you doing ?

Tell us: are you going to China?

– Yes, we do, Innocent,

For the divine land [43]. »

The mirages of North America

The Pacific raises a gigantic wall of seas and currents on the route of the Spanish fleets. At the extreme south of the American continent, Magellan discovered the only sea passage that connects the Atlantic to the Pacific. But it is the strait of all dangers. Was there a higher land passage to the north that would link California to Asia?

– *Francisco de Alarcón, the captain Viceroy Antonio de Mendoza had sent to California, did he believe he could find land connecting California to Asia?*

– For him, either these lands bordered on Greater China, or the sailing time between them and the Grocery Islands must have been very short [44].

– *Is it for this reason that the Viceroy organized a double expedition to North-West America, that of Francisco de Alarcón and that of Vázquez de Coronado, which were supposed to join?*

– In 1540, [Francisco Vázquez de Coronado] was appointed to lead the company [...]. This was called the Cibola expedition. The information came from fray Marcos de Niza, who was provincial of the Franciscan order.

– *Is it Cibola, and therefore the legend which tells that after the capture of Mérida by the Moors, in 1150, seven bishops would have left the city to take refuge in a region where they would have founded Cibola and Quivira, cities, it was said, entirely paved with gold?*

– Marcos de Niza claimed to have seen with his own eyes the Seven Cities and many other lands and provinces [45].

This Franciscan storyteller also spread the rumor that "the city of Cibola was so big that it could contain two Sevilles, and that the other cities were worth almost [46]". Everyone imagined that it was "the best thing in the world" and that they were on their way to the "earthly paradise ". The rumor of this Eldorado grew, it crossed the borders of the Monarchy, it even reached Istanbul, where it crossed the walls of the Topkapi Palace [48].

– What happened to Vázquez de Coronado's expedition?

- She got lost. With more than a thousand Spaniards, and nothing but beautiful people [...]. They have undergone all sorts of hardships during their wanderings in these deserted, remote and isolated lands, stretching as far as the eye can see and depopulated, but they have never reached any region which they could have occupied nor offered them land. livable, especially for a nation as presumptuous and warlike as ours.

Vázquez de Coronado traveled as far as Arizona, and in July 1540 he arrived at a place he identified as Cibola. His lieutenant reached the Grand Canyon and the Colorado River [49]. The distances are so gigantic that the survivors imagined that they were near the end of the world [50].

– Why did the viceroy send a second expedition under the direction of Francisco de Alarcón?

– The fleet would pass through the South Sea and the land invasion would cross [...] regions of California [...]. With the idea that, if Vázquez de Coronado made some good discovery, he would come into contact with our New Spain by sea.

– What was it in reality?

– Quite the opposite happened. Neither of them succeeded. Tired of having traveled through so much land, so vast and so empty of people, when Vázquez de Coronado reached the distance he was supposed to reach without encountering anything good, he turned back. He ended his expedition and returned to New Spain. As for Francisco de Alarcón, he had already returned to Mexico, failing to have been able to make his connection as planned. He had stayed longer than his instructions stipulated and wanted to prevent his men who fell ill from perishing. In addition, he was short of food [51].

Why walk north?

Throughout the century, the Chichimec Indians hindered the advance of colonization towards the northern lands, those which today correspond to northern Mexico and the southern United States.

– *Why do the Spaniards attack these populations?*

– The Chichimecs have vast lands very rich in silver ore. We hope that in the future God will want us to exploit them and explore them, just like other countries and other nations about which we are quite well informed, because these are the lands from which the ancient Mexicans come.

– *What resistance do these indigenous groups put up against the Spanish forces?*

– Many famous captains of our Spaniards have distinguished themselves by fighting against the Chichimecs: for the most part, these have perished, but the others continue to wage the most cruel and barbaric war in the world. They fight with bows and arrows, their bodies naked, with nothing to shelter and protect themselves [52].

– *Did the border advance under the successor of Viceroy Antonio de Mendoza?*

– We occupied the new kingdom of Biscay, which is called Chametla. [...] Villa de Santa Bárbara, Guadiana, Sombrerete, Chalchihuites, Mazapil, Tierra de Indehe and all those remote regions were also populated at this time [53].

– *How did the new viceroy react to this spectacular progression?*

– It was at the beginning of his government that the Royal Audience of New Galicia was created.

– *But the resistances – you speak of aggressions – would have resumed with renewed vigor under his successor, the viceroy Martín Enríquez, from 1568?*

– In his time, the Chichimecs did as they pleased. They committed massacres and robberies on the roads of Zacatecas and in cattle ranches to such an extent that it was very difficult to circulate in the region. We had to build forts and install garrisons in many places on the lands of the Chichimecs [54].

– *With what result?*

– With these garrisons, we compensated in part for the losses caused by the Chichimec bandits.

This is all that Diego reports on the situation of the northern frontier in the last leaves of the manuscript that we have and which dates from the end of the 1580s. And yet, in this region, the Indians of Tlaxcala directly participated in the success of Spanish expansion. Since the first years of the conquest, Tlaxcala has not contented itself with supplying soldiers to the colonial authorities, it has also delivered contingents of emigrants. In 1527, the conquistador Jorge de Alvarado led 6,000 indigenous allies from the Altiplano to Central America. Weddings then sealed the alliance of the Alvarados with a powerful family from Tlaxcala [55].

By sharing the risks and the spoils in these expeditions of conquest, the Tlaxcaltec Indians became emulators of their Castilian allies. Or at least that is the memory that their descendants tried to keep [56].

The colonization of the northern border seemed for a long time the only way to pacify the region and to settle the Chichimecs who were being Christianized. An attempt to settle (the first?) with the Tlaxcaltecs fizzled out in 1560. A thousand families should have gone north, to San Miguel. In 1576, there was again talk of asking the caciques of Tlaxcala for settlers [57]. But it was only after 1585 that a systematic policy of occupation of areas threatened or occupied by the Chichimecs was considered. These would be pacified with the help of "well catechized" Mexica and Tlaxcaltec Indians who would be installed with them [58]. At the end of 1580, the viceroy decided to send 400 Tlaxcaltec families. The deal was negotiated with the help of the Franciscan Gerónimo de Mendieta, then guardian of the convent of Tlaxcala. But the province is not letting it go. The operation comes up against the opposition of a fraction of the native authorities, who under the aegis of the lord (*tlatoani*) of Tizatlan, don Leonardo Xicotencatl, tries to sabotage the operation. In vain.

In 1591, Diego again assumed his role as privileged intermediary between the Crown and the Tlaxcaltec authorities. He found himself *proveedor and repartidor general de tierras* and founded San Miguel Mezquitic in the Guachichiles area (in the state of San Luis Potosi) [59]. For him, the displacement of an indigenous population is a new experience. Diego is no longer a chronicler of events; this time, he takes an active part in it. However, his writings remain silent on this enterprise carried out at an advanced age: Diego was then over sixty years old.

China and beyond

Throughout his story, one space after another, Diego draws the horizons of a new world; ocean and planetary horizons. Admittedly, he does not have a precise idea of all the worlds which surround him, and it is not he who will describe China or India of the Portuguese. He contented himself with marking the spaces which then mobilized the forces of the colonial elites, and set the scene on which his history of Tlaxcala henceforth accompanies that of a New Spain committed body and soul to the rise of the Catholic Monarchy.

In his eyes, the north-west of New Spain, China and Japan form a group of lands sufficiently close to become the stages of maritime and land traffic. His contemporary from Istanbul, the anonymous to whom we owe the first Ottoman chronicle on the New World, is from agrees. While recognizing that it is not easy to explore the north of New Spain (*Yeni Ispanya*), the cold and the violent winds making this region unexplorable, this Ottoman chronicler points out that from this region one could reach China and its southern part (*çin u maçin*) [60].

The supposed proximity of North America and the Asian territories also imposes itself on whoever takes a look at the map that the Antwerper Abraham Ortelius drew and published in 1570 in his Theatrum Orbis *Terrarum* . On this sheet, which belongs to one of the first atlases designed in Europe, two blocks face each other: one made up of Tartary, China and Japan, and the other which corresponds to northwestern America. from the North, inside which one of the sites evoked by Diego, Tiguer (Tiguas on the atlas of Ortelius [61]) can be found. Everything suggests that at one time or another, in Mexico City or Tlaxcala, Diego had this card in his hands.

Ortelius' atlas also features the Strait of Anian. Does Diego think about it when he recounts the crossing of a western strait by Chichimec groups who came to populate New Spain? In Europe, the idea of an easily passable strait has spread widely. It even appears on a map by Giacomo Gastaldi (1562), then on another by Bolognino Zaltieri (1567) [62]. But nothing in Diego's text allows us to advance this hypothesis. Our historian never ventures to identify the strait of Anian with that which the ancestors of the Tlaxcaltecs crossed to reach the "New World".

What does he know of China? His knowledge of the Celestial Empire remains quite nebulous when it is not paved with evidence or clichés. He repeats what everyone in Tlaxcala and in Europe knows: the colossal profits expected to be made from this part of the world and, for a Christian conscience, the even greater harvest of souls to be saved.

Diego does not seem to have consulted the first work published in Spanish in Seville on China, in 1577 [63], any more than he could not have seen the *History of the great kingdom of China* , published in Rome in 1585 [64]. Anyway, these books told the history of China and it did not concern him. He is equally silent on the political maneuvers of which the Ming empire is the target in Macau, Manila and Mexico City. The 1580s nevertheless resounded with a project of conquest of China that pushed lobbies installed in Mexico City and the Philippines. The ideologue of the project is a Jesuit, Alonso Sánchez. His initiative provoked fierce opposition from another Jesuit, José de Acosta [65].

Diego is not affected by this news. His attention remains anchored on the tangible, on the north of New Spain and its monotonous geography – "the plains of Cibola" –, and its gigantic herds of bison: "The bulls with humps, with small horns, which look like buffalo [...]. They occupy immense and endless lands, and especially the plains of Cibola. We always guess, in Diego, the breeder who slumbers.

– Why is this country so important to you? Is it because it is in contact with other big companies that look like us?

– Francisco Vázquez de Coronado plunged into the region towards the west with 300 men without finding any agglomeration [...], and he advanced more than a hundred leagues to the place where the "cows" were [= bison]. On the spot, through the signs and the information he gathered, he learned that ten days away there were people dressed like us, who were traveling on the sea in large ships. With signs, the Indians made him understand that they were wearing the same clothes as us [66].

– *Did Vázquez de Coronado go to meet these people?*

– He did not go past these villages because he returned with those he had left in the plains of the cows. The time fixed for his return had passed.

Apparently, Diego is content to reproduce the words of Vázquez de Coronado. Was it false news spread by the Indians to get rid of the Spaniards by pushing them to sink ever deeper into the American plains, or a still unknown reality: the chronicler López de Gomara points out the existence in the country of [a] king named Tatarrax, "who prayed with a book of hours, adored a golden cross and a statue of a woman "? Unless, more simply, it is a question of the companions landed with Francisco de Alarcón.

The road to Peru

– *You don't talk much about New Spain's relations with Peru, as if your gaze was mainly directed towards the Filipino and Chinese west or towards the north of New Spain?*

– It was under the government of Viceroy Antonio de Mendoza, so peaceful and so tranquil, that the road to Peru was discovered, passing through the South Sea.

– *Another initiative from New Spain?*

– We built ships that went as far as Callao, in Lima. This expedition and then this discovery, we owe them to Diego de Ocampo, a knight of condition, originally from the city of Cáceres, in the kingdoms of Castile.

– *Diego de Ocampo was a friend of Cortés and he left on ships built in the arsenals of Tehuantepec.*

– He spent enormously and suffered many setbacks [68].

Peru is increasingly asserting its presence on the horizon of New Spain, but Diego says little more. It is admitted that Cortés inaugurated this sea route by sending relief to his cousin Francisco Pizarro, who was busy conquering Peru. The leader of the expedition – which took place in 1536 – was called Hernando de Grijalva. Seven years later, in 1543, the Viceroy Mendoza sent three ships while Peruvian ships touched the Mexican coast. Trade was then limited to supplying basic necessities, arms, powder, horses and provisions to the Spaniards of Peru who were just beginning to settle in the Andes. With the discovery of silver from Potosi (1545) and mercury from Huancavelica (1559), trade intensified. Between 1550 and 1560, they reached a value oscillating between 100,000 and 120,000 pesos to exceed 200,000 pesos in the following decade [69]. From the 1570s, a regular connection was established with the Philippines. The Chinese outlet will upset the situation and the exchanges take on such a scale that in 1593 the Crown again prohibits any direct link between Peru and Manila [70]. The traders of Lima then fell back on Acapulco, where they disembark with silver ingots intended for Chinese merchants.

An axis of communication therefore exists between Peru and New Spain. Diego took notice. However, either he is unaware that merchants from Mexico City and Lima are laying the groundwork for a flourishing trans-Pacific trade with the Philippines, Ming China and even Macau since the union of the two crowns placed the two empires Spanish and Portuguese under the leadership of Philip II (1580); or – this is our hypothesis – he is aware of the bonanza that the South Seas are beginning to bring in, but he is careful not to mention exchanges that could cover smuggling activities [71].

Another silence from Diego, and this time it is less surprising: in the very years when he wrote his report, the colonial authorities of Peru launched a policy of recognition and occupation of the Strait of Magellan. In 1579, Viceroy Toledo sent Sarmiento de Gamboa at the head of a fleet of ships to explore the labyrinthine channels of the strait, then found a settlement and build fortresses to block the way to English or Dutch corsairs [72]. But, for the elites of New Spain, the real strait, the one that matters, if it exists, is always to be found in the northern hemisphere.

Florida Disasters

The umbilical cord that connects New Spain and Peru to the Castilian metropolis crosses the Gulf of Mexico. And it is the Florida peninsula that plays the role of advanced sentinel facing the Atlantic. It therefore occupies an exceptional strategic position in the geography of the empire.

– The fleet of the Indies which sailed laden with treasures towards the metropolis was supposed to pass off Florida. Often perilous surroundings?

– Under don Luis de Velasco, in 1553, the fleet that was going from these kingdoms [of Mexico and Peru] to those of Castile was shipwrecked on the coast of Florida. Many people died, many perished. Considerable treasure was lost and few ships in the fleet [survived].

– Do you remember the names of the missing?

– The Indians massacred many religious and well-known people. It was there that the Dominican Juan de Méndez, a very famous preacher, died [...]. They also killed doña Catalina, the widow of Juan Ponce de León, *encomendero* [74] of Tecama, who was on her way to Spain where she had been exiled because of the death of her husband, killed by the hand, it is said, of Bernardino de Bocanegra.

– Was Viceroy Luis de Velasco interested in Florida?

– It was he who, in 1559, sent a fleet to Florida.

– Suárez de Peralta says that Luis de Velasco insisted on accompanying the starters to your home in Tlaxcala [75]*. How did this expedition end?*

- She was shipwrecked.

– How did we deal with this new disaster?

– Angel de Villafaña went to the rescue of the fleet to collect the castaways.

– Villafaña had for this purpose received the title of general and governor of Florida.

– His intervention was very useful, because he picked up people who were starving in Florida. As all their supplies had been lost in the storm that had surprised them at sea, they had nothing to eat. They perished of hunger, because the country was not colonized, it was populated by Chichimecs.

– Suárez de Peralta says that the castaways ate their horses before devouring all the leather objects they possessed, seasoned with a little salt: it was for them "the best food in the world"–.

– Villafaña ended up coming back with all those he could bring back and he landed them in Havana.

" So this settlement has failed?"

– From there, [Angel de Villafaña] returned to New Spain, leaving Florida empty, for lack of instructions on what to do with so many women and children sent to occupy the country [...].

– Explain yourself!

"Had it been otherwise, he would have followed the advice of many captains and gone inland. It would have been the right decision and we would have occupied New **Mexico**.

– Who benefited from this disaster?

– The damage was considerable, because then the French and other nations tried to occupy Florida, but ours prevented them.

– For example, Pedro Menéndez de Avilés, General of the Indian Sea Fleet?

– The corsairs and in particular the French were very afraid of him, because he chased them and drove them out of Florida.

" Do you know more about these French people?"

– [Pedro Menéndez de Avilés] captured Juan Ribaud [*sic*], the general of the French, who had seized the tip of Santa Helena and San Matheo.

– La Punta de Santa Elena is now Parris Island, South Carolina. It is the only allusion to the kingdom of France which appears in your writings.

Seen from Tlaxcala, France appears with the unattractive features of a small aggressive nation populated by corsairs. Diego does not make Jean Ribault an Englishman like Suárez de Peralta [78], but he could at least have called him a heretic since the Dieppois was a Huguenot captain recruited in 1562 by Admiral de Coligny to colonize Florida. Accompanied by René de Goulaine de Laudonnière, Ribault founded Charlesfort on the "Pointe de Sainte-Hélène" in honor of King Charles IX. After his return to France, he made a second attempt in 1565, which came up against the seasoned forces of Pedro Menéndez. The Spaniard takes the colony of Fort Caroline and massacres all the occupants, including women and children. Taken prisoner, Ribault is executed as a "Lutheran [79]". Let us add that the "knight" that is Pedro Menéndez (in Diego's eyes) had led a long career as a corsair in the service of the Spanish crown before taking charge of the Indian fleet and becoming the architect of the resumption of Florida.

The rise of animal husbandry

New Spain is carried away in a continual movement. Maritime and land expansion beyond the borders is accompanied by spectacular agricultural growth. Diego is attentive to an economic activity that closely affects his interests, the rise of livestock farming. This source of wealth also strikes Suárez de Peralta, who does not fail to recall that meat is everywhere so abundant that it is often abandoned on the spot to the voracity of wild dogs and vultures [80].

– Do you associate the rise of animal husbandry with the dynamics of the rush to the north?

– As cattle herds increased considerably and wreaked havoc on the pacified Indians, this discovery became indispensable [81].

– You call "discovery" the recognition of new lands and their occupation. But did this advance in colonization have repercussions on the first activities of the Spaniards?

– In the process, we abandoned many farms in the valley of Tepepulco, Atzumpa [82] and Toluca [83], where the first ranches had appeared, and we left to occupy these plains where all the cattle farms in the country are now located. country.

– Have other regions benefited from the livestock boom?

– With the increase in the number of Spaniards, the coastal regions of Pánuco and Nautla began to be occupied, which are called the plains of Almería, and beyond that appeared the great ranches [...] of Veracruz and others in the hot lands of Tlalixcoyan, on the coast of Cohuatzacoalcos [84], which go to the Grijalva river.

– *You insist on the growth of breeding and you attribute to it an unprecedented scale.*

– If one cannot see it with one's own eyes, it is impossible to take the measure of it and appreciate it at its fair value [85] [...]. New Spain was enriched with new Spanish settlers and the herds of sheep grew in number [86].

– *With what impact on the country's economy?*

– It was at this time that the cloth and linen workshops began to operate. And the work of wool has experienced a great boom. [The viceroy] had merino sheep imported into Spain to improve the animals that had been introduced before, because they gave only coarse wool.

Crises

On the domestic political side, Diego is less talkative. Like his contemporaries, as a faithful servant of the monarchy, he weaves crowns for the first two viceroys of New Spain, Antonio de Mendoza and Luis de Velasco. The peace that reigns in Mexico is all the more appreciated as Peru is plunged into an interminable civil war. For the rest, the West Indies escaped the religious confrontations which ravaged the European continent.

– *What prestigious title was awarded to Viceroy Luis de Velasco?*

– His sagacity and maturity earned him the title of excellence of "father of the country" [87].

Plutarch explains to us that Cicero had received this honor [88]. Later, in Florence, Cosimo de' Medici would in turn be celebrated as "father of the country" and everything suggests that the scholars of Mexico were not unhappy to deposit an antique patina on the so recent institutions of New Spain. But what can the word "homeland" mean for the Creoles, and in particular for Diego the Tlaxcaltec? Our perplexity grows even more when we learn that the initiative to award this prestigious designation to the representative of sovereign power would come from the native nobility, and not from Creole circles [89].

Fatherland or not, and for whom? New Spain remains a fragile creation, brought to political boiling, even if the crises never turn into civil war as in the Andes. "As soon as the news arrived, Mexico City and the whole country entered into revolution, because the situation was unprecedented [90]. It is in these terms that Suárez de Peralta describes the changes brought about by the installation of the first viceroy, Antonio de Mendoza, in 1535. Nine years later, the inspection tour of the visitor Tello de Sandoval sows trouble again: he is the bearer of the royal orders which prohibit native slavery and put an end to the employment of Indians as *tamemes* – that is to say porters – which gave rise to all sorts of abuses. The country is young, but its elites are already clinging to their privileges.

– Major troubles broke out and the earth was on the edge of the abyss [91].

– *Who prevented the catastrophe?*

– It's Don Antonio de Mendoza. Thanks to his sagacity, he appeased the country, which remained calm.

– *How did he do it?*

– Several measures were not applied immediately, but were introduced gradually. We waited for the disappearance of the slaves that there were then and we used the means necessary to suspend the laws while giving them obedience.

– *In other words, the local administration invented one of the golden rules of the colonial order: "We obey, but we do not execute", without which Spanish domination would never have stood the test of American reality.*

This flexibility was not only opportune, it was essential because of the distance that separated the Mexican land from the metropolis. The fact remains that the powerful, here the *encomenderos* [92] and the wealthy colonists, were not the only ones to be agitated in the 1540s.

– We discovered a revolt that had tried to organize the black slaves of the Spaniards. These blacks had called the Indians of Santiago Tlatelolco to join them [93].

– *Obsessed by the possibility of collusion between Africans, mestizos and natives, the viceroy Mendoza goes so far as to evoke the election of a king by the rebellious blacks. How did the court react?*

– She intervened against the culprits and the country remained calm until another rebellion was brewing which would have been even more disastrous if it had gone further [...]. The culprits were also punished, and the leaders of the revolt executed with extreme rigor.

– *Who reported them?*

– Gaspar de Tapia and Sebastian Lazo de la Vega.

– *The chronicler Suárez de Peralta contradicts your version. The suspects are said to have paid with their lives for empty remarks or made in a state of intoxication: "I heard that they died innocent* [94]. *When do you date this conspiracy, in your eyes "more dangerous" than the slave revolt, no doubt because it involved Europeans?*

– It happened in 1549.

– *These are turbulent times for Spanish America. Was there a connection between Peru's civil wars and Mexican unrest?*

– Many people involved in this league, in this plot, fled the country for Peru which, at the time, had risen under the leadership of Gonzalo Pizarro and Francisco de Carvajal, his lieutenant general.

" *Did they have to go to a port on the Pacific coast?*"

– We arrested many men on the roads, especially in Tehuantepec and Oaxaca [95].

The port of Tehuantepec, at the mouth of the eponymous isthmus on the Pacific coast, was the gateway to Peru and the end point of the *camino real* which led from Mexico City to Oaxaca.

– *How did the power react to the civil wars that ravaged Peru under the government of Pedro de la Gasca at the end of the 1540s?*

– There would be many things to say about the help that Don Antonio de Mendoza, then viceroy of New Spain, sent to the *licenciado* La Gasca. This one had made the request from Peru at the time when we were fighting against Pizarro. From Mexico, the Viceroy then sent troops led by his son, Don Francisco de Mendoza [96].

– *What struck you most about these events dating back to 1548?*

– To arm this fleet, we have mobilized the finest troops in the world that we can muster, more than a thousand men, infantry, horsemen, nobles, squires, people of the highest nobility. All handpicked and illustrious, from across India, ready to serve their king and lord with loyalty and fierce determination. All set off with a lot of cavalry and went as reinforcements.

" *However, there was never a Mexican army in Peru?*

"Then news came that it was no longer needed because Peru was at peace and once again loyal to His Majesty. This is how this wonderful relief expedition ended. But that did not prevent many people from going to Peru [97].

In 1566, New Spain was shaken by a new crisis, the seriousness of which Diego did not hide, since he described it as new rebellion and even gives it a name: the "Mexico [98] rebellion". The triumphant return of Hernán Cortés' son, Martín, catalyzes discontent. The atmosphere is charged: the "passion for business" agitates the Creole world. Many begin to dream aloud, rumors lend the Cortés clan the intention of separating New Spain from the motherland. There is even talk of having Martín crowned by the pope to break definitively with the metropolis. But a brutal repression crushes the movement in the bud [99]. Scarred by the civil wars of Peru, the Crown does not mess with the desire for independence.

– *How can a political crisis of this magnitude be explained?*

– There would be a lot to say. But I'll stop there, because many have written about this rebellion.

– *Suárez de Peralta is more talkative or more courageous. In his* Treatise on the Discovery of the Indies *, he devotes several chapters to examining the facts and gives his own testimony. We understand your discretion, but what side did you take? That of Martín Cortés or that of the Audience?*

– I defer to what the Royal Audience did and to the procedures they followed.

Diego confines himself to giving the names of the Spaniards executed and banished. He also cites three men who are at the heart of the turmoil, Martín Cortés and his two half-brothers, including a half-breed like him. And he does not forget to mention the fatal fate that struck the two judges sent to Mexico by the Crown to organize the repression: one died during the outward journey and the other disappeared during the crossing of feedback. As if death, impartial, had struck both sides. Or, rather, as if divine justice had not spared the perpetrators of such fierce repression, which at least Diego wanted to point out. He adds that the viceroy sent to liquidate the case was forced to return to Spain, on the grounds that he was favorable to the party of the Marquis del Valle, Martín Cortés. Pierce between the lines the violence of the political hurricane that is beating down on this very young New Spain. We won't know much more. But do we feel the situation the same way in Mexico City or in Tlaxcala? This internal crisis has shaken people's minds all the more because the waters of the Atlantic are no longer safe. This time, the corsairs are not content to bite on distant lands [100].

– In 1568, the viceroy don Martín Enríquez succeeds don Gastón de Peralta. The fleet transporting him to Mexico has a nasty surprise.

– The Viceroy found the port of San Juan de Ulúa in the hands of Juan de Acle. This man of order brought the situation under control and the port and the island of San Juan de Ulúa were recaptured, but there were clashes and violent exchanges which left many dead on each side.

– Who is Juan de Acle?

– An English corsair.

" Isn't that John Hawkins, a wealthy merchant from Plymouth?" It was the uncle of the famous Francis Drake who was at his side during this attack. Suárez de Peralta, who calls it Juan Aquiens, explains that this port, near Veracruz, is "the key to this whole New World [101]".

– This situation has deeply disturbed the country because of the damage that [these corsairs] have committed and that they [still] commit every day, because of the rampages they perpetrate on the Ocean Sea, in Santo Domingo, in Cartagena of the Indies, at Puerto de Caballos, on the coast of the South Sea, on the route to the Philippines and on the shores of Peru [102].

- *What do you know about Drake?*

– Francisco Drack [*sic*] seized a ship that was coming from the Philippines near the port of Navidad and California [...]. And he captured other vessels laden with silver, gold, pearls, and other riches, not to mention other unbearable damage that one cannot speak of without experiencing immense pain and grief.

– *You're referring to what happened in 1579 when Drake reached the shores of California on his second circumnavigation of the globe in Western history. What do you blame the authorities for?*

– Of having taken no account of the corsairs and the affair of San Juan de Ulúa.

Diego's criticism is harsh. It reflects as much concern about the foreign threat as the interest shown in the maritime routes that connect the kingdom to the rest of the world. It is also sensitive to ongoing geopolitical transformations. Henceforth, the American continent, which Diego always calls the *Nuevo Mundo* , is surrounded and besieged by the corsairs of Elizabeth of England. At the beginning of the 17th century , "Spain, founded on water and surrounded by water, was, it was said, a galleon where all are in danger [103]". With the attacks of the corsairs, the Spaniards of New Spain, so far removed from European politics, began to become aware of what was happening on the other side of the ocean and of the fragility of Iberian domination. Suárez de Peralta relates that the English survivors of John Hawkins' expedition were sent to Mexico, where they were detained and tried. The inhabitants of the city thus had the opportunity to see closely these Europeans who were easily confused with the French and who aroused great curiosity. The prisoners, for their part, did not lead off on this land where the Inquisition reigned [104].

The Catholic Monarchy

The world before the Conquest was reduced to what the Indians called Anahuac, a mass of land surrounded by an impassable wall of water that rose to the sky, that is to say the Atlantic Ocean and the Pacific Ocean. With the Spanish domination, Anahuac finds itself included in a larger space which expands towards the north, the south and the west at the rate of the Iberian progression.

Diego is not the only one in New Spain to perceive this expansion of the New World. In 1584, in Mexico City, Balthazar Obregón besieged the monarch with the recall of his services and his requests for office. Engaged from the age of nineteen in the conquest of the northern immensities, from New Biscay and Cibola to California, he offered to direct the expansion of the monarchy towards such promising regions [105].

In his *Treatise on the Discovery of the Indies* , Juan Suárez de Peralta is just as attentive to the irresistible impulse which seems bound to push back the confines of New Spain indefinitely. The expeditions launched towards the north of the country and Florida, across the Pacific, or towards the Philippines interest this son of a conquistador as much as Diego [106]. The driving forces are always the same: the taste for lucre, the brilliant commercial prospects, the fortune at hand, "the gigantic hopes of obtaining what is best in the world ". Added to this are the multiplier effects of the mirages that inflame public opinion and unleash veritable rushes to the north or to the coasts of China. This excess mocks reality. This is the case for China, which we refuse to see for what it already is: no one has eyes for "the power of this country, the small number of starters and the multitude that lives [there]. Although expansion may often be a fiasco and a tragedy – and neither Diego nor Suárez de Peralta are men to delude themselves – it is part of the DNA of New Spain.

In October 1580, news of the conquest of Portugal reached the ears of the Archbishop of Mexico. Without waiting, the city began to resound with prayers and processions organized for the victory of its sovereign. Some time later, the union of the two crowns will be proclaimed.

Diego could have prided himself on belonging to the first European domination which coveted a planetary influence. Although he was not yet fully aware of this at the beginning of the 1580s, his trip to Spain and his stay in Madrid gave him the means to appreciate the greatness of the Castilian monarchy up close. At that time, Spanish propaganda went into overdrive. Mottos, such as the one appearing on a medal struck in 1580 for Philip II, " *Non sufficit orbis* " ("The world is not enough for him"), raise the bar of Castilian power as high as possible, that is to say at the height of the globe. Plans for the invasion of England (1588) or China (1583) – from Manila with the support of New Spain – testify to the euphoric climate and universal appetite that reigns from Madrid to the most remote provinces . The Bishop of Manila imagines Philip II on the verge of becoming the greatest monarch the world has ever seen [109]. Diego has China in mind when he himself predicts an unprecedented success: even more than the deal of the century, "it will be the best and most important commercial relationship that has existed in the world[110]". In 1582, the conquest of the Azores by the Marquis of Santa Cruz made the people of Madrid say that even Christ was no longer safe in paradise, for the marquis might well go and fetch him there and crucify him again. A reckless statement, but which says a lot about the state of mind of contemporaries. It does not matter that in these same years the attacks of Francis Drake (1585-1586) or the disaster of the Invincible Armada (1588) come to remind us of the principle of reality. The elites of the Monarchy grew accustomed to cultivating the image of a world given over to the appetites of their merchants, the ambitions of their soldiers and the dreams of their missionaries. Even to the bitter enemies of the Crown, Dutch, English or French, this domination appears without limit.

This open world draws the contours of the imagination shared by Diego. However, to believe that it would be reduced to the terrestrial globe and that it would henceforth be delivered into the sole hands of (European) men is still premature. The erasure of all transcendence is yet to come. Secularization is barely beginning. The globe retains solid metaphysical foundations: the prodigious rise of the Habsburgs, the miraculous sequence of the *Reconquista* and the *Conquista* , the diabolical actions of the Lutheran or Mohammedan enemy would be inconceivable without the eye and without the omnipresent hand of the divine Providence. Castilian imperialism remains shrouded in a messianic aura [111].

To tell the truth, the will of Heaven is a dimension to which Diego shows himself less sensitive as soon as he moves away from the Tlaxcaltec space: in his viewfinder, China is a commercial objective of the first magnitude more than a land of assignment. The colonization of northern Mexico is primarily linked to the protection of silver mines, ranching projects and prospects for quick enrichment. In the same spirit, his contemporary Suárez de Peralta drove home the point: "The day there are no more mines, it will be the end of India [112]. And if he comes to evoke hell, it is to describe the abyssal depths of the Mexican mines and, who knows, the fate reserved for black and indigenous minors. Each time he speaks of an expedition, it is to record the profits made or the losses suffered [113].

Science is the other pillar of the rise of the monarchy. Hence the importance that Diego attaches to the knowledge and mastery of maritime routes at a time when the Crown is launching great scientific firsts, such as the coordinated observation of lunar eclipses. Science transforms the Iberian domain into a gigantic open-air laboratory of which Madrid, Mexico City, Manila and Macao constitute the terrestrial relays.

Yet globalization is not limited to the lands of the Catholic Monarchy. "Cortés took with him a son of Moctezuma and many other chiefs from Tlaxcala and Cempoala, and in 1520 [sic *]* he arrived in Toledo in Spain -Who tells us about the conquistador's return to Europe by mentioning a detail, the Tlaxcaltec accompaniment, that Diego omits or ignores? A great Ottoman chronicle, the *Tarih-i Hind-i Garbi* , written in the early 1580s. The emergence of the planetary scene that Diego describes from his observatory in Tlaxcala is a phenomenon that can also be seen from Istanbul. Years ago the shock wave of the conquest of the New World reached the shores of the Bosphorus. Contemporary of Diego Muñoz Camargo, this anonymous chronicler close to the Ottoman court situates the event in the history of the world and strives to explain America - the "New India" - to his contemporaries who live in the land of Islam. Istanbul registers the upheavals of the geopolitics of the world and takes note of a gigantic widening which opens a global space common to the Iberians and the Turks. The globalization launched by the Iberians is now as noticeable on the Bosphorus as in the mountains of Tlaxcala. When the Tlaxcaltec authorities decide to found a new village, San Felipe Tequemecan, they give it the name of the sovereign, because its creation dates back to the year "where we left to occupy the Philippine islands of the Ponant [115]". Tlaxcala, Manila, Istanbul, same world.

Another manifestation of globalization, this one immediately deadly, throughout the sixteenth century, epidemics periodically struck New Spain. They decimated the native populations more surely than the war of conquest and the unbridled exploitation of the local workforce. These epidemics are now at the heart of all historical analyses, but they also figured prominently in the questionnaire that gave rise to the geographical relationships. Diego has already replied to this topic. It remained to indicate the celestial dimension of these calamities. This is an opportunity for him to express beliefs shared by Spaniards and Indians [116].

– In 1576, a very great plague struck the Indians of this country. It lasted over a year.

“ *You say she depopulated and destroyed most of New Spain.*

– A month before the epidemic, we saw a great sign in the sky, three wheels on the sun which looked like three very bloody suns from which came out flames of fire [117].

" *Like the wonders that preceded the arrival of the conquistadors?"*

– These three wheels had the same colors as the rainbow called the Iris arc. They lasted from eight in the morning to one in the afternoon.

1. Gruzinski (2017), p. 159-180.

2. D57v°.

3. D59r°.

4. C239.

5. C176 ; D158v°.

6. D158r°.

7. 7. C262.

8. C259.

9. C260.

10. Le franciscain Motolinía reports the same histoire he dates from 1527, in Motolinía, *Memorials or Book of the Things of New Spain and the Naturals of It* , Edmundo O. Gorman éd., Mexico, UNAM, 1967, p. 253.

11. Diego Muñoz Camargo, *Manuscrito 210 Historia de Tlaxcala* , National Library of France, Luis Reyes García ed., *Amoxcalli* , 381, https://amoxcalli.org.mx/facsimilar.php?id=210. [1]In the seventeenth century , a cacique recalls in his chronicle of Tlaxcala that a climate of terror maintained by the deaths of children and the executions of caciques preceded the great campaigns of baptism, in Martínez Baracs (2008), p. 120.

12. C221.

13. Boris Jeanne, "Papal diplomacy and sacraments: the dispute over mass baptisms in Mexico (1524-1584)", *Mixtures of the French School of Rome* , t. 121-1, 2009, p. 139-154, https://www.persee.fr/doc/mefr_1123-9891_2009_num_121_1_10581 [2].

14. C155/6.

---

1. https://amoxcalli.org.mx/facsimilar.php?id=210

2. https://www.persee.fr/doc/mefr_1123

15. D147r°.

16. *Ibid.*

17. D57r°-57v°.

18. C280.

19. Suarez de Peralta (1990), p. 167.

20. C280.

21. C157.

22. C265.

23. Marta Milagros del Vas Mingo, «The ordinances of 1573, their antecedents and consequences», *Quincentenary* , no ˙ 8, 1985, p. 83-102, https://dialnet.unirioja.es/servlet/articulo?codigo=80347.[3]

24. Martinez Baracs (1992), p. 200.

25. C268.

26. C269-270.

27. Bernal Díaz del Castillo, *True History of the Conquest of New Spain* , Mexico, Historical Research Institute, t. I, 1982, p. 605.

28. C270.

29. Spanish Municipality in the province of Zamora.

30. C272.

31. Martín Fernández de Navarrete, *Collection of trips and discoveries* , t. IV, Madrid, National Printing, 1837, p. X ; Enriqueta Vila Vilar, *Los Corzo and los Mañara: types and archetypes of the merchant with the Indies* , Séville, University of Seville, 2011, http://www.congreso.es/docu/PHist/docs/05rest/biblioteca_ejemplar_digit.pdf.[4]

3. https://dialnet.unirioja.es/servlet/articulo?codigo=80347

32. Luis María de Salazar, *Discourse on the progress and current state of hydrography in Spain* , Madrid, Imprenta Real, 1809, p. 24.

33. Alvarado García de Escalante, *Journey to the Western Islands* , Carlos Martínez Shaw ed., University of Cantabria, 1999, p. 17.

34. *Collection of unpublished documents for the history of Chile from Magellan's voyage to the battle of Maipo, 1518-1818* , José Toribio Medina éd., t. II, Santiago du Chili, Ercilla Press, 1988, p. 274.

35. *Ibid.* , p. 271 ; Luis Abraham Barandica Martínez, *From New Spain to the Western Islands: the organization and journey of the participants in the expedition led by Ruy Lopez Villalobos 1542-1549* , Mexico, UNAM, mémoire de maîtrise, 2004, chap. vii.

36. Michael C. Krivor, John de Bry et *al., Archival Investigations for Potential Colonial-Era Shipwrecks in Ultra-Deepwater within the Gulf of Mexico*, La Nouvelle-Orléans, U.S. Department of the Interior, 2011, p. 42, https://www.boem.gov/ESPIS/4/5109.pdf.[5]

37. C272.

38. Goa.

39. Ce sera le deuxième gouverneur des Philippines (1572-1575).

40. C272.

41. C288.

42. Dennis O. Flynn et Arturo Giraldez, « Born with a "Silver Spoon" », *Journal of World History*, vol. 6, n° 2, 1995, p. 201-221.

43. Fernán González de Eslava, *Spiritual and Sacramental Colloquies* , Othón Arróniz ed., Mexico, UNAM, 1990, p. 154. The enthusiasm unleashed by China does not escape Juan Suárez de Peralta (1990), p. 109.

44. C274.

---

4. http://www.congreso.es/docu/PHist/docs/05rest/biblioteca_ejemplar_digit.pdf

5. https://www.boem.gov/ESPIS/4/5109.pdf

45. C273.

46. Suárez de Peralta (1990), p. 150.

47. *Ibid* ., p. 153.

48. Thomas Goodrich, *The Ottoman Turks and the New World. A Study of Tarih-i Hind-i Garbi and Sixteenth Century Ottoman Americana* , Wiesbaden, Harrassowitz, 1990, p. 264.

49. Rebecca Carte, *Capturing the Landscape of New Spain. Baltazar Obregón and the 1564 Ibarra Expedition* , Tucson, University of Arizona Press, 2015.

50. Suarez de Peralta (1990), p. 158.

51. C274.

52. C44.

53. C288.

54. C291.

55. Pedro, Jorge's brother, received from the hands of Cortés a daughter of Xicotencatl, doña Luisa. One of Luisa's sisters found herself in Jorge's arms, whom she accompanied to Peru.

56. On the *Lienzo de Tlaxcala* , Tlaxcaltecs and Spaniards share the same white skin while that of the opponent is red or brown in color. The rudimentary armament of the enemy also contrasts with the Tlaxcaltec panoplies, which display emblems and adopt weapons of Spanish origin such as swords.

57. Martinez Baracs (1992), p. 204.

58. *Ibid* ., p. 205.

59. The village is linked to the *cabecera* of Tepeticpac and governed by the cacique Francisco Vázquez Coronado, namesake of the unfortunate explorer, *ibid* ., p. 215, 226; Charles Foin, "A peacemaker from northern Mexico, Rodrigo de Río de Losa (1536-1606?)", *Miscellanies from the Casa de Velázquez* , t. XIV, 1978, p. 173-214.

60 . Goodrich (1990), p. 146.

61 . Abraham Ortelius, *Americae sive Novi Orbis Nova Descriptio* , Antwerp, 1572. The Tiguas River flows from east to west to flow into the Gulf of California after crossing the city of Cevola (Cibola).

62 . Leo Bragrow and RA Skelton, *History of Cartography* , Harvard, Harvard University Press, 1966, fig. 43 ; Eviatar Zerubavel, *Terra cognita : The Mental Discovery of America* , Piscataway, Transaction Publishers, 2003, https://www.sanderusmaps.com/en/our-catalogue/detail/166642/antique-map-of-north-america-by -forlani-and-zaltieri.[6]

63 . *Discourse of the navigation that the Portuguese make to the Kingdoms and Provinces of the East, and of the news that is had of the greatness of the Kingdom of China.*

64 . Juan González de Mendoza, *History of the most notable things, rites and customs of the great kingdom of China* , Rome, Vicentio Accolti, 1585.

65 . Serge Gruzinski, *The Eagle and the Dragon. European excess and globalization in the sixteenth century* , Paris, Fayard, 2012, p. 373-403.

66 . C276.

67 . Jean-Pierre Sanchez, *Myths and legends of the conquest of America* , Rennes, University Press of Rennes, 1996, p. 66.

68 . Guido Munch Galindo, *La Organización social de Tehuantepec y Juchitán* , Mexico City, UNAM, 1989, gives the date as 1529.

69 . Francisco R. Calderón, *Economic history of New Spain in the time of the Habsburgs* , Mexico, FCE, [1988] 2005, p. 572, http://peruhistoriaglobal.blogspot.com/2011/03/acapulco-y-el-callao-siglos-xvi-xvii-1a.html.[7]

70 . Fernando Iwasaki Cauti, *the Far East and Peru in the 16th century* , Lima, Pontifical Catholic University of Peru, 1995, p. 241.

71 . *Ibid.*

6. https://www.sanderusmaps.com/en/our-catalogue/detail/166642/antique-map-of-north-america-by-forlani-and-zaltieri

7. http://peruhistoriaglobal.blogspot.com/2011/03/acapulco-y-el-callao-siglos-xvi-xvii-1a.html

72 . Sarmiento de Gamboa (1987).

73 . C287.

74 . See note 3, p. 165.

75 . Suárez de Peralta (1990), p. 179.

76 . *Ibid* ., p. 180.

77 . C286 287 .

78 . Suárez de Peralta (1990), p. 182.

79 . Mickaël Augeron, John de Bry, Annick Notter (dir.), *Florida, a French Dream (1562-1565)* , Paris, Illustria, 2012.

80 . Suárez de Peralta (1990), p. 39.

81 . C276 ; María Xóchitl Galindo Villavicencio, « The Lords of the Land and the Mechanisms of Meat Supply in Tlaxcala in the Sixteenth Century », *Complutense Journal of History of America* , vol. 40 , 2014 , p. 155-1

82 . In the Valley of Mexico.

83 . Southwest of Mexico City.

84 . Coatzalcoalcos, in the state of Veracruz, on the Gulf of Mexico.

85 . C277.

86 . C279.

87 . C286.

88 . Plutarch, *Lives of Illustrious Men* , Ricard ed., Paris, Furne et Cie, 1840 ("Life of Cicero", XXX); Pierre Grimal, *Cicero* , Paris, Fayard, 2014.

89 . Maria Justina Sarabia Viejo, *Don Luis de Velasco, virrey de la Nueva España (1550-1564)* , Seville, CISIC, Escuela de Estudios Hispanoamericanos, 1978, p. 473.

90 . Suarez de Peralta (1990), p. 147.

91 . C278.

92 . Holders of an *encomienda* , these Spaniards benefited from the labor of the Indians living on the lands granted to them.

93 . Other sources comment on this uprising which affects Mexico City and its suburbs, whether they emanate from the viceroy Antonio de Mendoza (a letter of December 1537) or from native literate circles (*Codex Telleriano-Remensis* and *Vaticano A*); Matteo Lazari, *Afromessicani e inquisizione: la questione della raza nella Nuova Spagna del xvi-xvii secolo* , doctoral thesis, Bologna, University of Bologna, 2019, p. 95-100.

94 . Suarez de Peralta (1990), p. 163.

95 . C279.

96 . D233r°.

97 . D233v°.

98 . C289.

99 . Gregorio Salinero, *The Treason of Cortés. Disobedience, political trials and government of the Indies of Castile, second half of the 16th century* , Paris, Presses Universitaires de France, 2014.

100 . C290.

101 . Suarez de Peralta (1990), p. 238.

102 . C290.

103 . Sancho de Moncada, *Restauración politica de España* [1619], Jean Vilar ed., Madrid, Instituto de estudios financière, 1974, p. 97.

104 . Suarez de Peralta (1990), p. 252.

105. Francisco del Paso y Troncoso, *Epistolary of New Spain, 1508-1518* , t. XII, 1576-1596, Mexico, Old Robredo Bookstore, by José Porrúa and Sons, 1940, p. 95-9

106. Suárez de Peralta (1990), p. 109.

107. *Ibid* ., p. 153 , 157 .

108. *Ibid* ., p. 184.

109. Geoffrey Parker, "David or Goliath? Philip II and his World in the 1580s", in *Spain, Europe and the Atlantic World* , Richard L. Kagan and Geoffrey Parker eds., Cambridge, Cambridge University Press, 1995, p. 255.

110. C288.

111. This will still be the case at the beginning of the seventeenth century when Tommaso Campanella will write his *Monarchy of Spain* .

112. Suarez de Peralta (1990), p. 177.

113. *Ibid* ., p. 158.

114. Goodrich (1990), p. 261.

115. Martinez Baracs (2008), p. 233.

116. Gerhard (1972), p. 24.

117. C291-292.

CHAPTER IX

"We should all be one"

Diego did not experience the Conquest (1519-1521). When he sets to work, more than sixty years have passed. This is the lapse that separates us today (2019) from the victory of the Cuban revolution. Assuming that time flows in the sixteenth century at the same speed as ours, we understand that these founding years can be surrounded by a halo of hagiography and heroism. The memory passed on by the Spanish elites has shifted into the epic gesture – Francisco de Terrazas writes his poem *Nuevo Mundo y Conquista* [1]– while deep in the Franciscan cloisters the beginnings of Christianization have taken on the appearance of an age of gold irretrievably lost.

Faced with the exaltation of the Spanish gesture or the Franciscan nostalgia, the condemnations of the Dominican Bartolomé de Las Casas continue to resonate in America and Europe. His *Very Brief Account of the Destruction of the Indies. Tyrannies and cruelties of the Spaniards* circulated in French and Dutch (1578). The German version will come out in 1597 [2]. The black legend is settling for several centuries. It associated the Conquest with an irreparable human cataclysm and inspired Montaigne to write lines that have become famous: "So many cities razed to the ground, so many nations exterminated, so many millions of peoples put to the sword, and the richest and most beautiful part of the world upset for the negotiation of pearls and pepper. This excerpt from the chapter "Coaches" will be published in 1588. Diego does not have the same interpretation of the Conquest.

Act I: "We were all to be one"

– *We know through Cortés and other historians that the Mexica were expecting an invasion from the East and that Moctezuma had resigned himself to it* [3]. *Can you remind us of the words of Xicotencatl, one of the Tlaxcaltec leaders?*

– "We have known, he said, since the time of our elders that people from the region of the rising sun must arrive [4]. »

– *What would they look like?*

– They would be white and bearded. They would carry small books on their heads as a sign of their authority and would have long legs [...] and very strong weapons, stronger than our bows.

– *No possible mistake about the identity of the intruders?*

– It was these people, they said, it was these people and no one else who would come looking for us.

– *What purposes were attributed to them?*

– They would match with us and we all had to do one [5].

– *This is also what Montaigne, your contemporary, would have wished; he had imagined that a fraternal society and intelligence might have arisen "between them and us ."* –

The arrival of visitors is therefore not unexpected. It has always been part of the local tradition. And the Europeans lead the game: "They are the ones who came to get us. Here, however, Diego departs from the usual narratives. He speaks no no "conquest" for Tlaxcala, but a merger. The Spaniards' goal was not belligerent. What Diego's informants (or Diego himself) express with words that are perhaps still familiar to us since "We must all be one" takes up the prayer of Christ in the Gospel of John (17, 21): "That all may be one, as you Father are in me, and as I am in you, that they too may be one in us, that the world may believe that you sent me. From the outset, the bar is set very high. Appeal to which Cortés echoes by answering that all together they will share the name of Christians. "And we will all be one, united in one whole [7]. Pierces again the spirit of the Scriptures, especially of the Epistle to the Galatians: "There is no longer either Jew or Greek, there is no longer either slave or free, there is no longer either man nor wife; for all of you are one in Christ Jesus [8]»

Words imagined from start to finish by Diego in the 1580s or, more surely, elaborated during the great half-century that separates him from events. Our author would then be the last link in a double tradition: that of the indigenous elites of Tlaxcala who, over the generations, reflected on the image of the past that they intended to exploit, and that of the Spanish chroniclers, who broadcast from Cortés to López de Gómara and from López de Gómara to Cervantes de Salazar [9].

That would be counting without the pre-Hispanic precedent. However, the memory of the invasion of the Chichimec ancestors, far from being extinguished, is the subject of constant re-elaboration. We knew that the conquerors had come to take women from the old Toltec cities. The nomadic ancestors there had gained the prestige and legitimacy associated with sedentary cities while the latter captured the warrior energy of the newcomers [10]. Isn't this exactly what the Tlaxcaltecs offered the conquistadors in exchange for the new strength they brought? Already, pre-Hispanic traditions had blurred the brutal dimensions of the Chichimec invasion. With the irruption of the Spaniards, the violence of the shock is always evaded, but the roles are reversed: the settled descendants of the ancient Chichimecs become the donors of women while the Castilians take on the role of migrants. The spring remains the same.

So many clues to think that Diego's interpretation also draws from the depths of local memories, as if he wanted to support the idea that not all intrusion ends in conquest and that conquest does not invariably lead to destruction or submission.

Let's get back to the facts. The Spaniards enter Tlaxcaltec territory at Tzompanzingo. According to most chroniclers, the Tlaxcaltecs and Spaniards immediately went to war.

– You give a slightly different version. Is it to cushion the memory of the shock or hide the double game of the Tlaxcaltecs?

– [Cortés arrived] at the borders, at the limits of this province [...], where from clashes to skirmishes he was welcomed by waging a very harsh war against him. The Otomian Indians of Tecohuactzinco, who were in charge of guarding this border, killed a Spaniard and two horses. But, as soon as the Tlaxcaltecs knew it, they sent messengers to them. They ordered [...] not to attack them to avoid angering them and letting them pass and go where they wanted [11].

– Moctezuma's lavish welcome to Cortés when he arrived in Mexico City-Tenochtitlan is remembered. How was the first meeting in Tlaxcala and who was there?

– The great lord Xicotencatl and his companions. The reception was the most solemn and the most famous that we have seen and that we have heard of in the world, for, in these countries so distant and so different from ours, no prince had ever been received in such a manner.

– In Mexico, the chroniclers mention tens of thousands of natives. How was Cortés' welcome to Tlaxcala exceptional?

– The four lords of Tlaxcala appeared in the greatest possible pomp and majesty, in the company of many other *tecuhtles* and *piles* [13], and of the great lords of the republic, with more than one hundred thousand men who filled the streets and fields. It seemed incredible [14].

– The entry of the Spaniards must have aroused enormous curiosity?

– In view of these novelties and these unprecedented situations, foreigners and Indians from elsewhere secretly came to see what was going on, to know who these people were who had just arrived, where they came from and what things they brought [15].

– *What did the Tlaxcaltec explain to them?*

"They were telling them more than what was happening, to scare them and scare them, and to spread these rumors all over the country, which indeed they did. It was claimed that our people were gods, that no human power was strong enough to fight against them, and that no one in the world could harm them .

– *In other words, the Tlaxcaltecs were already behaving like allies who sought to intoxicate their old adversary, the Indians of Mexico-Tenochtitlan. Relations with newcomers go through the exchange of presents. What importance did the Indians give to these gestures of cordiality?*

– The Indians have a hard time with people not accepting their gifts, even a flower, because for them this attitude is suspicious of enmity, a lack of love and trust between the one who gives and the one who receives [17].

– *Slaves are then offered to Cortés, who ends up accepting them and puts them in the service of his companion at the time, La Malinche. This immediately brings the two camps closer together.*

– Seeing that some slaves were well with the Spaniards, the *principals* themselves gave their own daughters [18].

– *For what purpose?*

– With the idea that, if by chance some of them fell pregnant, they would still have descendants of these valiant and courageous men [19].

– *Aren't you describing the origins of miscegenation?*

– Driven by this thought, many lords gave their daughters to the Spaniards, to keep their descendants and have a line in case the Spaniards left the country.

– Your answer suggests that the son of a Spaniard and an Indian of the nobility remains a Spaniard. That would explain why you can constantly present yourself as a Spaniard while your mother is Indian.

– This is how the good Xicotencatl gave one of his daughters, pretty and beautiful in appearance, to don Pedro de Alvarado: her name was doña Luisa Techquilhuastzin.

– In other words, the fusion of the Tlaxcaltecs with the Castilians was beginning to become a reality?

– The Indians gave Hernán Cortés the name of " *chalchiuh capitán* [20]" – it is as if we were saying "captain of great value and esteem" [...] – and don Pedro de Alvarado that of "Sun" because, they said they, he was son of the sun to be red and red. He had such a pretty face, such a beautiful look and looks. The Indians gave him no other nickname because, after Captain Hernando Cortés, no one was more loved and more cherished by the natives than Don Pedro de Alvarado, and even more by the Tlaxcaltecs [21].

At the time, the word *casta* meant in Spanish a "noble and unmixed lineage, one that is of good lineage and good ancestry [22]". The Indian elites do not at all have in mind to produce mestizos, but to preserve a physical trace of the passage of the Spaniards in order to appropriate some of their strength and energy. Doña Luisa Xicotencatl, who will be united to Pedro de Alvarado, will have two children from him, Pedro and Leonor: did these births meet the expectations of the Tlaxcaltec elites? In reality, it is Cortés, and not Xicotencatl – who gives Luisa in marriage to his lieutenant Pedro de Alvarado – a rite of which the pagan princes then had no idea and which the intruders did without difficulty [23].

Are the words that Diego attributes to the Tlaxcaltec chiefs authentic? Insofar as he writes partly under the control of indigenous elites, the substance of what he reports must correspond if not to the real scene, at least to what the local tradition has made of it, which has gradually crystallized in Tlaxcala.

Politically, the staging of an immediate and enthusiastic collaboration with the Spanish invader was essential, because part of the local elites quickly understood that they thus had an exceptional card to save what could still be saved. . The active collaboration of the Tlaxcaltecs has historical roots. Driven out of Mexico-Tenochtitlan, the conquistadors were on the brink of being annihilated when the Tlaxcaltecs saved them the day. It is on this alliance that the privileges granted to the province of Tlaxcala are based. It gains there a privileged tributary situation, the protection of the grounds against the invasions of the Spaniards, the administrative autonomy and the maintenance in place of the local elites. Not to mention the symbolic capital: the good conscience and the pride of those who not only helped the Conquest, but made it possible, would for a long time distinguish the Tlaxcaltecs from all the other peoples of New Spain.

Diego's art consists in imagining, staging and making plausible the primitive scene where these first relationships are established. The speeches alternate and follow one another, the reasoning and the arguments put forward answer each other on both sides, in the course of a progression which inevitably leads to the victory of Cortés and to the adhesion body and soul of the Tlaxcaltecs. This restitution is disconcerting, as it contrasts with the usual vision of a pitiless confrontation punctuated by inhuman violence.

The saviors of the Spaniards

– You do not miss an opportunity to insist on the dependence of the Spaniards on the Tlaxcaltecs. These are not content to bring presents, to offer women. They supply their hosts whom the Indians called the white men [24].

– They offered Cortés food in large quantities, birds, hens, partridges, hares, rabbits, deer and all kinds of game [...] not to mention corn, beans and other vegetables from the country [25].

– You describe in detail the welcome given to Spaniards fleeing Mexico City, while Suárez de Peralta limits himself to writing "that they were well received by the Tlaxcaltecs [26]*".*

"As they began [...] to enter the city, people came out to see them and, as the Spaniards were in a sorry state, they were taken with great pity.

– How did the Tlaxcaltec women react?

– Mounted on the roofs of the houses and on the terraces, they cried to them while weeping: "Poor of you! who tricked you into going to Mexico, throwing yourself into the hands of such cruel and perverse traitors? Poor you! after the mistreatment they subjected you to [27]. »

– How did they encourage the future conquistadors against their adversaries?

– "Do not be afraid of these bad people and these traitors" [they said of the Mexicas]. They comforted them with gestures of love and other marks of tenderness.

The attitude of the women of Tlaxcala shows a reversal of positions: the invaders of the day before become fugitives, vanquished, since women come to bring their comfort to routed warriors. It is therefore Tlaxcala, men and women alike, who have the best role. We better capture the singularity of the situation by listening to the words that Diego puts in the mouths of the Tlaxcaltec princes.

– *How do they address Cortés from the first meeting?*

– They made an effort to have convincing, sweet and loving words for him, they prayed and begged him with great insistence [28].

" *But to tell him what?"*

– "For us, you are brothers, true friends and even sons [...]. We are at peace with you, we are at your disposal. Our friendship is pure and sure. You have our word that we will have you as friends, and our word is inviolable and faithful ·»

On both sides, diplomatic rhetoric will no longer cease to emphasize the same values, friendship, fraternity, sincerity and loyalty.

Act II: blackmail at conversion

These principles guide the questions the Indians ask about the intentions, identity and origin of their visitors. Cortés replies in the same tone, imbued with chivalrous courtesy, but he quickly insists on the need for conversion. He preaches Christianity to them: "I have come to bring you [...] another law which is better than yours, that of the true God [30]. The offer has its counterpart: "Since you have so much friendship for me, I want to destroy your idols [...], that is the priority goal of my coming [31]. The conversion of the Indians will be their greatest proof of love: "It will give me the assurance that you love me well. This bond of love will confirm our friendship forever and you will call yourselves Christians like me and like all my companions who say and call themselves Christians [32]. »

The fusion by women on the mode of the matrimonial alliance envisaged by the princes becomes in Cortés a project of spiritual union which will erase the gap between Castilians and Indians. What distinguishes the former is not their divine nature, but their Christian faith. She makes them men apart: "Yes! we are indeed humans and mortals like you, but the advantage we have over you is simply to be Christians. »

Will we radically oppose the indigenous project to the Cortesian project, as if one essentially implied the union of bodies, and the other the salvation of souls? In the 16th century, becoming a Christian was much more than a matter of faith and salvation: it was a political gesture and a societal choice, it was unreserved adherence to a new way of life, with its procession of commitments and servitudes. But the indigenous position is just as calculated: thanks to the marriages proposed by the Tlaxcaltec chiefs, the elites hope to capture the magical force or the aura of the newcomers in order to keep the trace of it alive within them, like a graft. Such is their conception of miscegenation. Still, all this happens in the head of Diego, a half-breed who wants to be Spanish and Christian.

Act III: the reactions of the elites

The conversion process is too complex for Diego to rush into a few formulas. It is a question both of not concealing the resistance and of highlighting the sincerity of the Tlaxcaltec leaders and the journey which leads them to accept the Christian faith. It is the strength of conviction, the "effectiveness" of Cortés' reasoning that must win acceptance. It is not once a question of imposing beliefs. The conversion is therefore shown in an ideal light.

– *How do the native leaders react to the "sermon" of Cortés?*

– The four lords of the four princely houses of the lordship of Tlaxcala stood dumbfounded, surprised and perplexed by what the good captain had said to them and answered.

– *What effect could Cortés' "sweet words of love" have had on them?*

– They insinuated themselves into their hearts, miraculously infusing them with the grace of the Holy Spirit. Filled with this plenitude, they reacted to these profound words with extreme tenderness and tears in their [eyes].

– *Do you remember their answer?*

– "How do you want [they said] that we so easily abandon [our divinities] and that we consent to let you profane with your violent and sacrilegious hands the gods that we esteem and appreciate so much? »

– *These words are not anonymous. They come from the four lords of Tlaxcala, including Xicotencatl and Maxixcatzin, who will very quickly take the lead in the collaboration. He is also the ancestor of your daughter-in-law, Francisca Maxixcatzin.*

– He was the wisest and the youngest of the four caciques [35].

The dialogues follow one another with such vivacity and such precision that one has the impression of having the scene under the eyes. The scenario has been skilfully calculated so that Christian faith (= truth) ends up winning out over error, but without the Tlaxcaltecs losing face at any time. These will rely on reason since Cortés recommends them to "look with the eyes of understanding [36]". However, Diego does not evade the misunderstandings and misunderstandings that surround the conversion.

– *Why do the lords tell the population that Cortés wants to give them another god?*

– This is how I explain this way of saying that he wanted to give them another god. When these people knew of a god endowed with estimable qualities and morals, they received him and admitted him as a deity. And this because other peoples from elsewhere had brought them many idols they adopted into their pantheon. That's why they said Cortés brought them another god.

" *Does it look like the princes tried to manipulate Cortés?" You lend them injunctions which seem to insinuate it...*

– "Let no one stand in his way [...], let us do what he wants and what he wishes, let him take responsibility for it, it is their business: both are gods , over there everyone will understand each other, and everyone will take care of themselves and what concerns them [37]. »

– *The princes end up accepting the faith. With or without resistance?*

– Many have shown themselves to be hardened, rebellious and stubbornly resistant to conversion. And even today, in 1576, many elderly notables have asked for the water of baptism because, ashamed and embarrassed as they were, they had not wanted to be baptized [at first]. Later, out of pure shame, as they were notables, they did not dare to come to holy baptism [...], even though they were married before our holy mother the Church, even though they bore Christian names and [...] went to confession and communion every [year].

– *You conclude with a laconic and perhaps ironic observation: "And that year, in a few days, they finished as Catholics. But what happened in popular circles?*

– There were those who said to their lords: "Speak to the captain and ask him why he wants to take away our gods that we have served so long, us and our ancestors. They can well put their god among the others without having to remove them or remove them from their sacred places [...]. We will make him dwellings and temples apart and for him alone. He will also be our **god**. »

– *Montaigne writes almost the same thing when he imagines the response of the Indians to the conquistadors: "As for a single God, the discourse pleased them, but they did not change their religion, having used it so usefully for so long, and that they were accustomed to taking advice only from their friends and* **acquaintances**. »

– Their lords and caciques told them that there was no way to satisfy their demands and that we had to do exactly what the captain asked: we weren't going to go back on that.

– *What forms did the resistance of the populations take?*

– It happened that they were immediately silent. And they started hiding and secretly concealing many idols and statues [...] in places where many of them served and worshiped them as before. The demon advised them not to lose heart and not to be deceived by the intruders. He told them in dreams and by appearing to them in other forms

Despite this resistance, the dialogue at the top ends well: the princes accept the Christian faith "forever and ever" while Cortés receives carte blanche. "And the worst of idolatries has come to an end, that which had been raging for so many centuries among these populations [42]. » Mixed parties (half-Castilian, half-Indian) celebrate first baptisms. Everything is for the best in the best of all worlds.

This series of episodes and the *happy ending* of the final scene remind us that Tlaxcala has been a center of theatrical experimentation for a good half-century and that Diego, at the age of nine, was able to attend one of the most spectacular achievements of the Franciscan theatre, *The Conquest of Jerusalem* (1539). This theater of evangelization invariably leads to the apology of conversion and the rout of the pagans. In 1578, the Society of Jesus had *El triunfo de los santos* represented in Mexico , the action of which took place at the court of the Emperor Diocletian: Faith and Hope there triumph over Idolatry and Gentileness [43]. Diego may have been among the spectators.

These exchanges can take other forms. The famous colloquy between the Franciscans and the priests of the idols that the Franciscan Bernardino de Sahagún wrote down and recomposed is the counterpart of the dialogues that Diego offers us, with two differences [44]. First, in Tlaxcala, the Christian message is entirely entrusted to the conquistador, without the missionaries getting involved. Then, if they are not the direct inspiration of Diego's dialogues, the descendants of the indigenous interlocutors are still sufficiently present in the Tlaxcaltec society of the end of the 16th century for their memory and their version to be respected.

These exchanges were made possible by the intervention of a woman, the companion of Hernán Cortés, doña Marina, also known as La Malinche. Not only does Diego not ignore it, but he is one of the columnists who tells us the most about it. He is close in this respect to Bernal Díaz del Castillo, the author of the *True History of the Conquest of New Spain* [45]. It relates his origin, his abduction, his tribulations on the Gulf Coast. This pretty woman is offered to a cacique by merchants anxious to obtain her good graces. Then links are forged between Malintzin and a Spanish castaway, Jerónimo de Aguilar: a first communication is then established before Marina is offered with about twenty other women to Hernán Cortés [46]. Once she had become the companion of the conquistador, La Malinche would play a decisive role in the first exchanges that the conqueror would establish with the Tlaxcaltec lords. This female intervention has undoubtedly fascinated Diego interprets her like the painters of *Lienzo de Tlaxcala* who always represent her alongside the conquistador.

– *Who was the one you call Marina or Malintzin?*

– She was of Mexican origin, because she knew this language very fluently.

- *What else do you know?*

– Those who have written about the conquest of these lands have dealt with the question at length. In particular Bernal Díaz del Castillo. This very ancient author spoke of it extensively as an eyewitness, for he was everywhere. He is one of the first conquistadors of this New World. I defer to him.

- *But still?*

– Malintzin was an Indian of character, great courage, great intelligence [47].

– *How to explain the influence it has acquired?*

– When she arrived in these countries, she was already a woman capable of explaining who King Moctezuma was, who were his enemies and adversaries, what were his great empire and his great monarchy, without forgetting his immense wealth and treasures.

– *The Spaniard Aguilar had received her as his wife and the two had learned the Mayan language on the land where fate had brought them together.*

– Husband and wife got along very well and spoke this language to each other as if it were their own language. It was through this that Jerónimo de Aguilar knew and understood the great secrets of all this land and of the lordship of the great Moctezuma.

– *How to understand the place of La Malinche in this story?*

– It is divine Providence which wanted these people to convert to our holy Catholic faith and to have a true knowledge of God: of all this, Marina was the instrument and the means.

dialogues of love

In *Repúblicas del mundo* , the Augustinian Jerónimo Román y Zamora praises Tlaxcala, that republic which is home to an oligarchic government where, he says, the most virtuous are rewarded. But the city also gives the example of a smooth transition from paganism to Christianity: "Those of Tlaxcala before or after [the Conquest] governed their republic on their own account: for before they lived in a very orderly way and afterwards they persevered in all things of the Christian religion and of the service of the king. Conclusion: "They lived peacefully under a good government [...] surrounded by much peace and love [48]. »

"Peace and love": the formula appears as the leitmotif of the chapters devoted to the encounter. It alternates with another doublet: "love and friendship". Each side seems to have only these three words in their mouths, which they decline anyway. The Indians to Cortés: "You see, we love you very much [49] [...]. The friendship we took for you [50] [...]. They had given him their hearts and their friendship, the best of their people. Cortés to the Indians: "This bond of love will confirm our friendship [...]. The love and friendship you bear to me without any malice of any kind [51]. »

But "love and friendship" are false friends. Nothing could be more misleading than these seemingly familiar words, which in fact carry more complex emotional messages and resonances than we imagine. The secularization of our lifestyles and our imaginations, the transformations of family ties and forms of dependency, the popularization of the ideas of medicine in the 19th century and of psychoanalysis in the last century, the sequels of all romanticisms render opaque the categories and emotions of the early modern age. With Diego, the case is complicated since he evolves not only within an American society of the Renaissance, but also in an entourage whose emotions and transport feed on reflexes and habits sedimented during the long Amerindian millennia.

" *Amor y amistad* ". On the European side, we are spoiled for choice. Let's start with the author of *Parallel Lives* because, when he thinks of love and friendship, Diego may have Plutarch's writings in mind. He reflected "on the great number of friends" and on fraternal friendship; he composed a *Dialogue on love* in the Platonic tradition, *Erotikos* [52]. In the *Life* he devotes to the Theban strategist Pelopidas, friendship and alliance go hand in hand, which reminds us that the agreement concluded at Tlaxcala is first and foremost a military alliance sealed between Indians and Castilians [53].

Many centuries after Plutarch, who scrutinizes the Platonic dimensions of love, a mixed race contemporary of Diego, the Inca Garcilaso de la Vega, will examine the theories of universal love and harmony by tackling the translation of the *Dialogues of Love* by Leo the Hebrew, precisely during these 1580s. The idea of Eros as the organizing principle of the world in its cosmic and social dimensions commands the chain of love that unites all beings. At the same time, the Inca explores the duality of the lover and the beloved [54]. From his reading of Leo the Hebrew and Neoplatonism, he will draw the framework philosophy and the arguments from which he will build his social and political vision of the Inca Empire on the eve of the Spanish conquest.

The shadow of Plutarch, omnipresent in the 16th century , the European vogue of Leo the Hebrew and the curiosities of Garcilaso therefore encourage us to link "love and friendship" to Renaissance humanism. Noting however that, unlike the Inca Garcilaso, Diego does not have pre-Hispanic society in mind. He reserves the use of these concepts for the scene of the Conquest to describe the relationships that develop between invaders and invaders.

From one knighthood to another

However, isn't it excessive to reduce everything to Plato? Love and friendship according to Diego are supposed to unite fighters against a common enemy, the Mexicas. The chronicler even uses a technical term, *comilitón* , which points to military camaraderie. What does it tell us about the links between Cortés and Prince Maxixcatzin? "He was for him and all his *comrades in arms* a very faithful friend [55]. Medieval chivalry never ceased to exalt the relationships between men who risked their lives together on the battlefields [56]. This tradition was still alive enough at the end of the 16th century for Cervantes to make fun of it in *Don Quixote* and to instil in *amor y amistad* a social and emotional charge [57].

Diego venerates everything that refers to *hidalguía* , to nobility. He is not for nothing the son of a conquistador father linked to Creole circles. Admittedly, the world of knights is more of a bygone ideal than reality, but the novels in maintain worship and remembrance on American soil to the chagrin of the authorities. When we quote Claude Élien, Plato et Végèce, Alexandre le Grand and Hercule [58], we have every chance of having had some of these best-sellers in our hands, as widespread among individuals and booksellers as the works of law and theology. *Amadis de Gaule, Trapisondas de Don Reynaldos, Espejo de caballerías* are among the many titles waiting, by the hundreds of copies, in the warehouses of Seville's printers to be loaded onto the Indian fleet [59].

The transcontinental vogue for this literature among the conquistadors and the colonists is dazzling, and the success of series like *Game of Thrones* can today make us touch the extent of the phenomenon. In any case, it escaped neither the moralists nor the Crown, who worried about the "toxic" effects of this reading on the Europeans of India and feared even more their influence on the minds of the Indians.

From the 1540s, the young Diego dreamed of the exploits of the valiants, of their cavalcades in marvelous lands and of the unfailing friendships which bound them. In his father's house, the reading aloud of these works brightened the cool evenings of the Altiplano. And perhaps, with his Indian and Spanish comrades, he imagined an Old World populated by paladins ready to fight for their beauty and to perish alongside their best friend? A bit like a Europe of legends enchanted the young American spectators of Disney in the 1930s. The mirage of the Seven Cities of Cibola has nothing to envy to the enchanted palaces of Castilian novels.

But, after all, Diego reminds us, didn't the Indians also have their knighthood? Both Mexicas and Tlaxcaltecs used to arm knights [60]. This was the case with the most valiant men in battle and the best-advised in politics. Diego is inexhaustible on the ceremonies of dubbing, the forms of initiation and apprenticeship, the fasts and the physical tests through which the future knights passed [61]. They were required to show proof of "great humility to win a reward and a prize of this value [62]". However, in Diego, indigenous chivalry is never a copy of Christian chivalry, but it shares its values and provides, as in Europe, one of the means of affirming social hierarchies and distributing privileges.

And how not to have in mind the “Nueve de la Fama”, our “Nine Preux”, one of the great frescoes that decorated the town hall in Tlaxcala? Each week, Diego had these portraits in front of his eyes, "full of nuances and colors, most of them on horseback [63]". Inspired by the *Golden Legend* , Jacques de Longuyon had imagined a cohort of nine heroes, Jews, pagans and Christians, to give faces to the ideal of chivalry. Hector, Alexander and Julius Caesar for the Greco-Roman world, Joshua, David and Judas Maccabee for the Bible, Arthur, Charlemagne and Godfrey of Bouillon for the Christian Middle Ages paraded before the eyes of the Indians. In Europe, this iconographic program was everywhere favored by aristocratic houses and this fashion did not spare New Spain.

Chivalric and diplomatic friendships

These chivalrous friendships built on relationships of vassalage and exchange of services require fidelity and reciprocity. They are inherited from generation to generation and invariably contain a strong emotional charge that runs through the harangues of Cortés and his interlocutors [64]. Diego describes the establishment and strengthening an emotional bond between the two parties. The best knight is able to inspire the deepest attachments. In Tlaxcala, Cortés' superiority was due less to the triumph of his arms than to his ability to rally the Tlaxcaltecs to his convictions by arousing unfailing support among them.

By establishing social and political responsibilities, friendship is also a component of international relations [65]. It appears in the title of embassies. In 1580, some time before Diego began to write his account, Philip II addressed the Emperor of China claiming his "friendship" and offering his own, in the tone of a preacher who had nothing to envy to that of Cortés by Diego Muñoz Camargo [66]. Friendship is synonymous with collaboration in agreements between States. Logically, the term *amigo* appears in the Spanish sources to designate what we would call, in an anachronistic and stigmatizing way, the indigenous "collaborators".

Here, Diego's thought draws from multiple sources. We find there as much the echo, direct or indirect, close or distant, of legal texts – *las Partidas* [67] – as of treatises on ethics inspired by Aristotle [68]. "The friend is another me [...], he is a great happiness than to be twice a man when you have a true friend" – the formula floats in the air of the times [69]. In turn, she explains to us "this desire to become one" that Diego ascribes to Cortés and his interlocutors, " *para que todos seamos uno* ". Like others, the humanist Cristobal de Villalón insists on the benefits of friendship for the prosperity of the world: "It is through it that kingdoms are preserved and possessions are increased. As "this love is completely free, because it rests on the will" (Villalón), the response of the Tlaxcaltecs to the solicitations of Cortés can only be the expression of their free will. Diego has probably not read Villalón, but these neighborhoods confirm the importance that Iberian societies, in Europe as in America, accord to this conception of human relations. In these worlds, friendship in the strongest sense still structures social relations. This leads Diego to interpret the first relations between Tlaxcaltecs and Spaniards in the ideal framework of the *compañía that the amigos* must form . This, of course, implies that all should be Christians – a recurring argument in the mouth of Cortés.

The Tlaxcaltecs "got fucked" by the Spaniards

This detour was necessary to learn about the paths that allowed Diego to portray indigenous collaboration in a light that is as irreproachable as it is inevitable. That it paints an ideal framework, it is obvious. His way of conceiving and justifying the alliance between the two groups inspires him with an argument contrary to the idea of the "clash of civilizations", dear to Samuel Huntington. He draws from it an exemplary and peaceful picture which could not deceive anyone since other sources, of wider circulation, delivered a much less refined version.

However, the past that Diego took up married the political and economic interests of the Tlaxcaltec elites. The Crown, for its part, had no reason to doubt these claims of unshakeable fidelity: the colonial order demanded that things should have been done properly. And Diego had personal motives for thinking and writing that between Spaniards and Indians everything had gone off as well as possible.

Our columnist however introduces a discordant point of view when he relates a tragic moment of the Conquest: the massacre of Cholula. We are in October 1519. The Spaniards have left Tlaxcala and set out for Mexico-Tenochtitlan, where Moctezuma awaits them. Cholula stands in their way. It was one of the commercial and spiritual capitals of the Amerindian world, famous for its pyramid, the most massive in the Americas, the cult of Quetzalcoatl and its political aura: it was in Cholula that the future leaders of the region were enthroned. .

– The troops approaching Cholula are made up of Spaniards and Tlaxcaltec allies. How did the Choultecs react to this invasion?

– The Cholutec had such confidence in their idol Quetzalcoatl that they felt that no human power could subjugate or attack them [70].

– *What do they say about the Tlaxcaltecs?*

– "Look at these ignoble Tlaxcaltecs, these cowards, who deserve punishment. [...] And they would add other things like that [...]: "They are crazy about who they trust. These effeminate sodomites are only the bearded women of these bearded men, it is out of fear that they gave themselves up to them [71]. »

– *No doubt we must make allowance for the ritual insults (or not) that precede any fight, in Europe as in Mexico. Can you repeat the infamous words of the Cholultecs?*

"What fate awaits you? You are lost! [...] Where did you get these intruders from, where did you hire them to satisfy your revenge? Wretches of you who have lost the immortal fame passed on to you by your ancestors, these men of the illustrious blood of the ancient Teochichimecs. »

The Tlaxcaltecs would have first tried to rally their neighbors of Cholula to the Spanish cause. But they categorically reject any form of collaboration and shower them with insults. This reaction can be understood in two ways. It reveals as much the state of mind of the Choultecs at the time of the Conquest as the contempt still aroused by the rallying of the Tlaxcaltecs to the Spanish cause sixty years later. Recalling the insults hurled at his friends in Tlaxcala, Diego also knows he is bringing out the boundless devotion of the native allies.

The Choultecs mock the submission of the Tlaxcaltecs to their Spanish "husbands" [72]. Among the ancient Mexicans, as in other regions of the world, association with the female sex was experienced as a form of humiliation and belittlement. At one point in their history, the Mexica experienced their defeat as if their winners had forced them to "wear women's petticoats [73]". In the eyes of the Indians of Cholula, the privileged relations established between Tlaxcaltecs and conquistadors, love and friendship, no longer have anything. to do with the virtues carried to the pinnacle by the two camps. They mask degrading bonds.

In fact, the remarks attributed to the Cholustecs associate a practice hated by Christians, sodomy – which essentially relates to anal coitus –, and a humiliating condition, that of bardache. *Bardache* is a term derived from the Persian *bardah* (captive/slave) [74]. In the Mediterranean and in the rest of Western Europe, "bardache" reduces the subject to an infantile stage and to an exclusively passive role [75]. It connotes a set of humiliating occupations for the male adult, denounces effeminate conduct and appearance, involves the exercise of prostitution and merges with the condition of slavery. These insulting qualifiers lead to the grotesque image that the Choultecs have of their Tlaxcaltec rivals: "They are nothing more than the bardache women of these bearded men [76]. These are the images that Diego has in his head and that he transmitted to us.

Hermaphrodites or bardaches

There is no reason to think that this information does not have an Amerindian basis, even if Christian and Mediterranean prejudices here seem to cover it up and stifle it. How to find the local version? Diego was interested at least twice in sexual behavior that the Indians disapproved of. A long-reported anecdote concerns a "bisexual" hermaphrodite. Diego recounts the fate reserved for this teenager who looked like a young girl. The son of Xicotencatl, one of the four lords of Tlaxcala, fell in love with it and introduced it into his "harem".

- *What happened in the harem?*

– By establishing relationships and speaking with the other women of his companions, he fell in love with them and used the male sex in such a way and with such frequency that he impregnated more than twenty of them. He had taken advantage of the absence of his master, who had remained away for more than a year [77].

- *The pregnancy of these women did not go unnoticed?*

– As the master had returned and had seen that his women were fat, he was distressed and burst into anger. He sought to know who in his house had committed an act of such impudence.

– *What did he discover?*

– We ended up knowing that this woman, their companion, had made them pregnant, because she was a man and a woman.

– *The victims were purely and simply repudiated. But what about the culprit?*

– They publicly exposed the miserable hermaphrodite in a sacrificial place reserved for the punishment of wrongdoers to show that he had gravely betrayed his lord, his master and his husband. And while he was alive and his flesh bared, they cut open his left side with a very sharp flint knife. Once wounded and his side open, they freed him to go where he wanted, where his fate would guide him. He fled while bleeding. The children pursued and stoned him for a quarter of a league until the unfortunate fell dead, and the birds of the sky devoured him.

– *Is this story the origin of a saying?*

– A maxim circulated among the great lords: "Beware of the one who has impregnated the women of such and such, and be careful of your women: if they use both sexes, beware of them, that they do not you do not fatten them. »

The explanation saved the honor and respectability of the native prince, who had perhaps not mistaken the identity sex of his new wife [78]. For homosexuality, or rather relations between men, was obviously not absent from Tlaxcaltec society.

– *How were the sodomites considered among them?*

– [The Tlaxcaltecs] held in great abomination the abominable sin and the sodomites were discredited, despised and treated like women [79].

– *What punishment was reserved for them?*

– There was no punishment for these unnatural sins. But they were abhorred. They did not punish them, but they said to them, "Accursed and wretched men, is there a shortage of women in the world? And you who are bards, who take the place of women, wouldn't it be better if you were men? »

– *What should be understood by* "bardajas "?

– Bardache women, effeminate sodomites...

– *Did the Indians give this behavior a religious meaning?*

– They saw in it an omen and something superstitious [80].

bardajas twice , Diego may have had in mind the Amerindians that several chroniclers of the Indies referred to by this name. Some indigenous societies assigned a special status to men who did not enter the group of warriors and shared the tasks devolved to women without suffering social rejection [81]. The chronicler Gonzalo Fernández de Oviedo and the Dominican Las Casas report a few cases. Who knows if, when Diego took care of the education of the young Indians brought back from Florida, he did not hear Cabeza de Vaca describe the "bardaches" of the island of Mal Hado, in Galveston Bay (Texas). Unless he had read what the chronicler López de Gómara had taken from Cabeza de Vaca in his *General History of the Indies* [82].

In general, the little that comes to us from the colonial era concerns distant and peripheral populations. The attitude of the big Indian companies of the Altiplano remains opaque. We sense Diego's embarrassment in the face of Tlaxcaltec practices. While the Europeans hostile to the natives did not hesitate to raise the specter of sodomy each time it was necessary to justify the misdeeds of the Conquest, other testimonies, just as peremptory, agree in celebrating the pre-Hispanic condemnation of this practice. and the rigor of the punishments reserved for the deviant. Diego does not follow them, but neither does he risk evoking ritualized behavior within the framework of religious ceremonies, therefore in the already abominable context of idolatry.

Still, some information leaked out. An observer as well-informed as the Franciscan chronicler Torquemada, who is also an attentive reader of Diego, recalls celebrations that took place in Mexico City and Tlaxcala on the occasion of the month of *Quecholli* . "Effeminate men dressed as women" performed there. They were discredited and despised people who had exchanges only with women, and who tattooed and scarified their [flesh]. The Franciscan takes up the words de Diego, which he extends to Mexico-Tenochtitlan, and openly suggests ritual and therefore idolatrous practices.

Diego shared the ideas and prejudices of the Spanish milieu to which he flattered himself that he belonged. And it is doubtful that, in the 1580s, his native interlocutors thought differently. They had had plenty of time to internalize the Iberian repulsion and condemnations of the Church, and therefore to adopt the prevailing vocabulary and stereotypes.

Like the straw that broke the camel's back, the insults received come just in time to justify the intervention of the Tlaxcaltecs in the massacre that bloodied Cholula. Today, she draws our attention to the hidden reverse side of love and friendship in ancient societies. In the Middle Ages, friendship was "a totalizing relationship with its own rules". Above any other form of social and affective bond, it constitutes "the supreme bond between men [84]". One imagines that it is still the same in the sixteenth century . And that the connection sometimes reaches an intensity and a depth that the condemnation of homosexuality and the taboo of relations between men have subsequently rendered incomprehensible. So much so that one can slip from the ideal to the caricature, like the Choultecs. All told by a man who claims to be Spanish and who translates into his language, that of New Spain, what was said and happened (or not happened) in Cholula.

What happens when we refuse love and friendship?

– *A member of the Tlaxcaltec elite would have opposed collaboration with the invaders and even defended the alliance with Mexico City?*

– A cacique by the name of Axayacatzin Xicotencatl, to whom his father had given the government of his lordship, making him captain general.

– *What was he accused of?*

– This man accepted the idea that our people died and that we killed them to the last one.

" *Why didn't he get his way?"*

– Maxixcatzin, who was of the opposite opinion, got very angry with him. He was so pissed off, he was so angry that he verbally abused him, calling him a coward, a woman and a sissy.

" *What kind of man was Xicotencatl?"*

“He was said to be mad, unreasonable and very inconsistent in his opinions. He was a seditious who disturbed the republic...

- *You are ruthless. What was his fate?*

– The majority and the authorities of the republic followed the advice of Maxixcatzin, and Axayacatzin Xicotencatl was condemned, and executed.

– *A decision of Tlaxcala?*

– Cortés had him hanged with the consent of the Republic of Tlaxcala [85].

How can we imagine what is going on in Xicotencatl's head and the remarks he may have made in front of his people, if not by resorting, like Diego, to the classics? But this time it will be those of the 20th century . For example :

"For others, we are the stranger. They come to us, assimilate us, and our paths become theirs. We, on the other hand, follow their paths and their plans, until our loss. Our death is their design. And we follow them in death. And, following them, we are immediately separated from those who are dear to us and who for us become others [86]. »

The Austrian Elfriede Jelinek makes the dead speak as well as Plutarch the Greek. But Malcolm Lowry, author of *Below the Volcano* , is more expeditious [87]:

"At this place the young Xicohtencatl [*sic*] harangued his soldiers, telling them to fight the conquerors to the limit, dying if necessary: "... *no pasarán* ." »

– *Morality?*

– They supported Maxixcatzin's conduct. It was not necessary that other young madmen be emboldened to follow the opinion and the party of Xicotencatl Axayacatzin.

Through the phraseology of love and friendship as in sexual insults or in the punishment of the traitor Xicotencatl, it is the very nature of the relationship between Tlaxcaltecs and Spaniards that is at stake. Their alliance, supposed to be eternal and boundless, establishes the unique position claimed by Tlaxcala in New Spain. The Tlaxcaltec case raises the question of the integration of the colonized and the limits set by the colonizers. While the Dominican Las Casas denounces the destructive effects of the European conquest, at the antipodes of this argument, Diego pleads love and friendship, even fusion. While the Dominican blackens the line, the spokesman of the Tlaxcaltecs idealizes at all costs. Listening to him, one can imagine what a European colonization of the Americas could have been like, playing the interbreeding card to the fullest. Still, this ideal excluded any religious tolerance: for Diego, as for the Spaniards and the Indians who had become Christians, conversion was not negotiable. And if the merger is played out as equals, it is exclusively between conquistadors and local aristocrats [88].

1. Cabrera Pons (2015).

2. *La Destruction des Indes by Bartolomé de Las Casas* , Jean-Paul Duviols ed., Paris, Chandeigne, 2013. The text was translated into Flemish by Jacques de Miggrode in Antwerp in 1579.

3. Hernán Cortés, *Cartas y documentos* , "Segunda carta, 30 de octubre de 1520", Mario Hernández Sánchez-Barba ed., Mexico City, Porrúa, 1963, p. 59.

4. C197.

5. C197; D183v°.

6. Montaigne (1965), l. III, ch. vi, p. 142 ("Checkmarks").

7. C213.

8. C212; Galatians 3.28; see Plotin (VI, 5, 7, 6): "We are therefore All and One", in Pierre Hadot, *Plotin ou la Simplicité du regard* , Paris, Gallimard, 1997, p. 66.

9. In the 1550s and 1560s, friendship was the key word to describe the relationship between Tlaxcaltecs and Spaniards. After López de Gómara, the chronicler Cervantes de Salazar confirms the atmosphere of concord that would have reigned in Tlaxcala by highlighting the demonstrations and professions of friendship towards the invaders: Francisco Cervantes de Salazar, Crónica de la Nueva España, *Mexico* , Porrúa, 1985, p. 238, 240, 241.

10. Gruzinski (2017), p. 133-141.

11. D184r°.

12. C199.

13. The *stacks* denote the nobles and the *tecuhtles* are the head of the ruling class.

14. C199; D184v°.

15. C204; D186r°.

16. C205.

17. C207.

18. D187r°.

19. C207; D187r°.

20. That is to say "emerald captain", "precious captain".

21. C207; D187v°.

22. Sebastian de Covarrubias, *Tesoro de la lengua castellana o española* , Seville, 1611, p. 409.

23. « Provança del Adelantado D. Pedro de Alvarado and Doña Leonor de Alvarado his daughter », *Annals of the Society of Geography and History* , vol. XIII, 4 (Guatemala), June 1937, p. 475-487 ; Florine GL Asselbergs, *Conquered Conquistadors . The Lienzo de Quauhquechollan: A Nahua Vision of the Conquest of Guatemala* , Boulder, University Press of Colorado, 2008, p. 22 ; Patrick Lesbre, "Juan de Cuéllar, a married conquistador with a Tezcocan princess", October 2016, https://journals.openedition.org/e-spania/26041. [1]Plusieurs cas d'Espagnols unis à des femmes de la noblesse indigène: Luis Reyes García, *Historia de Tlaxcala, ms . 210 of the National Library of Paris* , Mexico, CIESAS, Autonomous University of Tlaxcala, 1998, p. 30.

24. C204.

25. C203.

26. Suárez de Peralta (1990), p. 134.

27. C246.

28. D188r°.

29. C209 ; D188r°.

30. C211.

31. C212 ; D189v°.

32. C212 ; D189v°.

1. https://journals.openedition.org/e-spania/26041

33. C213 ; D190v°.

34. C213.

35. C214-216.

36. C216.

37. C217-218.

38. C219.

39. C218.

40 . Montaigne (1965), t. III, p. 143 ("Des cars").

41 . C218-219.

42 . C220.

43 . Fernando Horcasitas, *The Nahuatl Theater: New Spanish and modern times* , Mexico, National Autonomous University of Mexico, 1974, *passim* ; *Mexican theater. History and dramaturgy* , t. IV, Armando Partida ed., Mexico, Conaculta, 1992, p. 37 *sq* .

44 . Bernardino de Sahagún, *The Dialogues of 1524 according to the text of Fray Bernardino de Sahagún and his indigenous collaborators* , Miguel León-Portilla éd., Mexico, UNAM, 1986.

45 . Bernal Díaz del Castillo, *Historia verdadera de la conquista de México* , Joaquín Ramírez Cabañas ed., Mexico City, Porrúa, 2 vols., 1968.

46 . C193.

47 . C190.

48 . Román (1595) evokes the 1540 embassy to Charles V (fol. 158).

49 . C215.

50 . *Ibid.*

51 . C217, 212, 216.

52. Robert Flacelière ed., Paris, Belles Lettres, 2008.

53. Plutarch uses the Greek term *symmachia* ; see *Life of Pelopidas* , http://remacle.org/bloodwolf/historians/Plutarch/pelopidas.htm.[2]

54. Carmen Bernand, *A Platonic Inca. Garcilaso de la Vega* , Paris, Fayard, 2006; Antonio Cornejo Polar, «The discourse of impossible harmony», *Latin American Literary Criticism Magazine* , vol. 19, 38, 1993, p. 73-80 ; Eduardo Subirats, «The empty continent: the conquest of the New World and modern consciousness», *Bulletin of the Institute of Argentine and American History «Doctor Emilio Ravignani»* , vol. 13, 113, January 1996, https://www.researchgate.net/publication/
273059229_Eduardo_Subirats_El_continente_vacio_La_conquista_del_Nuevo_Mundo_y_la_co
[3]

55. C91.

56. Paul Dingmar, *Ethics and Emotions : A Cultural History of Chivalric Friendship in Medieval/Early Modern Times* , Rochester, University of Rochester Press, 2012.

57. Alain de Libera, "Sexual life and friendship", in *Thinking in the Middle Ages* , Barcelona, Anthropos, 2000, p. 166 *sq.* ; Concepción Company Company, *Love and culture in the Middle Ages* , Mexico, UNAM, 1991.

58. D67v°.

59. Irving Leonard, *The Books of the Conqueror* , Mexico, FCE, 1996, p. 84, 101.

60. C56 ; D155r°.

61. C57.

62. C58.

63. D11v°.

---

2. http://remacle.org/bloodwolf/historiens/Plutarque/pelopidas.htm

3. https://www.researchgate.net/publication/
273059229_Eduardo_Subirats_El_continente_vacio_La_conquista_del_Nuevo_Mundo_y_la_conciencia_Moderna

64 . The couple formed by Roland and Olivier embodies chivalrous friendship: "The strength of [this friendship] manages to neutralize the hostility resulting from belonging to two opposing camps", in Maciej Abramowicz, "Chivalrous friendship in the mirror of French medieval literature", Acta Universitatis Wratislaviensis no ˙ 3774, *Romanica Wratislaviensis* , Wroclaw, vol. LXIV, 2017, p. 11-21.

65 . G. Althoff, « The amicitiae [friendships] as relations between states and peoples », in LK Little et BH Rosewein (dir.), *The Middle Ages at Debate* , Madrid, Akal, 2003, p. 304-336 ; Bruno Paradisi, "The International Amicability of the Upper Middle Ages", *Writings in Honor of Contardo Ferrini* , p. II, Milan, Società Editrice Vita e Pensiero, 1947, p. 178-2

66 . Carmen Y. Hsu, « Writing on Behalf of a Christian Empire : Gifts, Dissimulation and Politics in the Letters of Philip II of Spain to Wanli of China », *Hispanic Review* , vol. 78, 3, summer 2010, p. 323 344 .

67 . The *Siete Partidas* are a body of legislation drawn up in Castile during the reign of Alfonso X the Wise in the 13th century .

68 . See the *Breviloquio de amor y amiçiçia* by Alfonso Fernández de Madrigal (1437-1441) or the *Breviloquio de virtudes* by Diego de Valera (1461). This literature regulated the conduct of individuals and states by distinguishing various forms of love and friendship. On the circulation of these topoi, Josué Villa Prieto, "La amistad en la mentalidad medieval: análisis de los tratados morales de la Península Ibérica", *Lemir* , no 20 , Valence, 2016, p. 191-210, http://parnaseo.uv.es/Lemir/Revista/Revista20/06_Villa_Josue.pdf [4]; Jacqueline Ferreras, *Los Diálogos humanísticos del siglo xv en lengua castellana* , Murcia, Universidad de Murcia, 2008.

69 . She figures in *El Scholástico* by Cristóbal de Villalón (1550).

70 . C224.

71 . *Ibid.*

---

4. http://parnaseo.uv.es/Lemir/Revista/Revista20/06_Villa_Josue.pdf

72. Guilhem Olivier, "Conquerors and missionaries faced with abominable sin: an essay on homosexuality in America at the time of the Spanish conquest", *Caravelle. Notebooks of the Hispanic and Luso-Brazilian World* , No. 55 , 1990, p. 19-51, https://www.persee.fr/doc/carav_1147-6753_1990_num_55_1_2438 [5].

73. *Relación de las ceremonias y ritos y población y gobierno de los indios de la provincia de Michoacan (1541)* , José Corona Nuñez ed., Mexico City, Balsal Editores, 1977, p. 259.

74. Then from Arabic *bardaj* , "captive", an origin disputed today. It is also derived from the Greek by adding an *r* (*badas* giving *bardas*) and it circulates in Italy in the form *bardassa* , https://dle.rae.es/bardaje?m=30_2 [6]: Michel Masson, "Barda, Bardache and Bredindin: the BRD "base" in the Romance languages", *Linguistics* , 51, 1, 2015, p. 41-88.

75. Covarrubias (1611), p. 122.

76. C224; D197v°.

77. C163; D151r°.

78. C163. On the Conceptions of Christianized Indians Provided by Bernardino de Sahagún, Alfredo López Austin, *Cuerpo humano e ideología . Las conceptions de los antiguos Nahuas* , t. II, Mexico, UNAM, 1980, p. 266.

79. C149. On this chapter, Diego contradicts himself (D37r°: "Those who were in it died because of it").

80. C150.

81. This is the case of the Indian peoples of the Great Plains. Traces of this institutionalization can be found in Cuba, among the Siboneys, and in other Amerindian societies; see Francisco Guerra, *The Pre-Columbian Mind: A Study into the Aberrant Nature of Sexual Drives, Drugs affecting Behaviour, and the Attitude towards Life and Death* , London, Seminar Press, 1971.

---

5. https://www.persee.fr/doc/carav_1147

6. https://dle.rae.es/bardaje?m=30_2

82. Alfredo Mirandé, *Behind the Mask : Gender Hybridity in a Zapotec Community*, Tucson, The University of Arizona Press, 2017, p. 167 ; Ramón Gutierrez, *When Jesus came, the Corn Mothers went away. Marriage, Sexuality and Power in New Mexico, 1500-1846*, Stanford, Stanford University Press, 1991, p. 26 ; Richard Trexler, *Sex and Conquest : Gendered Violence, Political Order and the European*, Cornell, Cornell University Press, 1999, p. 259.

83. Torquemada (1976), t. III, p. 427.

84. William Burgwinkle, « Modèles médiévaux de l'amitié masculine », *Itinéraires*, 2008, p. 23, https://journals.openedition.org/itineraires/2201.[7]

85. C246-247.

86. Elfriede Jelinek, *Totenauberg* , Paris, Points, 2011, p. 48.

87. Paris, Gallimard, 1987, p. 503.

88. The Tlaxcaltecs are not the only ones to claim their role as allies and collaborators. The Nahuas of Quauhquecholan, in the Puebla Valley, similarly invoked their participation in the conquest of Guatemala and claimed the privileges they expected from it (Asselbergs [2008], p. 22).

7. https://journals.openedition.org/itineraires/2201

CHAPTER X

The time of the crime

"The Cholutecs hadn't planned anything!

It was neither with swords nor with shields that they faced the Spaniards.

It was simply out of treachery that they were killed, they simply died like blind men, they simply died without knowing it.

By simply trapping them, the Tlaxcaltecs pounced on them. »

Florentine Codex (1569) [1].

From the first moments of the Conquest, the Tlaxcaltec way was far from arousing unanimity, in particular among the indigenous groups who chose to resist, such as the Choultecs and the Mexicas. In October 1519, the massacre of Cholula gives them a taste of the fate that awaits them. It claimed 3,000 victims in a few hours according to Cortés or 6,000 in five hours according to the chronicler López de Gómara [2]. It inaugurates the chain of violence that will lead to the conquest of Mexico and this is why the episode struck the chroniclers, who interpreted it variously [3]. In his *Very Brief Relation* , the Dominican Las Casas bitterly denounced the killing, but a Spanish Creole like Suárez de Peralta refutes the Dominican and defends the version provided by Cortés. The execution of a hundred lords, the 5,000 to 6,000 victims, the Indians being burned alive and other appalling cruelties "never existed". No more than Cortés would have sung a famous Spanish *romance :*

"Look, Nero, from the Tarpeian rock,

Rome in flames [4]. »

The controversy surrounding the event is part of the history of Europe and the West. The black legend, then philosophical criticism took hold of it. The Cholula massacre sounds like what Peter Sloterdijk called "the hour of crime [5]" in the sense that the unlimited appetite of Europeans appears to him as an inaugural stage of modernity, captured in its darkest light. The criminal act would be distinguished as much by its monstrosity as by the way in which its perpetrators assume responsibility for it.

A founding stage of the Conquest

– *What place does the Cholula stage occupy for the Tlaxcaltecs and their Spanish allies?*

– We began [then] to discuss the progress of the conquest [6]: how we could enter Mexico, how we could take it and seize the other provinces so that they could access the knowledge of God.

" *Events then precipitated?* "

– We entered through the province of Cholula, which was destroyed in no time.

– *What was the fate of the inhabitants?*

– The massacres and destruction that took place in this city are beyond imagination [7][...]. So many people died, or were robbed and their property ransacked [...]. The Choultecs have been defeated and cut to pieces. Most of them were killed and reduced to nothing in a very short time.

" *Is that what the Tlaxcaltecs asked for?*"

– They said to Cortés: "Lord, [...] we want to go with you to destroy this nation and its province so that no one among this people so harmful, so obstinate and so stubborn remains alive. »

– *"Obstinate, stubborn": you would think you were talking about the pharaoh of the Exodus who remained deaf to Moses' warnings. How did Cortes react?*

– Cortés told them [...] not to worry. He promised them that they would be avenged.

– *What effect did this massacre have on the populations of Mexico on the plateau* ?

– Our armies then advanced, spreading terror and terror wherever they went until the news of the destruction spread throughout the country [8].

– *Can we speak of a panic?*

– All these people then asked a lot of questions. They offered great sacrifices and made offerings to prevent the same from happening to others. They lamented and sighed. It was sad to see them in such disarray.

– *Has the policy of terror shattered any hint of resistance?*

– It cooled the surrounding populations [...]. And, from then on, they lived on their guard, waiting to see what the newcomers would do. The Indians hid their children, their wives and their possessions in the remotest depths of the mountains.

The trigger

Diego joins the camp of those who legitimize the killing and who claim their responsibility, including in the outbreak of the massacre. If the Tlaxcaltecs had the best reasons in the world to exterminate the inhabitants of Cholula, did they not supply them?

– The province of Cholula [...] was destroyed for very serious reasons related to the Indians of the city [11].

– What do you mean by "very serious reasons"?

– Before the beginning of the war, messengers and ambassadors from the city of Tlaxcala had been sent to the Cholultecs to beg them and summon them to make peace, letting them know that it was not theirs we were talking about. wanted, but to the Culhuas, to the Mexican Culhuacanenses [...]. I say Mexicans because that is the name of the city of Mexico where they lived and where their supreme power was.

– What did the Tlaxcaltec envoys offer them?

– They asked them as friends to receive the Spaniards peacefully. If that were the case, they would be treated well [...]. Otherwise, if they angered them, they would be very ferocious. They were valiant men, ready for anything, equipped with superior, very solid, white metal armament (they said that because there was no iron among them, but copper) [...] and who wore garments and breeches of iron.

– Did they convince the Cholutecs to be reasonable?

– [The Tlaxcaltecs] thought it was the best way to avoid huge losses and, as friends, they advised them to comply. But [the Choultecs] made no case of their advice. They decided to die rather than surrender.

– Is this plea of inadmissibility sufficient to explain the massacre?

– Instead of following this good advice and giving the right answer to the Tlaxcaltecs, they skinned alive the face of their ambassador Patlahuatzin, a very esteemed and very courageous person. They did the same with his hands, which they scratched up to the elbows. They cut his hands off at the wrists, and he had them hanging down. And it was in such a cruel way that they sent him away.

– How did Tlaxcala react to the cruelty of the gesture?

– The poor ambassador was received with tears and expressions of pain. It was a terrible and intolerable spectacle for the republic, for he was one of the handsome and elegant men of this seigniory, very well formed and handsome. The Tlaxcaltecs were indignant to see such presumptuousness and the abject fate that caused the death of Patlahuatzin. He died as a servant of his country, a country where his reputation will survive forever among his people.

– What sources do you have?

– Their "enigmatic metaphors" and their *cantares* .

– Meaning songs composed in memory of Patlahuatzin. The attack would therefore be the trigger for the famous massacre of Cholula?

– The Tlaxcaltecs found this unprecedented act in the world very offensive.

– Is the violation of diplomatic immunity as serious a crime as the ensuing massacre?

– Ambassadors of this kind were always respected and honored by foreign kings and lords who negotiated with them peaces, wars and the various conflicts that might arise between provinces and kingdoms [13].

In Diego's mind, such an unheard-of package violates universal standards. Perhaps he has in mind ancient examples, such as the killing of the heralds of Darius [14]. The ambassadors of the Great King had been thrown into a well in Sparta, and this crime unleashed the wrath of the gods, who demanded the punishment of the guilty.

– What was the reaction of the Tlaxcaltecs?

– "That a people so harmful, so stubborn and so stubborn in its wickedness and its tyranny does not remain alive [...]. They deserve eternal punishment [...]. They wanted to despise us and put us down because we love [you]. »

– How to explain the stubbornness of the Choultecs?

– The Cholutecs placed such confidence in their idol Quetzalcoatl that they thought [could] quickly finish with ours [16]. With the idea that these were few in number and that the Tlaxcaltecs had brought them there by deception so that they would finish them [17].

– So the Choultecs would have counted on a reflex of indigenous solidarity? Or on a miracle?

– They were so confident in their idol that they believed that with lightning and fire from heaven they would consume them, annihilate them and drown them under the waters [...]. They expected them to be ablaze with the flashes of fire that were to fall from heaven upon them, and from the very temples of their idols would spring mighty streams of water that would flow down to drown the Tlaxcaltecs with ours. .

– The conflict then takes another turn: we go from settling scores between indigenous cities to a confrontation between cosmic forces. Did the Tlaxcaltecs believe in it?

– This greatly appalled the Tlaxcaltec friends who believed that things were going to turn out as the Choultecs said [18].

– These would then have begun to unseal the stones of the temples to release the providential sources which would annihilate the enemy.

"They did, but it didn't help them. What they found themselves very wrong. They were like distraught.

– *What form did their despair take?*

– Most of those who died in this Cholula war threw themselves into the void; they launched themselves headlong from the top of the temple of Quetzalcoatl [...]. Most of them perished in despair, killing [themselves].

– *In other words, the Choultecs perished victims of themselves much more than the Spaniards or the Tlaxcaltecs. After all, they didn't all voluntarily kill themselves?*

– A very cruel war was waged against them in which a multitude of them perished.

– *We would like to know more!*

– Just read the chronicle of the conquest that was written.

– *According to Bernal Díaz del Castillo, the Tlaxcaltecs threw themselves into the fighting with such fury that the Spaniards would have had trouble calming them down. The Tlaxcaltec captains are said to have claimed that the Cholultecs "deserved even worse because of the betrayals that this city had committed against them".*

– It is for this and for other betrayals that we began to make a very cruel war against them [20].

– *These betrayals (which you mention with Bernal Díaz del Castillo [21]) suggest that there was a quarrel between the two Indian cities. The Tlaxcaltecs would have taken advantage of the passage of the conquistadors to settle their accounts. What lesson did the Choultecs learn from this disaster?*

– They understood, they realized that the god of the white men was stronger and that his sons were more powerful.

– *Did the god of the Whites intervene?*

– When they saw themselves in great danger during the battles and the massacre, our Tlaxcaltec friends called and invoked the Apostle Saint James, shouting very loudly "Santiago" [22]!

– In Spain, Santiago Matamoros often appeared in battles between Christians and Muslims. What did this cry mean for the Tlaxcaltecs?

– From that moment on, they didn't feel like they were committing great crimes. Everything was guided by the divine will since Our Lord thought it good that this land be conquered, that it be taken back and that it escape the grip of the demon [23].

Tlaxcaltec version versus Mexican version

In the second half of the century, contradictory versions of the Cholula massacre circulated in Mexico, Spain and Europe. The camp of the Spaniards who denounce it as an atrocity without name and share the accusations of Bartolomé de Las Casas is opposed to that of the sons of the conquistadors, like Suárez de Peralta, who play down or justify the act accomplished. But there are also several indigenous versions. The painters of Tlaxcala, authors of the *linen cloth* of the same name, left us an image of the massacre. Spaniards and Tlaxcaltecs fight side by side amid horribly mutilated corpses.

To this vision is opposed that of the future victims of the fury of the conquistadors, the Mexicas. While Diego's version draws on the oral memory of the nobles of Tlaxcala and the *cantares* they still remembered, the Mexica version, collected by the Franciscan Bernardino de Sahagún, has comparable origins. It is a mixture of oral history and commemorations that are expressed in songs and dances that periodically bring together the survivors of the nobility of Mexico-Tenochtitlan. Except that, in the years 1560-1570, the Indians of Mexico City, or more precisely those of the neighboring city of Tlatelolco, were still angry with the Tlaxcaltecs. It is they and no one else, it is their calumnies which would have driven the Spaniards to the massacre. The accusation could not be more categorical: the attack was indeed carried out at the instigation of Tlaxcala. The nobles of Cholula fell into a trap: "It was then that the knives spoke, there were deaths, there were beatings. The Cholutecs hadn't planned anything! It was neither with swords nor with shields that they faced the Spaniards. It was simply out of treachery that they were killed. They just died blind, they just died without knowing it. By simply trapping them, the Tlaxcaltecs threw themselves on them [24]. »

The plurality of versions of the massacre sweeps away any binary vision that would oppose the camp of the winners to that of the vanquished. It expresses the multiple and contradictory interests of groups that compete for power or crumbs of power within colonial society. On one point, however, everyone agrees: the awareness of being faced with an event in which the legitimacy of colonial domination is at stake. The drama will quickly appear as the beginning of the Spanish influence on the Mexican world. By sharing the virulent denunciation of Las Casas and making the Cholula massacre and atrocities Spanish in America the harbinger of the fate that awaits the enemies of the Catholic Monarchy, Dutch, English, French, Protestants and anti-Spanish Catholics will give a transoceanic scope to this massacre. Is it a coincidence that, to illustrate the massacre of Cholula in his compilation on America, Théodore de Bry from Liège chooses an engraving that evokes both the first Christian martyrs and the atrocities of the Wars of Religion [25] ? Diego disagrees with this interpretation, but he attaches to the event the importance it deserves.

1. Bernardino de Sahagún, *General History of the Things of New Spain* , Angel Maria Garibay ed., Mexico, Porrúa, t. IV, 1977, p. 99-1

2. Francisco Lopez de Gomara, *General History of the Indies* , Saragossa, Augustine Millan, 1552, chap. lx, « The punishment inflicted on those of Chololla for their treachery » ; online : artHistory/Board of Castile and Leon, http://www.arthistory.jcyl.en/chronicles/contexts/10192.htm.[1]

3. Michel Graulich, *Montezuma* , Paris, Fayard, 1994, p. 360, chap. xiii, "The Cholula Controversy."

4. Suárez de Peralta (1990), p. 126.

5. Peter Sloterdijk, *The Hour of Crime and the Time of the Work of Art* , Paris, Calmann-Lévy, 2000.

6. C223.

7. C225.

8. C227-229.

9. C229.

10. *Ibid.*

11. C224.

12. C226.

13. C227.

14. The story is taken up by Pausanias and Plutarch; see Louise-Marie Wéry, "The murder of the heralds of Darius in 491 and the inviolability of the herald", *L'Antiquité Classique* , vol. 35, 2, 1966, p. 468-486; Laurent Gourmelen, "The murder of the Persian heralds (Hérodote, t. II, p. 133-137)", in Gérard Jacquin (dir.), *Tales of embassies and figures of messengers* , Rennes, Presses universitaire de Rennes, 2007, p. 21-45.

1. http://www.artehistoria.jcyl.es/cronicas/contextos/10192.htm

15. C227: the Tlaxcaltecs address Cortés.

16. The Spaniards.

17. C224.

18. C225.

19. C228.

20. C227.

21. Bernal Díaz del Castillo, *Historia verdadera de la conquista de México* , t. 1, chap. lxxxi-lxxxiii, Joaquín Ramírez Cabañas ed., Mexico, Porrua, 1968, p. 234-249.

22. C228.

23. C225.

24. Sahagún (1977), t. IV, p. 99-100.

25. Théodore de Bry, *Travels in the East Indies and the West Indies, published in 13 parts by Theodore, Joan-Theodore de Bry and Mathew Merian* , Frankfort-sur-le-Main, 1590-1634.

CHAPTER XI

Local and global

How to define Diego? Is he an "organic intellectual" supposed to put his knowledge of colonial society at the service of the circles he represents, the indigenous elites? Or is it a new type of observer, capable of reacting to the transformations imposed by transoceanic domination and learning lessons?

Throughout the chapters he devotes to pre-Hispanic times, Tlaxcala appears as the culmination of a centripetal movement that starts on the shores of Mesoamerica to come to a standstill in the heart of the Altiplano. The Tlaxcaltec domain was shaped by the rhythm of the occupation of the Mesoamerican area by the Chichimec invaders. Then, after the conquest of Cortés, the dynamic is reversed. Tlaxcala becomes the focus of a centrifugal movement which, at the time Diego writes, borders on the edges of Spanish domination: to the south, Diego is eyeing Peru; to the north, his gaze extends to California, New Mexico and Florida; to the west, it crosses the Pacific Ocean, reaches the Philippine archipelago and touches Greater China; finally, to the east, he catches a glimpse of the coasts of the Iberian Peninsula, where the Tlaxcaltec embassy which he has escorted has taken him.

Diego connects several modes of representation of the world which each correspond to distinct historical processes. Nothing is frozen, nothing is out of time. Tlaxcala before the Conquest has nothing of a city of immemorial origins. With its factional struggles and its repeated conflicts, it has all of a endless building game. Under Spanish domination, Tlaxcala learns to live in an exponentially growing environment that goes beyond the Altiplano and the American continent [1].

The patria or the local according to Diego

In the 1580s, the Tlaxcala that Diego had before his eyes was no longer that of the mid- 16th century. Throughout Mexico, the indigenous population has melted away like snow in the sun. At the same time, the native authorities constantly reacted to the pressures of colonial society, and in particular to the encroachments of Europeans and mestizos who hoped to take advantage of the voids left by the demographic hecatomb to appropriate the lands in disherence. Far from remaining passive, the authorities endeavored to incorporate the land threatened by the Castilians into the properties of the city. They intensified the occupation of the bordering areas on which the intruders were biting, so that the administrative influence of the city was redeployed around new chief towns (*cabeceras*). The authority of the Indian *cabildo* was thereby strengthened and power more centralized.

In the 1580s, two forces shared power locally: the Indian government, installed in the city of Tlaxcala, and the order of the Franciscans, which reserved the ecclesiastical administration of the province [3]. This tandem succeeded in a unique undertaking on American soil: preventing the fragmentation, even the territorial and political explosion of the province, while the other lordships of the Altiplano did not resist the onslaught of colonization.

Diego seems to have played an active role in this exceptional context. It is with the approval of the Indian government and the advice of the Franciscans that he sets out a policy of redistribution of populations, made essential by the demographic fall. and crop abandonment. Its geographical description can therefore be read as the manifesto of a new politico-territorial order and a plea to guarantee the hegemony of the city of Tlaxcala over the whole province. There is reason to think that this program would have been written with four hands, in concert with an influential member of the order of Saint Francis, Gerónimo de Mendieta [4]. The attitude of this Franciscan, who occupies and has occupied important functions within the order in Mexico, is better understood when we remember that he always sought to save the monopoly of his co-religionists on the province and to maintain in place the *señores naturales* .

Unity is strength. The monks and the native lords agree that the hierarchy between *cabeceras/doctrinas* and *subjects/visitas* should not be questioned [5]. The *cabeceras* (or capitals) and the *subjects* (or subjects) come under the civil administration, while the *doctrinas* (or parishes) and the *visitas* ("treves") form the ecclesiastical districts. It is therefore planned to divide the space into a series of hamlets and villages: the *visitas* of each monastery will become *aldeas* , these *aldeas* will be grouped around the eight villages to which the rank of *villas will be granted* , and all these *villas* will return to the movement of the "city" of Tlaxcala [6]. One will gather the populations dispersed around the *aldeas* and the *villas* , by distributing the grounds again, even if it means modifying the social structure in the campaigns since a class of small farmers and small owners will thus be born.

This program is not a simple ersatz of colonial domination. It is on the spot that the space is redesigned to better preserve it by associating the forces attached to it, the regular Church and the native aristocracy. The repeated efforts to justify the privileges granted by the Crown and to ensure the future testify to the weight of local particularisms. A Castilian word synthesizes this influence of the local: *patria.* He expresses a a strong sense of belonging and applies a western, even ancient, varnish to an entity whose origin owes nothing to New Spain. Because Tlaxcala can claim to have an "antiquity", unlike Puebla, the neighboring city created from scratch for the Spaniards in 1531.

– Can we speak of homeland among the ancient Chichimecs, so in the distant times of the origins?

"They were one. They formed only one line, allies and relatives, because all came from the same country and the same land [7].

– By adopting Tlaxcala, they therefore changed their homeland over the ages [8]. *But isn't this also the case of Cortés when he fled Mexico City?*

– Tlaxcala was already considered his homeland, his home; it protected and defended the small number of surviving Christians [9] [...]. Ours were received with great enthusiasm and they were offered all the conveniences as if they were in their homeland and in their native land [10].

– But a homeland can also be torn apart, as in the civil wars before the Conquest?

– It was because they mixed their own blood with that of their country [11].

– Does love of country also apply to the allies and vassals of Tlaxcala?

– They never wanted to betray their former lords [...] on the contrary, they would have come to give their lives for their country and their republic.

– Under your gaze, Tlaxcala looks as much like a Roman republic as a pre-Hispanic lordship!

In Diego, "homeland" is equivalent to *nación* and *tierra natural* [12]. In the 16th century , in Castilian and in other European languages, the fatherland designates the place where one is born and where one spends one's days. As he writes, on the other side of the ocean, the idea of Spain is beginning to make its way into historical literature as a leaven that inspires a sense of belonging, continuity and pride. . This is the time when the *History of Spain* by Juan de Mariana [13 is published]. The great authors of the Golden Age, Cervantes, Lope de Vega, Quevedo, each in turn and in their own way, contribute their stone to the construction of this ideal. But Diego's homeland is neither Spain nor New Spain. It was always Tlaxcala that he had in his sights, convinced that the indigenous societies before the Conquest were already homelands.

The universo mundo or the global according to Diego

These projects of local reorganization are carried in Madrid by a Diego who at the same time has in mind the grandiose scene that invests men, ideas and beliefs of the Monarchy. Several times, Diego uses the word “world”. Flanked by the adjective "new", the term encompasses the new lands invaded by the native ancestors, which constitute "another new world", before designating the Indies discovered by the Spaniards: it is our "New World" (*Nuevo World*). When the horizons of Diego merge with the surface of the globe, it is then a question of *mundo* and universo *mundo.*

– *What happened after the Flood?*

– People came out of [Noah's] ark. They began to breed and grow. This is how they spread to various parts of the world until the populations covered the entire surface of the earth.

– *When did the names of the continents appear?*

– Men were so driven by subversive ambition and covetousness that they came to divide and distribute the world into three parts by giving them the names of Asia, Africa and Europe.

– *What do Africa, Asia and Europe have in common?*

– We have always known these three parts with the limits and confines we gave them; they were related and communicated. All the nations of the world knew [it].

– *Why three continents and not four?*

– Even if, since the beginnings of which we have spoken, people have made a lot of efforts to continue to expand in the universe, they never thought that there were lands left for them to discover.

" *So Europeans can be as wrong as Indians?"*

– How many kings and monarchs, how many philosophers and cosmographers have fallen into this deception! How many mistakes have those who have spoken and written on this subject committed! And how many different views and opinions among those who knew the most on this point!

– *When did we get out of the error?*

– These errors lasted for centuries until it pleased God our lord to enlighten us to the truth of all that we did not know, until in our time we discovered this New World, which had remained so unknown, so distant and so foreign to our knowledge.

– *For a man who apologizes for being born in the New World, you don't spare European scholars!*

What does this *universo mundo correspond to* ? The expression refers first of all to a universality of a political and religious order since Diego is attached to a Christian humanity which claims a biblical past and is moving towards Redemption. He is also the subject of a prince who reigns over the four parts of the globe. In 1585, a contemporary of Diego, Alonso de Zurita, addressed Philip II by counting the lands of his empire: the prince reigned over part of Europe, Africa and Asia, he is "universal king and the supreme lord of all the Indies of the Ocean Sea, and every day a multitude of people are discovered and mobilized in his service, numerous and vast lands, a superabundance of infinite riches, hitherto never seen and never known. With each reading of a *cédula real* , members of the city council in Tlaxcala are entitled to the ritual utterance of the emperor's titles. Like that of don Giovanni's amorous conquests in the air of the catalogue, the list of distant lands is as endless as it is geographically incoherent: Castile, Leon, Aragon, the Two Sicilies, Jerusalem, Navarre, Granada, Toledo, Valencia, Cadiz , Majorca, Seville, Cordoba, Sardinia, Corsica, Murcia, Jaén, the Algarves, Algeciras, Gibraltar, the Canary Islands, the county of Flanders, the Tyrol, without forgetting India [16]. We bet that more than one member of the city council will have asked to see on a map the location of these distant lands with sometimes strange denominations.

This political cartography is, however, out of step with the globalization that is taking hold and whose dynamics Diego intuitively senses. An unprecedented set of common structures, circulations, exchanges, shared economic, spiritual and political interests organizes the first major transoceanic network between Europe, Africa, America and Asia. More than an anecdote, the journey of ginger that we have spoken about is an illustration of this. Mastering the Pacific, in which Diego is so interested, isn't it one of the major stages in an expansion that will eventually bring all the societies of the globe into contact with each other? At first exceptional or episodic, these circulations will quickly become routine. The trivialization of routes marks a threshold beyond which the prowess of the soldier or the adventure of the discoverer give way to systematic enhancement. The one, precisely, what Diego thinks about when he tells the story of ginger.

The nets of globalization are also those of European science: the cosmographers of the Old World are developing a new image of the Earth, intended to replace that of Ptolemy, by assigning to cartographic representation the entirely political task of depicting the progression of Iberians (then Europeans) in different parts of the globe. A new relationship to the world is established through systematic appropriation in the form of images. Because the world is first of all, for Europeans of course, its flat and cartographic representation or its reduction to the size of a world map [17]. In the 16th century , the European elites experienced a revolution. They conquered the privilege of being able to look at the world, whereas, for millennia, this fringe of humanity had trembled under the omniscient gaze of the pagan divinities, then of the god of the Christians.

Putting the world into images and words

The Diego who climbs the mountains between the valley of Mexico and that of Puebla and who draws a striking geographical evocation from it, or the one who undoubtedly observes the position of *Tiguas* on the map of Ortelius [18], is in the process of living and even take part in this transformation. The times are right. In 1582, Philip II founded the Academy of Mathematics in Madrid. Between 1577 and 1584, the first Iberian scientific expeditions set out to observe and measure lunar eclipses from three different continents, Europe, America and Asia. They organize experiments supposed to improve the still very approximate calculation of longitude. The Iberian domain has become a systematic object of knowledge and the route of the experts passes through Mexico City.

The *De* s *cription de Tlaxcala* is accompanied by dozens of images of Tlaxcala and the conquest of Mexico, as if the rich pictographic tradition of the *Tlacuilos painters* intersected with the new interest of Europeans for the image. What better way to make King Philip II aware of the fate of the Tlaxcaltecs than to show him, and almost show him, the "film" of the Conquest? The art and virtuosity of Indian painters echo the new requirement of the modern West, formulated by Martin Heidegger: "The fundamental process of the modern age is the conquest of the world as an image conceived [19]. »

This putting into images of the world is then as much a putting into words. Almost contemporary with Diego's texts, the work of the Augustinian Jerónimo Román, *Républicas del mundo* , delivers an astonishing application of them. Román takes his reader on a world tour of "States", which casts a spell on both Tlaxcala and the Chinese Empire, Ottoman domination and the Swiss cantons. Such projected encyclopedic design on a planetary scale leads to a geopolitics of the globe in twenty-seven books and three volumes [20].

Diego does not have this universal ambition. This does not prevent him from contributing to this embryonic modernity by transforming indigenous memories into a past accessible to European readers and, above all, to its sovereign. A time which had no existence for the Spaniards, or which remained extremely nebulous to them, acquires, from the pen of this committed observer, the consistency and familiarity of a story by Plutarch. The matter that Diego brews is rationalized and historicized. As facts and dates accumulate, the indigenous past is revealed like photographic film. And, later, this past, modeled by the grid of Aristotelianism, the values of Christianity and the rules of the Castilian language, will leave to join others in the libraries of Castile and Europe, starting with that of the Escorial. Less bloody than war, this painless form of conquest never ceases to prolong it [21]

.

Putting into words is also putting into numbers.

– *You explain that the Tlaxcala market is one of the richest in New Spain. Do you have any idea how much money is spent there?*

– This is where cochineal is traded and, for this trade alone, more than 200,000 pesos in one-real coins are invested by the Spaniards in the purchase of this product [22].

– *What about consumption figures?*

– In this city, 14,000 to 15,000 sheep are slaughtered each year and 3,000 to 4,000 steers in public butcheries; more than 2,000 pigs are consumed, as well as liquidambar resins [23], quantity of vegetables and various cereals [...] and all kinds of things that the Indians sell by bringing them to this market [24].

– *Everything is calculated, even the losses. How much did the 1583 flood cost?*

– It took more than 500 houses and we lost more than 50,000 pesos in cochineal and other property belonging to the Indians. This happened at the end of May [25].

Diego evolves between multiple backgrounds without the diversity of traditions, languages, social organizations and origins being an obstacle, any more than the immensity of distances, time lags and discordances, even reciprocal ignorance. This global reality is in the process of furnishing its *universo mundo* , it is losing the abstract or virtual dimension implied by the idea of universality. Everywhere human beings, who do not share the same trajectory or the same beliefs, come into contact or collide brutally, even if they do not all interest Diego, very discreet about Africa or the worlds of Islam if except for a handful of sartorial comparisons. On the other hand, at home the Chinese colossus already stands behind the Philippine archipelago, and inevitably the India of the Portuguese appears on the route of navigators who dare to cross the Pacific.

So what is the global for Diego? The perception of ever-expanding horizons, the prospect of gains picked up all over the planet – the journey of the ginger –, the launch of military operations on a continental scale – the American North – or across the Pacific. His contemporary, Suárez de Peralta, would no doubt have emphasized the incessant discoveries – "daily", he insists – of silver mines and the spectacular nature of these undertakings [26].

For Diego, the global is also the arena of power where Tlaxcala's affairs are settled by crossing an ocean and visiting another continent. The global sets in the background a prestigious imaginary: the Antiquity of the Old World, which its prologue summarizes in three names (Plato, Végèce and Artaxerxès) and which can be read implicitly in the gesture of the Chichimec invaders. Finally, the *universo mundo* draws its ultimate meaning from the redemptive mission of which it is the theatre. Diego's world is populated by a humanity to be redeemed and converted to the Christian faith.

Local versus global?

Local and global are first of all representations, constructed and experienced by actors in given circumstances; they are two competing perspectives that can, depending on the case, harmonize or enter into conflict. They are neither locations nor orders of magnitude, still less scale ratios.

On the side of the *patria* , the recognized singularities or the "acquired advantages" – let us translate the privileges granted by the Crown – are periodically questioned. The local sphere is constantly exposed to forces that go beyond it: this is the reason for Diego's trip to Spain. But the global itself is not only the sprawling expression of the colonial administration. Nor is it just a matter of perception. The global is also the arena of profound transformations that elude humans, such as the circulation of viruses that decimate Amerindian populations and upset the demographic landscape, or deforestation due to the rise of extensive livestock farming. The global sphere mobilizes forces external to the Catholic Monarchy: circulation on the Asian seas or the immoderate taste of the Chinese for the white metal, silver, are two examples. Chinese demand (unpredictable for Europeans) stimulated the predatory greed of Spanish miners, which were discountable. The global conceals a good part of the unpredictable.

The relationship between the local and the global cannot therefore be reduced to the tensions between the colonized land and the metropolis. If only because the grip of Iberian globalization goes far beyond the occupied territories and it is exercised differently depending on where you are. The sights of Mexico or of Lima on Asia diverge from those of the Crown – not that they are radically opposed, but because one envisages the globe differently from the shores of the Pacific. Global history is not the history of empires.

An interior global

When local elites read Las Casas or Jerónimo Román, they discover their own image, composed and recomposed from the metropolis. The paper mirror held up to them materializes on the spot the invisible intervention of an outside world, what the novelist Juan José Saer describes as the *innominado* [27], the nameless.

Everyday life continues to welcome Hispanic institutions, practices, fashions and imaginaries that are embedded in it. All link it to the rest of the Iberian world. Christianity and its clergy are present on site, materially and physically: Flemish-inspired art introduces the outside world into the city council chamber; the frescoes in the Municipal Palace dramatically display the discovery of America and the conquest of Peru alongside that of Mexico by Cortés.

Within the new administration, the nobles as well as the popular sectors become familiar with the workings, rules and rhetoric of the empire. All go to mass in churches that replicate European models; all are supposed to practice Christian monogamy and adopt the saints of the calendar, henceforth dedicated to punctuating work and days; all owe obedience to an invisible sovereign who resides on the other side of the ocean and rubs shoulders with more men and women of Spanish or African origin every day, when they are introduced by the slave trade. The mestizos and mulattoes who were born of these contacts embodied, even within the hearth, the irruption and the living presence, sometimes disturbing, henceforth inevitable, of these elsewhere unknown before the Conquest. The invasion of alphabetic writing – all the faster than the noble natives have understood the urgency of mastering this new technique – testifies to the emergence of this "inner global". The market of Tlaxcala exhibits all kinds of goods imported from Spain and, if the Indians were officially allowed to buy wine from Castile, the whole Spanish fleet would not be enough to transport it. The global is taking up residence everywhere, at the very heart of the local sphere. Adhesion to Hispanic modernity goes through this gigantic process of internalization.

The historian of colonization has learned to scrutinize the often subtle forms taken by Westernization. It remains to understand how Westernization manages to become effective, to take root and to persist. Taxation then rhymes with local appropriation: taxation when it comes to paying tribute to the Crown or providing labor to Spanish masters; appropriation when natives spy on European craftsmen and seize their tools and techniques. Imposition at the same time as appropriation each time the Spaniards arouse a demand and the Indians rush on the novelty. The success of Spanish wine has caused untold havoc, destructuring and ruining indigenous families. But the meat, wool and salt that Diego trades are just as popular with new consumers. As for the Indian elites, they only dream of mounts, swords and fashionable hats from Castile, when they are not personally in business relations with Spaniards[28].

The waves of monastic constructions which break over a part of Mexico can be explained in the same way. The religious feel the need to replicate in a more or less standardized form the environment they left in Spain. This new architectural space is intended to be both a place of life, spiritual anchoring and symbolic deployment of a Christian conception of the world and beyond. The nave and the vaults of the churches, the cloisters of the convents are so many small spheres, familiar shelters, protective envelopes that close in on the monks and their faithful. These spheres are not only a reproduction of the Church; they physically integrate the Indians into the lap of the universal community of believers. Palpable presence of the stones, technical prowess of the new architecture: in its unavoidable materiality as in the acrobatic dash of its arches, the local sanctuary opens directly onto the metaphysical universe that the sermons describe to the neophyte crowds. In this sense, the local space has changed. This does not mean that the ancient divine presences that permeate the land, the landscape and the toponymy have disappeared, nor the ancestral relationship to the environment and the rhythm of the seasons. But, everywhere, everyday space is taken over by new presences that have spread from Mexico to the Andes and, everywhere, they look alike.

The links of globalization

Circulations, networks and human beings: local and global interpenetrate. The Franciscans of Tlaxcala, who built the convent of the Assumption and the open chapel in the middle of the city, belong to an order with a planetary vocation, whose general resides in Rome, therefore in the heart of Catholicity, and whose many provinces prosper on several continents. The religious orders, the Secular Church with its bishoprics and archbishoprics, the Holy Office of the Inquisition and its American courts stretch their webs over part of the globe, crossing their networks of information, training, control and repression.

Diego the historian would not exist without the school networks set up by the Franciscans. Nor would it exist without the business networks that colonization developed in New Spain and on the seas that surround it. Diego is informed of commercial circulations on a planetary scale. And if he takes the trouble to answer a questionnaire, it's because the crown of Castile has created the first bureaucracy in the world that can boast of intervening in all four parts of the globe. Its representative in Tlaxcala is the *alcalde mayor* . It is up to him to enforce the laws that are current from Manila to Buenos Aires. It is before the Audience of Mexico that the Indian cities now settle their disputes according to principles developed for centuries on the other side of the ocean. Even if, in everyday life and for small matters, Indian custom remains in force, major issues for the community are now handled and resolved according to Castilian law. It is not just a change in content, nor even a story of laws replacing other laws. The new and "modern" idea is imposed, even for Europe, that the same rules can be exported from one end of the planet to the other.

Other networks, more discreet but no less efficient, worked to connect the Indian nobility to the Iberian nobility – and to the European nobility in general – by granting them recognition and visibility in the form of coats of arms. To the indigenous lord, the task of proposing motifs of local origin

which would articulate with the dominant language of European heraldry[29]
.

The city of Tlaxcala received a coat of arms featuring the double-headed eagle of the Habsburgs which reappears, even more majestic, on the *Lienzo of Tlaxcala* . The double-headed eagle is undoubtedly a colonial imposition. But the proud raptor is also a power of pre-Hispanic origin charged with cosmic resonances. Heraldry therefore maintains a mutual recognition: power and tradition according to the Habsburgs espouse the power and tradition of the native city. Two worlds interpenetrate in what they have both in common and what is distinct. And since, from the indigenous perspective, the eagle embodies a divine presence that makes it more than a sign or a symbol, however prestigious it may be, the link between global and local is strengthened.

The allegories decorating the walls of the city council chamber use another language, also on the way to becoming intercontinental, around a classic trilogy: Death which shoots its arrows against "all humanity", Memory surrounded of all sorts of books and stories "that have happened all over the world", and Fame[30]. The medallions brought together the municipal elites of topoi from ancient literature, but reread by medieval and Renaissance Europe. It remains to be seen what they captured, beyond the undeniable fashion effect that carried these images to the heart of Tlaxcaltec power. Death, memory and fame revealed to native eyes the keys to Time as understood by the European scholars of the Renaissance.

At that time, the illustrated editions of the *Emblems* of Alciati disseminated throughout Europe and as far as America the same didactic and moralizing message, as much for decorative purposes as for political propaganda purposes. The global is already deploying its languages and its codes, and with heraldry and emblems everywhere, alphabetical writing, Latin and Spanish are imposing themselves.

Clocks, bridges and journeys

Let's go for a walk in Tlaxcala in the middle of the 16th century . The indigenous town council then deliberates on whether to build a clock. A minority of the council questioned the need for such a machine and feared the cost. The majority considers that the clock is a matter of prestige for the city [31]. And the native annals record the installation of this machine in the year 1560.

To adopt the European rhythm of the hours, after having become accustomed to the ringing of the bells of the monastery, is to take another step towards a sphere governed by a uniform flow of time wherever one is on the planet. As well as displaying a concern for urban standing worthy of an Iberian city, the clock connects local time to the time of the Monarchy. The clock has nothing symbolic about it. It interests all the workshop owners of the city. Time on the dial can give rhythm to colonial work. In 1554, the Cathedral of Mexico received a clock from Emperor Charles V. In 1559, it was the turn of Puebla Cathedral. Tlatelolco, San Gabriel Cholula, Tepeaca follow in their footsteps [32]. Penetration is gradual: it starts in the middle of the century. By tradition, the monks keep their sundials for their community uses, but these are usually arranged inside the convents, as in Churubusco, at the gates of Mexico City [33].

The city has become a very busy place of passage: carriages, carts and convoys, horsemen and mule drivers crowd there [34]. In the countryside of Tlaxcala, teams of indigenous workers take turns to build stone bridges with one or two arches : [35] the depths of the province must be linked to Mexico City, the capital of the viceroyalty, to Spanish neighbor, but also at the port of San Juan Ulua (Veracruz), because it is from there that one joins Havana or that one embarks for Seville, from where one goes up on Madrid, Barcelona,

Antwerp or Roma. Mexico has an imperative need for bridges, like Castile at the time.

It is these bridges, these roads and these vessels that the Tlaxcaltec deputations use on their way to Spain and to the court. Despite the obstacles that hamper communications between America and Europe, the local elite soon proved willing and able to establish a direct relationship with the heart of power. The bond becomes almost cyclic. The first indigenous delegation left Tlaxcala in 1527. The second arrived in Spain in 1534. A third met Charles V in 1540. And others followed in 1562, then in 1584: this time, Diego was there as 'interpreter. The delegation brings together representatives of the four lordships of Ocutelulco, Tizatlán, Quiahuixtlán and Tepetícpac.

The group set off in April 1584 and was granted a reception by Philip II between March and May of the following year. He returned to Mexico with, in his trunks, nearly fifteen *cédulas reales* which ratified existing privileges or added new ones. Any communication with the sovereign is materialized by a written order that the Tlaxcaltec delegates can possibly receive in Spain and in person. The document must then be presented to the viceroy in Mexico, then to the municipal council of Tlaxcala, before being preciously preserved in the safe with the five keys available to the indigenous government [36]. The campaign of 1585 proved to be a success and Diego had the opportunity to deliver to the prince a calligraphic copy of his account of Tlaxcala, enriched with a number of drawings which celebrate the aid given to the Spanish conquest [37].

Moving from one world to another is certainly not an easy task. Organizing a transatlantic crossing requires extensive skills and contacts in mainland France. You have to meet all sorts of expenses, starting with food and clothing: hose, doublets, silks, shirts, hats and shoes [38]. Housing, travel, salaries of lawyers and of all those capable of " *agilizar las cosas* ", that is to say, of facilitating things for a fee, everything cost the Tlaxcaltec taxpayer. Without forgetting the presents for the sovereign, such as these luxurious images made of feathers, these large cornflowers or these necklaces that the city council had made at the expense of the city [39]. Despite this, there is a rush to take the boat and the authorities are forced to remember that only the nobles they have designated will travel [40]. Once overcome the change of scenery, the envoys must make allies in Spain, and these steps are also expensive. We also learn to take advantage of the dead time of the trip and to exploit the promiscuity on the ship. The endless crossings often become conducive to encounters: at the end of 1535, Diego Maxixcatzin returns to Mexico in the company of the first viceroy, Antonio de Mendoza. A less expensive solution is to take advantage of the religious who pass through Tlaxcala on their way back to Spain. They will be entrusted with the requests which they will submit to the Council of the Indies.

Those who cross the ocean will not forget the seasickness or the storms of which certain *cantares* have preserved the echo:

"The wind rises, roaring and whistling,

the ocean is boiling,

and the ship creaks forward [41]. »

1. Martinez Baracs (2008), p. 101-107; in the second half of the century, a term of indigenous origin – *altepetl* – came to designate a new entity integrated into the colonial society in the making.

2. *Ibid* ., p. 249: Sempat Assadourian gives the figure of 80%.

3. *Ibid* ., p. 245.

4. *Ibid* ., p. 247.

5. D54v°.

6. Martinez Baracs (2008), p. 248.

7. D96v°.

8. As Aeneas did when he exiled himself from his Trojan homeland for Italian soil; see KB Fletcher, *Finding Italy: Travel, Nation and Colonization in Virgil's Aeneid* , Ann Arbor, The University of Michigan Press, 2014, p. 185.

9. C241.

10. C244.

11. C66.

12. C42, 66, 74, 102, 125, 132, 140, 241, 244 ; 150 pour *nation* ; 310 pour *natural soil* ; 141.

13. The first edition (in Latin) was published in 1592 ; Mateo Ballester Rodriguez, "On the Genesis of a National Identity: Spain in the Sixteenth and Seventeenth Centuries," *Journal of Political Studies* (Nueva Época), n ° 146, October-December 2009, p. 149-178 ; Xavier Gil Pujol, « A Provincial Court Culture. Fatherland, communication and language in the Hispanic Monarchy of the Austrians », in Pablo Fernandez Albaladejo ed., *Monarchy, empire and peoples in modern Spain* , Alicante, University of Alicante, 1997, p. 225-257 ; id., « One king, one faith, many nations. Fatherland and Nation in Sixteenth and Seventeenth Century Spain", in Antonio Álvarez-Ossorio Alvariño et Bernardo J. García García ed., *The*

Monarchy of Nations. Fatherland, nation and nature in the Monarchy of Spain , Madrid, Fundación Carlos de Antwerp, 2004, p. 39-76.

14. D66r°-66v°.

15. Alonso de Zurita, *Los Señores de la Nueva España* , Mexico City, UNAM, 1993, p. 3.

16. Celestino Solís (1985), p. 358.

17. Twenty- first century society , which delights in the contemplation of screens of all sizes and in the individual and collective production of images in unlimited numbers, forgets the debt it has contracted with its Renaissance ancestor.

18. See footnote 2, p. 155.

19. Martin Heidegger, *Paths that lead nowhere* , Paris, Gallimard, "Tel", [1962] 2006, p. 123.

20. See footnote 1, p. 28.

21. Gruzinsky (2017).

22. D9v°.

23. Deciduous tree whose resin, likened to liquid amber, is used in perfumes.

24. D10r°.

25. D7v°.

26. Suarez de Peralta (1990), p. 177.

27. Gruzinski (2017), p. 9-14.

28. Don Carlos Ometochtli – although executed at the stake under the double accusation of idolatry and infidelity to the Spanish crown – devoted his time and his money to developing on his lands, with the help of the colonizers, the cultivation of plants imported from Spain; see Gruzinski (2017), p. 119-120.

29. Inclusion in a global space and imagination does not always involve erasing the native. On the contrary, it is by manifesting the particularities of his origins that the "natural lord"

joins the transoceanic club of gentlemen with coats of arms, whether they live in London, Goa or Tlaxcala.

30_ D11v°. Sur les sources probables, *Los Emblemas de Alciato traduzidos en rhimas españolas. Añadidos de figuras y de nueuos emblemas en la tercera parte de la obra* , Lyon, Guillaume Rouillé, 1549 [ou Lyon, Macé Bonhomme, 1549]; *Francisci Sanctii Brocensis In Inclyta Salmaticensi Academy of Rhetoric and Professor of the Greek Language, Comment. in And. Alciati Emblemata* , Lyon, Guillaume Rouillé, 1573; Sagrario López Posa, "L'emblème en Espagne au xvi e et au xvii e siècle: actualité et perspectives futures", *Littérature* , n o 145, 1, 2007, p. 19-137, https://www.cairn.info/revue-litterature-2007-1-page-119.htm#n [1]o 2 ·

31. Gibson (1952), p. 147.

32. Ramón Sánchez Flores, *History of technology and invention in Mexico* , Mexico, Fomento Cultural Banamex, 1980, p. 77 ; Guillermo Bois Morales, « Iron at the beginning of New Spain », *Bulletin of Historical Monuments* , 3rd period, 35, September-December 2015, p. 70-99, http://boletin-cnmh.inah.gob.mx/boletin/boletines/BMH%2035-%205%20BR.pdf.[2]

33. Ross Hassig, *Time, History and Belief in Aztec and Colonial Mexico* , Austin, Texas University Press, 2012, p. 146.

34. Cervantes de Salazar (1985), p. 245.

35. Gibson (1952), p. 135.

36. *Ibid* ., p. 16, 168.

37. It's not just the elites who have a say. Other sectors of the population, less favored, complain in Madrid of the bad treatment inflicted on the common people (*macehuales*).

38. Diaz Serrano (2012), note 11, p. 1055.

39. *Ibid.* , p. 1066.

1. https://www.cairn.info/revue-litterature-2007

2. http://boletin-cnmh.inah.gob.mx/boletin/boletines/BMH%2035-%205%20BR.pdf

40. Celestino Solís (1985), p. 369, 584-585.

41. "Cantar mexicano LXVIII", in Serge Gruzinski, *La Pensée métisse* , Paris, Fayard, 1999, p. 225.

CHAPTER XII

Who, today or tomorrow, will still think of you?

"Who, today or tomorrow, will still think of you? »

Elfriede Jelinek, *Totenauberg*[1].

– *Do you realize that your approach is exceptional?*

– There are not many who dare to take up the pen, for they dread the criticisms and opinions that others give on things which have cost them no effort.

– *So why did you start such an "enterprise", since that's the word you use?*

– Sometimes, the famous phrase of the divine Plato gave me courage: "Man is not born only for himself, but also to serve his sweet country and his friends [2]. »

– *Did you hesitate a moment before accepting the challenge?*

– It is not once, but many times that the limits of my poor intelligence have stopped me in an arduous task which requires philosophy, but also knowledge of geometry and arithmetic.

" *You went to work anyway because the order came from the king and the viceroy. But why you?*

– That someone wanted to entrust me with this task remains a great mystery. But this stroke of fate disarmed my understanding[3], I who am only a man born in this New World.

– *For you, fate is shrouded in mystery, it is unpredictable and capricious like the "wheel of fortune"*[4]*. Did you feel fit to write the relationship?*

– We could have entrusted it to someone more erudite, because I was sure to fail and fall into a thousand mistakes [...] I, who am a man born in this New World, insufficiently prepared for such an enterprise.

This man who escapes us

Is his condition as an American, a "native of the New World", a handicap, a reproach that could be leveled at him, or on the contrary an undeniable asset since he puts forward a field experience of more than thirty -five years ?

Diego unpacks with us a modesty of circumstance. He takes refuge behind the humility of the believer and the obedience of the courtier. We will not dissipate this opacity covered with rhetoric and pious thoughts, but we can circumvent it. The time does not lend itself to autobiography and Diego is not Michel de Montaigne. Moreover, the genre chosen, story or administrative report, hardly encourages confidence, even if from time to time Diego has found a way to stage himself, if only through childhood memories or the occasion of a mountain excursion.

We know nothing about his love life, his illnesses. We know little of his culinary tastes. But by what right, after all? And what about his artistic interests? The relationship he offers to Philip II is accompanied by the reproduction of the great frescoes of Tlaxcala without know if the rapprochement is intentional, in other words if he himself took this initiative. Mexican painters seem to have been freely inspired by the *Triumphs of Charles Quint* [5]. Dedicated to Philip II, the series of twelve engravings was published by Hieronymus Cock in Antwerp in 1556. Engraved from drawings by Maarten Van Heemskerck, these images exalt the reign of Philip's father by spreading the glory of a domination extended to the entire globe [6]. The illustrations that conclude the *Description of Tlaxcala* are too sloppy for us to be able to draw any precise ideas about Diego's eye. Except that, still sensitive to the pre-Hispanic tradition, he would have remained convinced that the image brings as much as the text. Let's not neglect either the eye of wonder at the beauty of the landscape that he discovers from Mount Tlaloc, nor the eye of an antiquarian that he casts on the Olmec ruins. Finally, nothing about his musical tastes, not even the indication of the hymns that were sung during the native elections and that the Augustinian Jerónimo Román – who, however, never set foot in Tlaxcala – takes care to record . However, in the middle of the century, according to the Dominican Las Casas, the province had at least a thousand musicians and singers: chalumeaux, saquebutes, dulzainas (a kind of oboe), trumpets, drums resounded everywhere in the festivals, and in Tlaxcala , in the main church, polyphonies alternated with plainsong[7].

As for his literary tastes, the shadow of Plutarch seems to hover over his writing. The Greek historian would have provided him with a model and words to organize the mass of information that his native interlocutors provided him with. The words: perhaps it is from this side, if we follow Marguerite Yourcenar, that we get closer to the inner man.

love of country

Diego borrows from a letter from Plato the motto that adorns the first lines of his *Descriptio* n: "Man was not born only for himself, but also for his sweet homeland and his friends [8]. Is it there by pure writing convention? I do not believe that. Nor should we see in it a philosophical message analogous to that which slips into the correspondence between two humanists like the Frenchman Guillaume Budé and the Spaniard Juan Luis Vives [9]. On the other hand, this motto applies like a glove to his dedication to the Republic of Tlaxcala. If only by counting the hours, the days, the months spent collecting testimonies to record their history.

"Man was not born for himself..." Erasmus placed this injunction among his *Adages* (*Nemo sibi nascitur* [3581]), one of the bestsellers of the 16th century . Admittedly, the quotation is not enough not to make Diego a disciple of Erasmus [10], but his presence with the humanist of Rotterdam offers one more reason to adopt this rule of life for anyone claiming to hold a pen in Renaissance Mexico [11]. Diego also wishes to serve his "friends". However, when we know the place it attributes to love and friendship, this group of elected officials had to include its European and Métis partners as much as its indigenous allies. This entourage spared him the blows of fate, and in particular the exile to which he should have been condemned by a royal certificate banishing the half-breeds from Tlaxcala [12].

By placing himself under the authority of the "divine Plato", our author stands out from the Franciscan chroniclers he has read and who work for the greater glory of God and the Church. In Western Europe, the formula "the divine Plato" first had the favor of Neoplatonic circles: it appears in the writings of Marsilio Ficino, one of the most influential philosophers of the Italian Renaissance. She then faded away. So much so that it slips into Mexico under the pen of another Métis historian, Alva Ixtlilxochitl, when he extols the merits of a former indigenous sovereign [13]. Not that a neoplatonic vein secretly runs on American soil, but humanism in New Spain gives more importance to Plato than we imagined and that this "cult" was still very much alive at the end of the 16th century .

The expression *dulce patria* ("sweet" does not appear in Plato's letter) is a cliché in the 16th century . We meet it in Spain with Pérez de Hita [14], the author of the *Civil Wars of Granada* (1595): he explains to us that the Moriscos forced into exile "preferred to die rather than abandon their sweet homeland [15]". Cervantes de Salazar, to whom we owe a *Chronicle of New Spain* , is among the first to associate it with Tlaxcala by putting in the mouth of Cortés the reasons for the Tlaxcaltec alliance: "The friends who surround us do not know how to fail us [...] because they would lose their sweet homeland and their beloved freedom . What confirms that Diego thinks of his Tlaxcaltec homeland when he speaks to his king and that he has undoubtedly read Cervantes de Salazar.

When he claimed service to his country, Diego unwittingly approached the great historians of Renaissance Italy, Leonardo Bruni or Ludovico Guicciardini, to name but a few, so devoted to their Florentine homeland. Did Diego hope, like Bruni in Florence, to receive from Tlaxcala a token of recognition for having served "the eternal fame of the city"? In any case, he too conceived of history as a means of exalting local [pride].

Plato's phrase was taken up by Cicero in his *De officiis* . The Latin speaker was also able to appear in Diego's eyes as a figure to identify with. Hadn't Cicero received the title of "father of the country ", [18] a distinction known to our author, which indicates that it was awarded to Viceroy Luis de Velasco in homage to his talents as a ruler?

These clues reveal to us a man who has thought about the meaning of the task assigned to him and the magnitude he intended to give it. He questioned himself. His involvement in the life of Tlaxcala and the analyzes that we have shared with him prohibit reducing his references to formulas of circumstance or to a simple cosmetic operation. The antique dealer that we discovered also knows how to slip into the skin of the humanist.

"The Thirst to Command, Own and Lead"

The homeland is "sweet", but the world has not always been so. Diego has a singularly black image of social relations and politics. According to him, as Plautus wrote long before him, "man is a wolf to man". Even the Native American man.

– *How did the Indians treat each other before the Spanish domination?*

– They tried to submit to each other to seize each other's wealth and possessions by forcibly snatching them away, making themselves feared by their cruelties and their perfectly unjustified tyrannical acts.

– *What were their motives?*

– They listened only to their thirst to command, to possess and to direct.

– *According to you, the Indians would have been as ambitious as the "men of reason".*

– Some fled submission and sought to remain free; the others, mad with ambition, strove to subjugate the whole human race by dint of wars and cruel acts.

– *Is the state of war of all against all valid for all humanity or is New Spain an exception?*

– [After the Flood] men gave free rein to their subversive ambition, each one had the claim to dominate his region and even to subject the world to his domination. It is from this that civil wars and cruel enmities between father and son, between brothers, parents, friends and neighbors were born, in order to despoil each other [19].

– *Are you talking about the whole world?*

– From East to West, wars and conflicts have never ceased, just and unjust, led by bloodthirsty and cruel tyrants. They provoked the cowardly and frightened flight of defeated and beaten peoples, and these, in order not to see the victorious face of their victorious enemies, preferred to flee and go and populate foreign lands rather than returning to live humiliated on the their [20].

"But, in your time, was not New Spain at peace?"

– All this would have lasted until the end of the world if the Spaniards had not arrived to put an end to it [21].

– The conquistadors are therefore the great peacemakers, contrary to what one of your contemporaries, Michel de Montaigne, asserts when he denounces the Conquest: "Never did ambition, never did public enmity push men against each other. the others to such horrible hostilities and calamities so miserable [22]. »

an american subject

Diego's work refracts the shadows and lights of the distant European Renaissance. It reveals what Mexico City on the American continent captures and even a miraculously preserved Indian city like Tlaxcala. But New Spain was also exposed "to the currents and winds" of the rest of the world. The humanism of this Tlaxcaltec by birth and adoption is the fruit of his American experience. It is never a lesson learned in Europe and exported to America, unlike that of Cervantes de Salazar, this Latinist emigrant trained at the University of Salamanca.

The Tlaxcaltec tropism differentiates Diego from his contemporary, crossed and recrossed over the course of these pages, Juan Suárez de Peralta. Even returning frustrated to Spain, this Creole is full of praise for "his homeland", but this time it is New Spain [23]. His positions constantly distinguish him from Diego [24]. Thus he does not hide the terror he felt when the Crown hunted down all those believed to be involved in the plot of the Marquis del Valle, son of Cortés. Diego has neither these Creole emotions nor this neo-Hispanic patriotism, even if twice he claims to have been born in the New World. And he does say the "New World", never the "New Spain"!

Its originality lies elsewhere. Here, European humanism can no longer serve as a guide. By forging a whole arsenal of benchmarks, by being attentive to the changes he observes everywhere around him, Diego learns to measure himself against an unprecedented form of domination which is intended to merge with the globe and which is at the origin of five centuries of Western hegemony. And he does it in a way that is uniquely his.

It is alone that Diego builds his marks, in the sense that there is no roadmap for a man of his dual origins. It is in his own way that he envisages the pre-Hispanic past, a past which he never recognizes as his own, but which he approaches as closely as possible. It was also in his own way that Diego steered his boat in the empire of Charles V and on the waters of the Catholic

Monarchy after 1580. The Tlaxcala account presents him as *vecino y natural* . However, Diego never poses as an heir to the local past or to anyone. Another loneliness. Nothing to do with the Christianized nobles who cultivate their lineage memories like a precious asset that is passed on from generation to generation, even when you have nothing else left.

It is surprising that a half-caste can have such an intimate and at the same time distanced relationship with the city where he was born and where his mother's parents were born. But, basically, what is a half-breed or what is it to be half-breed? A contemporary of Diego, Diego Valadés, with the same first name and born in the same years (around 1533), also sees his name attached to Tlaxcala. Author of a treatise famous in his time, the *Rhetorica christiana* , this Franciscan passes for being a native of the Tlaxcaltec city [25]. For a long time, we believed him to be half-breed. Some claim today that he was born in Spain, and therefore Spanish. So, mestizo or spanish? But Spanish, isn't that also the belonging claimed by our half-breed Diego Muñoz Camargo?

The vagueness that surrounds the origins of the two characters probably only exists in our still so Cartesian heads. These natural sons of conquistadors are socially integrated into the paternal and dominant group, whether or not they are biologically mestizos, they are not considered *mestizos* and can, if necessary, like Diego Valadés, make a career without hindrance in Europe and within the order of Saint Francis [26].

So let's take things another way. Because he spends his time examining them, synthesizing them, putting them down in writing and interpreting them, the two worlds – native and European – become for Diego objects of reflection that he constantly brings back to himself to have them before the eyes. It is from the knowledge and experiences accumulated in Tlaxcala, Mexico City and no doubt Madrid that he acquired this dual awareness of the indigenous world and the colonial world, but also of the local and of the global. This world-consciousness is the fruit of his personal journey, his analyses, his choices as much as his refusals and his silences. Or its dead ends. Diego is not the Indian from whom he always differentiates himself. Nor is he the Spaniard he claims to be.

Diego relates everything to himself, to his biases, to his interests, to his curiosities, whether he is in the process of constructing the pre-Hispanic past, whether he is staging the first moments of colonization or even reporting of colonial history up to 1590. When he reports the massacre of Tlaxcala, he is able to do so as much from the Spanish point of view as from the native point of view. About a Spaniard who supports Hernán Cortés and a native who would identify with a Tlaxcaltec nobleman, "friend" of the invaders. Diego is the one who, in the last instance, decides what he takes or does not take from the pre-Hispanic world as well as from the colonial world.

However, this unique position in the face of worlds that are both distinct and henceforth inseparable makes it an actor of a new type. Nothing to do with the construction of the modern subject that we usually salute in Montaigne, because here this process is specifically American. By writing that "the sixteenth century marks the birth of subjectivity ," [27] we have forgotten that the world cannot be reduced to Western Europe. You have to be anchored elsewhere to reach this distanced subjectivity. And what's more, in Diego's case, living alongside and not among the indigenous elites. Diego's vision is not the vision of the vanquished [28]. It is an American vision.

Landmarks

An American subject, why not? But does this bring us closer to the inner man? His interpretation of the Conquest – a veritable literary show, crowned by the macabre brilliance of Cholula – deserves to be revisited. By endeavoring to restore this great theater of friendship and cruelty, Diego reaffirms loud and clear the vital need for a commitment of the two groups, one alongside the other, one for the other. . Forever, Cortés will be the friend who has come to the aid of the honor of the Tlaxcaltecs. No trace here of conquest, defeat or submission, but the ideal of perfect reciprocity between Indians and Spaniards in the perspective of a merger "so that all are one".

However, Diego's "we" never refers to the Indians, and not for a moment does he consider questioning the validity of the Conquest. Diego ardently wishes for the fusion without however imagining himself to be (or to propose himself as) the product of this fusion. Or, at least, report it personally. What to understand?

This fusional ideal brings us face to face with the inner man. Couldn't these dreams and these fixations have to do with his personal history, with the choices he made, with the role he gave himself in Tlaxcala and in Mexico City, with the impasses he found himself in? is found ? Let's imagine that the "so that all may be one" points to the goal (caressed, but veiled and finally achieved) towards which Diego would have strived all his life. Son of a conquistador and an Indian woman, he always appears and thinks of himself – despite his bastardy – as Spanish. This does not prevent him from marrying a Tlaxcaltec lady before pushing his son into the arms of an heiress of the native aristocracy, which son will end up at the head of the republic of Tlaxcala, a position hitherto reserved for noble Indians. What better way to be, through his son, both Indian and Spanish?

But, to slalom between the two worlds without losing his bearings, he had to reduce the gap between the conquistadors and the native nobility as much as possible, without ever reducing it. Certainly the two worlds are not as distant as they appear to us today. Suárez de Peralta, Diego's contemporary, likes to recall that the Indians considered the Creoles, that is to say the Spaniards born in Mexico, brought up by Indian nurses 29 , as "sons of the earth and natives [30]". The two groups maintained ties of familiarity, especially when the Creoles knew the language of the country, which further strengthened harmony and mutual friendship: "There are Indians so 'Spanishized' [we would say Hispanized] that they are alike in many things [31]. The Indians and Creoles in question here obviously belong to the elites of New Spain.

How to maintain the equal balance without which there can be no question of fusion? Diego the historian and Diego the antiquary agree in giving the New World a past on a par with Greco-Roman antiquity. The great events of pre-Hispanic times are assessed on the scale of world history, and the unshakeable Tlaxcaltec fidelity at the time of the Conquest celebrated in all tones. Intellectually, Diego even recognizes that the indigenous society has its own way (" *al modo indico* [32]"), its logic, "its order [33]". And he takes up the certificate of rationality that the Dominican Las Casas generously distributes in his plea for indigenous societies: " *orden y concierto* ".

However, the reflex that pushes him to identify implicitly with the Spaniards (*los nuestros*) invariably ranks him on the side of the dominant. Still need to know who he has in mind. The *encomenderos* , the ecclesiastics, the civil servants, the inhabitants of the Iberian Peninsula? Or is he thinking of the conquistadors, long out of the political scene, or even of the first Creoles? Still misses him the neo-Hispanic patriotism of a Suárez de Peralta to connect with the Creole milieu.

Where is Diego in the colonial society? Diego is elusive. Unless the indetermination that surrounds him and this way of sticking to the indigenous world without renouncing to being his father's son signals his true place to us. A special place from which he can impose himself as the spokesperson for an entire province and the interlocutor of his sovereign. At the crossroads of the local and the global, the inner man undoubtedly finds there the balance essential to the accomplishment of his multiple tasks.

And the strength to circumvent the obstacles that obstruct his path: for the Spaniards, he is a bastard; for the Indians, a commoner. He writes about a society and a past that are not his own and for a world, the Iberian Peninsula, which is just as foreign to him since he only discovered it during his trip in 1584. Diego looks like an electron free moving between the Tlaxcaltec sphere and the Spain of Philip II, between an Indian land which "welcomed" his father and where he was born, and a distant peninsula which gave him the order to write and to which he directs his thoughts.

Does the close and distanced relationship that Diego maintains with the indigenous world reveal a more intimate debate? Absent from his stories, Diego's mother is an invisible woman, doomed to anonymity. It is true that in the sixteenth century on Iberian and European lands, without being either bastards or half-breeds, the men who write are usually not very eloquent about women in general, especially about their mothers. It would, however, be inaccurate to think that Diego ignores the fairer sex: La Malinche, the companion and Indian interpreter of Cortés, occupies a remarkable place in his account of the Conquest, and he does not fail to recall the prowess of a Spaniard, María de Estrada, who fought alongside the conquistadors, "as if she were one of the bravest men in the world".

If Diego always maintains a space between him and the (indigenous) world of his mother, if he never tries to appropriate this past and these glorious origins as a little later the Inca Garcilaso de la Vega, the reason is perhaps very simple. Not only is her mother not a princess, but her origins remain obscure. Nothing that would refer to the aristocratic elite that he describes with undisguised admiration. The spirit of caste that has been discovered in him would dictate silence. We will answer that he is hardly more verbose about his Hispanic origins, even if indirectly. In any case, Diego has nothing of a native Spaniard who would have taken to Mexico, clinging to his boots, a bit of his distant native land. This is what distinguishes him from his father. But, we know only too well, the writing of a geographical relationship is not an exercise that lends itself to personal confession.

The fact remains that, in order to exist in this developing society, everyone needs strong benchmarks and, in order for these benchmarks to stand, they first need a base on which to anchor themselves, they need to take root in a land, even if it now belongs to a new world. This explains Diego's prodigious interest in Tlaxcala's past, constructing it well beyond what the order addressed to him requires. But these local ties – his "homeland" – are not enough for him. They would run the risk of bogging him down in a provincial vision if they were not coupled with an exceptional openness of view, nourished by his knowledge of New Spain and its transformations within the empire.

So what's in Diego's head? If we wanted to use the anachronistic but revealing language of artificial intelligence, we would write that his knowledge of the societies of New Spain, added to the privileged position he occupies, is explained by a double apprenticeship: that of "scripts from the indigenous world and the Spanish world. It keeps transcribing one of its databases into the other and *vice versa* ; he masters distinct recognition codes, he deciphers words, objects, concepts that belong to different memories. This form of human intelligence reminds us that an artificial intelligence which would only be a clone of Western intelligence, incapable of stepping over societies and civilizations, would remain a decoy.

Finally, loyalty. In a society in the making where uprooting is the rule for practically everyone, invaders and colonized alike, ties and loyalties are the *sine qua non* conditions for integration and social success. The Crown and the Church do not tolerate deviation. Diego understood this well. Suspected of rebellion, Martín, the son of Hernán Cortés, paid dearly for his disloyalty in 1566. Twelve years later, the rector of the University of San Marcos, the Dominican Francisco de la Cruz, perished at the stake. Diego always measures what he says. His remarks and his silences are molded in a political and religious framework of impeccable orthodoxy. And Diego succeeded. In our time, he would be one of the "first of the rope [34]" so prized by our authorities.

1. Jelinek (2011), p. 18.

2. Porphyre de Tyr, *Letter to Marcella* , Paris, Belles Lettres, 2019, p. 22-23.

3. I would like to thank Louise Bénat-Tachot for her insights.

4. The same idea in Plutarch: "ἐν πυκνῷ θεοῦ τροχῷ", in *Lives of Illustrious Men* , t. II, *Life of Demetrius* [45], trans. Alexis Pierron, Paris, Charpentier, 1853, http://remacle.org/bloodwolf/historians/Plutarque/demetriuspieron1.htm.[1]

5. Our interpretation is based on the representation of caparisoned horses, the motifs that adorn the "front", the gestures of Charles V, the symbols that he and his son bear: the tripartite globe, the golden fleece, heraldry.

6. The Flemish series inspired a sumptuous illuminated manuscript, produced by the artist Giulio Clovio at the request of Philip II in the third quarter of the 16th century ; see Juan Francisco Pardo Molero, "Los triunfos de Carlos Quinto. Transferencias culturales y políticas en la exaltación de la monarquía", in *Las Monarquías española y francesa (siglos xvi-xviii)* , Anne Dubet and José Javier Ruiz Ibáñez (eds.), Madrid, Casa de Velázquez, 2010, p. 17-30.

7. Bartolomé de Las Casas, *Apologética historia sumaria* , Edmundo O'Gorman ed., t. I, Mexico, UNAM, 1967, p. 333-335.

8. The quote is taken from Plato's letter IX to Archytas of Taranto: "You must reflect that we were not born for ourselves alone, that our life is shared between our homeland, our parents and our friends", https:// fr .wikisource.org/wiki/Lettres_de_Platon_(trans._Victor [2]Cousin). Plato's formula circulates everywhere in Europe as in Spain, and in the most diverse works: for example, the prologue of Ruy Díaz de Isla, Tractado *contra el mal serpentino* , Seville, Andres de Burgos, 1542. See also Plato, *Works complete* , Joseph Souilhé trad., t. XIII, Paris, Les Belles Lettres, [1931] 2003.

9. *La Correspondance de Guillaume Budé and Juan Luis Vivés* , Gilbert Tournoy and Monique Mund Dopchie ed., Louvain, Leuven University Press, 2015, p. 76.

---

1. http://remacle.org/bloodwolf/historiens/Plutarque/demetriuspieron1.htm

2. https://fr.wikisource.org/wiki/Lettres_de_Platon_(trad._Victor

10 . http://ihrim.huma-num.fr/nmh/Erasmus/Proverbia/Adagium_3581.html. [3]On the influence of the humanist in the Iberian world, Marcel Bataillon, *Erasmus and Spain* . *Research on the spiritual history of the sixteenth* ^{century} , Geneva, Droz, 1988.

11 . The meaning of the motto in Cicero (*De officiis* , I, 7, 22). The Hispanic world has a translation by Francisco Tamara, *Libro de los officios* (1545), then two others in 1549, published in Alcala de Henares and Antwerp; Esther Martin, "Ciceronian eloquence as a weapon of war in the *Philippians* ", in Emmanuel Dupraz and Claire Geerhaert-Grafeuille ed., *The Civil War: representations, idealizations, identifications* , t. I, Rouen, University Presses of Rouen and Le Havre, 2014, p. 17.

12 . Morner (1962).

13 . Andrew Laird and Nicolas Miller eds., *Antiquities and Classical Traditions in Latin America* , Bulletin of Latin American Research Book Series, Hoboken, John Wiley & Sons, 2018, p. 94-95.

14 . Ginés Perez de Hita (1544?-1619?) is the author of the *Historia de los bandos de los Zegríes y Abencerrajes* , known as the *Civil Wars of Granada* , the first part of which relates the events leading up to the fall of the Kingdom of Granada.

15 . Part II, chap. xxv in *Novelistas anteriores a Cervantes* , Biblioteca de Autores españoles, t. III, Madrid, Ribadeneyra y Compañía, 1846, p. 686.

16 . Cervantes de Salazar (1985), ch. xxxix, p. 568.

17 . Like the author of the prefaces to the *History of Florence* (1418) and the *First Punic War* (1419), in *Medieval and Renaissance Texts and Studies* , The Renaissance Society of America. Renaissance Texts and Series, vol. 10, Binghampton, New York, Center for Medieval and Early Renaissance Studies, 1987, p. 175, 181.

18 . *Ibid* ., p. 187.

19 . D66r°.

20 . *Ibid* .

---

3. http://ihrim.huma-num.fr/nmh/Erasmus/Proverbia/Adagium_3581.html

21 . D73v°.

22 . Montaigne (1965), vol. III, ch. vi, "Checkmarks", p. 142.

23 . Suarez de Peralta (1990), p. 159.

24 . And not only his passion for horses or his knowledge of gambling houses: Suárez de Peralta (1990), p. 172, 162.

25 . Palomera (1988), p. 54.

26 . Juan Manuel Valadés Sierra, "Diego Valadés, a barcarroteño in the conquista of México", *Revista de estudios extremeños* , t. LXVII (III), 2011, p. 1293-1346.

27 . *The Problematic of the Subject in Montaigne* , proceedings of the Toronto colloquium compiled by Eva Kushner (October 20-21, 1992), Paris, Champion, 1995, p. 59.

28 . Miguel Leon-Portilla, *The Vision of the Vanquished. Indigenous Relations of the Conquest* , Mexico, 1959 ; Nathan Wachtel, *The Vision of Victors. The Indians of Peru before the Spanish Conquest (1530-1570)* , Paris, Gallimard, 1971.

29 . Suárez de Peralta (1990), p. 25 and chap. xv.

30 . *Albeitería book* , ms. 4255, National Library Madrid, chap. i, quoted in Suárez de Peralta (1990), p. 25.

31 . Suárez de Peralta (1990), p. 27, 58.

32 . D15v°.

33 . See his description of the pre-Hispanic war, D92v°.

34 . Emmanuel Macron, October 15, 2017.

CONCLUSION

The interbreeding of the 16th century

"This man alone and moreover connected to everything. »

Marguerite Yourcenar, *Notebooks of" Memoirs of Hadrian* " [1].

Intercontinental interbreeding is one of the decisive turns that the Iberian expansion imprints on the history of humanity in the 16th century . Regular links now unite Europe and Africa to America, and the latter to the Asian continent – and this fabulous reduction in the distances between the worlds results in an often brutal and unprecedented rapprochement between human beings. Maritime borders are no longer impassable and communications are experiencing an acceleration that will know no bounds. Even the most isolated islands of the Pacific discover strange visitors. These journeys and these encounters which excite the imagination of the European reader immersed in the atlases, quantities of beings experience them all over the world, often reluctantly.

But interbreeding does not only involve bodies, nor can they be reduced to "cultural epiphenomena". They affect all dimensions of social life, bite into politics, mobilize and question power relations, transform modes of exploitation as much as they stir up subjectivities and beliefs.

All this we have explored [2]. It remained to situate these phenomena in their proper context. Interbreeding is best observed at the local level. All kinds of constraints and contaminations are exerted there, emanating from other worlds. It is on the spot, more exactly at the *intersection* of the local and the global, that they take shape. They appear as the fruit and the manifestation of multiple interferences between an indigenous way of life, brutally exposed to the blows of the outside, and the dynamics of integration and homogenization set in motion by globalization. Interbreeding is born, transformed and exhausted within the balance of power orchestrated by this unprecedented setting.

Usually, for those concerned, the origin of these pressures remains of the order of the "Unnamed" (Juan José Saer [3]). Local perception is far from accounting for all the forces in action, and even less for their global character. Some of these processes are the object of a clear consciousness, others of a confused comprehension, still others remain opaque. It is because one can only apprehend these awakenings (or these opacities) on a local scale and by questioning individuals that I have devoted so many pages to Tlaxcala and to a "man born in the New World", Diego Muñoz Camargo. To watch for the meeting of the ancient world and the colonial world, the clash and concordance of times in an American spirit. To scrutinize the forces acting on man, his trajectory and his commitments.

On the clear conscience side, Diego, the inland man, has grasped the importance of the seas and maritime globalization. In principle, from this time, one can go by sea to any part of the globe. From now on, the space of the planet is broken down into a myriad of points that the Iberian man is able to connect together with the help of his ships. Europeans, mestizos, blacks and Indians living in America are probably more aware of this than others. Printing in Mexico in 1587 of a guide to navigation, a first, reveals the keen interest of the elites for naval construction, the technique par excellence of Iberian expansion [4]. Publishing in the New World is never an insignificant gesture. For Diego's generation, he explained to us, the lightning progress of maritime navigation is obvious and an irrevocable achievement.

All globalization invites excess: adventurers invade continents, destroy civilizations, pile up ruins. In Diego's time, in Manila and Mexico, they even toyed with the project of subjugating China. Why not ? No wonder Diego saw the conquistadors as unstoppable invaders. From globalization, Diego also captures what it conceals in terms of compulsive mobility. How else can we explain what he recounts of the irresistible "fidgeting" that gripped the Spaniards in the Indies, whether they were going to Peru with the intention of sharing this new fortune, whether they were trying to reach China by crossing the Pacific or to sink into the lands of the North to seize the fabulous riches of the Seven Cities?

It is also with Diego that we can penetrate the other side of interbreeding. From what he says or does not say, from what he suggests and even from what escapes him, we detect what these mixtures contain of resistance, adjustment and negotiation with the " Unnamed", always coming from elsewhere. How did it forge its defense mechanisms? How did he build his own memory while building a collective memory? Negotiation plays a major role here. But just as much the reparation: Diego has become the interpreter of a group which tries to stay afloat in a society broken by the irruption of the West. To repair then means to recover everything that can be repaired, starting with a founding memory by creating a pre-Hispanic past.

The inner man must therefore react to the challenges launched by a new transoceanic order, to its global repercussions as than to the shaking of the structures of indigenous societies. He then invents all sorts of landmarks in the face of a local society fighting for its survival and a multifaceted elsewhere: it can be the globe – *el universo mundo* – or the distant metropolis, or even the frontiers of Iberian expansion. The indigenous universe is thrown back into a bygone "antiquity", but carefully inventoried and always treated with the respect one has for the things of yesteryear. The Christian world which succeeds it can only be the last of the worlds. It is enough, like Diego, to be there on the good side.

We still lack the tools to analyze these multiple pathways. This is why, as far as I could, I let Diego speak instead of reducing his testimony to more or less faithful paraphrases or substituting my interpretations for him. The state of the manuscripts that have come down to us, the limits of our knowledge of sixteenth - century Castilian , his own relationship to the language of New Spain undermine the transparency of his testimony [5]. I found only one way to reduce all these obstacles. The repeated conversations between Diego and I ended up creating a certain familiarity which often helps to understand him half-word, even to interpret his silences. In my career as a researcher, I had never spent so many hours with a 16th century man , born on the other side of the ocean.

But how do you escape the tunnels of political correctness? They abound in these pages written to be made public. And yet, in our last conversation, under the veneer of ready-made phrases and occasional alibis, shouldn't we read the expression of the faith of a half-breed, a form commitment that has become more disturbing to so many of us today than the beliefs of the ancient Mexicans?

– *Why was the Spanish conquest successful?*

– Since God guided the course of things and Cortés knew he would succeed, nothing he undertook seemed impossible to him [6].

– *Was the project excessive?*

“Everything seemed easy to him. And, for them, to brutally attack and conquer the world in an hour was nothing.

– *As for Alexander?*

– When the conqueror reached the Ganges [*sic*] with his armies, having subjugated most of the world and reduced it to his power and mercy, what did he think when he arrived there, if not that the whole world was his and that he had nothing more to conquer, except the earthly paradise and Greater **India** ?

– *But how do you explain the Conquest?*

– The secrets of God are impenetrable. Let's put them aside and just give Him our praise and eternal gratitude.

- *But still?*

– The demon was the master of these nations. God wanted to put an end to his infernal tyranny by sending them Cortés and his companions to make them the instruments of their salvation.

– *What is the ultimate meaning of this whole story?*

– Our holy mother the Church wants to sink ever deeper so that all the nations of the world come to know their Creator [...] and that she obtains universally the conversion of all these new peoples.

– *Without forgetting China?*

– This is seen clearly every day today, since the Holy Gospel is preached in the Philippines and part of Greater China.

– *Was it the occupation of these islands that opened up this gigantic horizon?*

– Less than fifteen years ago, we cared very little about the priceless gift that God gave us [8].

– *That was my last question. What do you think of our conversation?*

– Opus laudat artificem [9]...

1. Yourcenar (1982), p. 519.

2. Gruzinsky (1999).

3. Gruzinski (2017), p. 9-14.

4. Erika Elizabeth Laanela, *Instrucción nautica by Diego García de Palacio . An Early Nautical Handbook from Mexico* , Master's Thesis, College Station, Texas, A&M University, 2008.

5. Sur les influences manifestes du nahuatl et de la rhétorique des *cantares* sur le style de Diego, María Inés Aldao, *Indigenous tradition, western tradition : Tensions in the mestizo chronicles of Juan Bautista Pomar, Diego Muñoz Camargo and Cristóbal del Castillo. Mexico, 16th century* , mémoire de maîtrise, Buenos Aires, University of Buenos Aires, 2015, p. 51-52.

6. D122v°.

7. D67r°.

8. D68v°.

9. D234v°. « À l'œuvre, on connaît l'artisan. »

CHRONOLOGY

1519: Charles V elected emperor.

1521: fall of Mexico-Tenochtitlan.

1524: the first Franciscans in Tlaxcala.

1530 (?): birth of Diego Muñoz Camargo.

1533: birth of Michel de Montaigne.

1535: Antonio de Mendoza, viceroy.

1537: Cabeza de Vaca returns to Mexico.

1550: Luis de Velasco, viceroy.

1551: creation of the University of Mexico.

1556: Philip II, King of Spain.

1565: Miguel López de Legazpi lands in the Philippines.

1571: the Inquisition is established in Mexico.

1581-1584 : *Description of Tlaxcala* by Diego Munoz Camargo.

1584: Departure for Spain of the Tlaxcaltec embassy.

1592 : Death of Michel de Montaigne.

1600 (?) : Death of Diego Munoz Camargo.

Also by Jensen Cox

Historia Americana: ¡Circunstancias históricas, personas importantes, sitios importantes y más!
Investing in Cryptocurrencies: The Fastest Strategies for Becoming a Crypto Millionaire
Criptomonedas: invierta sabiamente en las criptomonedas más rentables y confiables para ganar dinero
Cryptocurrencies: Invest Wisely in the Most Profitable and Trusted Cryptocurrencies to Make Money
Invertir en Criptomonedas: Las estrategias más rápidas para convertirse en un criptomillonario
The Armed Nation: American Culture and Guns at the Core
Y Genedl Arfog: Diwylliant Americanaidd a Gynnau wrth y Craidd
President Ronald Reagan: The President who Changed American Politics
Trump: A President's Life Against all Odds
The United States: Nation that Needs to be Rebuilt Itself, Joe Biden, and Kamala Harris
Dragon's Head: New China's Aspirations and Identity
The Decline of the West
Today's China: Why it is Crucial to Know How Dragons Think
Presidente Ronald Reagan: El presidente que cambió la política estadounidense
Trump: La vida de un presidente contra viento y marea
Cold War II
La decadencia de Occidente
The USA: A Journey to Rediscover a Country
Ukraine: Criticism of International Politics
Guide to Flawless Budgeting: Get Out of Debt and Learn How to Save on a Budget

The Great Forgotten: The Erasure of Women in History
29 capítulos para hablar bien en público y hablar con confianza
29 chapitres pour bien parler en public et parler avec confiance
29 Chapters for Public Speaking and Talk with Confidence
29 Kapitel für gutes öffentliches Reden und selbstbewusstes Sprechen
Guía para un presupuesto impecable: sal de deudas y aprende a ahorrar con un presupuesto
Discussion with a New Spanish Mestizo

Milton Keynes UK
Ingram Content Group UK Ltd.
UKHW020703310723
426074UK00017B/1093

9 798223 083757